# Internet Communications Using SIP

# Internet Communications Using SIP

**Delivering VoIP and Multimedia Services with Session Initiation Protocol**

Henry Sinnreich
Alan B. Johnston

Wiley Computer Publishing

John Wiley & Sons, Inc.

NEW YORK · CHICHESTER · WEINHEIM · BRISBANE · SINGAPORE · TORONTO

Publisher: Robert Ipsen
Editor: Carol A. Long
Assistant Editor: Adaobi Obi
Managing Editor: Geraldine Fahey

Text Design & Composition: Thomas Technology Solutions, Inc.

Designations used by companies to distinguish their products are often claimed as trademarks. In all instances where John Wiley & Sons, Inc., is aware of a claim, the product names appear in initial capital or ALL CAPITAL LETTERS. Readers, however, should contact the appropriate companies for more complete information regarding trademarks and registration.

This book is printed on acid-free paper. ⊚

**Published by John Wiley & Sons, Inc., New York**

Published simultaneously in Canada.

This publication is designed to provide accurate and authoritative information in regard to the subject matter covered. It is sold with the understanding that the publisher is not engaged in professional services. If professional advice or other expert assistance is required, the services of a competent professional person should be sought.

*Library of Congress Cataloging-in-Publication Data:*

Sinnreich, Henry.
    Internet communications using SIP: delivering VoIP and multimedia services with
    session initiation protocol / Henry Sinnreich, Alan Johnston.
        p. cm.—(Networking Council series)
    Includes bibliographical references and index.
    ISBN: 0-471-41399-2 (cloth : alk. paper)
      1. Computer network protocols. 2. Internet telephony. 3. Multimedia systems. I. Johnston, Alan. II. Title. III. Wiley Networking Council Series

    TK5105.55 .S56 2001
    004.6'2—dc21

                                                        2001045525

Printed in the United States of America.

10 9 8 7 6 5 4 3 2 1

*We could not have written this book without the support of our forgiving spouses, Fabienne and Lisa, who held the fort while we were working on SIP. And to both our family members shouting: "Your SIP phone is ringing!"*

# *Wiley Networking Council Series*

## *Series Editors*

Scott Bradner
*Senior Technical Consultant*, Harvard University

Vinton Cerf
*Senior Vice President*, WorldCom

Lyman Chapin
*Chief Scientist*, BBN/GTE

### Books in series:

- ISP Liability Survival Guide: Strategies for Managing Copyright, Spam, Cache, and Privacy Regulations
  Tim Casey
  ISBN: 0-471-37748-1

- VPN Applications Guide: Real Solutions for Enterprise Networks
  Dave McDysan
  ISBN: 0-471-37175-0

- Converged Networks and Services: Internetworking IP and the PSTN
  Igor Faynberg, Hui-Lan Lu, and Lawrence Gabuzda
  ISBN: 0-471-35644-1

# Contents

# Networking Council Foreword

The Networking Council Series was created in 1998 within Wiley's Computer Publishing group to fill an important gap in networking literature. Many current technical books are long on details but short on understanding. They do not give the reader a sense of where, in the universe of practical and theoretical knowledge, the technology might be useful in a particular organization. The Networking Council Series is concerned more with how to think clearly about networking issues than with promoting the virtues of a particular technology— how to relate new information to the rest of what the reader knows and needs, so the reader can develop a customized strategy for vendor and product selection, outsourcing, and design.

In *Internet Communications Using SIP: Delivering VoIP and Multimedia Services with Session Initiation Protocol* by Henry Sinnreich and Alan B. Johnston, you'll see the hallmarks of Networking Council books—examination of the advantages and disadvantages, strengths and weaknesses of market-ready technology, useful ways to think about options pragmatically, and direct links to business practices and needs. Disclosure of pertinent background issues needed to understand who supports a technology and how it was developed is another goal of all Networking Council books.

The Networking Council Series is aimed at satisfying the need for perspective in an evolving data and telecommunications world filled with hyperbole, speculation, and unearned optimism. In *Internet Communications Using SIP: Delivering VoIP and Multimedia Services with Session Initiation Protocol,* you'll get clear information from experienced practitioners.

We hope you enjoy the read. Let us know what you think. Feel free to visit the Networking Council Web site at www.wiley.com/networkingcouncil.

Scott Bradner
*Senior Technical Consultant,* Harvard University

Vinton Cerf
*Senior Vice President,* WorldCom

Lyman Chapin
*Chief Scientist,* NextHop Technologies

# Preface

This book is less about explaining the protocol details and how SIP works, but rather what SIP does and the new services enabled by SIP. Protocol details are kept to a minimum and mentioned only to the extent necessary to understand how the respective services can be built.

The book *Internet Communications Using SIP: Delivering VoIP and Multimedia Services with Session Initiation Protocol*[1] deals with *redefining communications* over the Internet, and is of interest to everybody in the telecommunications and Internet industry working in technology companies, for service providers and for students in the areas of communication and networks.

The authors of this book have had the privilege to closely monitor and contribute to the development of the Session Initiation Protocol in the Internet Engineering Task Force and to its deployment for new IP communication services in WorldCom, Inc.

Working in the telecommunications industry, we discovered SIP and were struck by the same thought: SIP will revolutionize telecommunications!

SIP will also considerably enrich the Internet. To quote Vint Cerf: SIP is probably the third great protocol of the Internet, after TCP/IP and HTTP.

---

[1]The authors would like to credit Teresa Hastings from WorldCom for coining this expression.

Two factors drove us to write this book: IP communications based on SIP is a rising tide for all ships and we want to convey the message. At the same time many concepts from legacy telephony networks are still trying to make it to the Internet, such as H.323 signaling and the "softswitch" type of central control, and we believe this requires a better understanding of SIP.

The exciting and very demanding protocol development work in the IETF SIP and other Working Groups has provided an incredible environment for critical assessment and open discussion of many detailed aspects of IP communications. SIP has generated so many contributions, that overload is one of the main challenges of the SIP working group. SIP is spilling over into several new working groups in the IETF and is also pursued in other international standards organizations.

Finally, this book is about practical implementation and network design. For the past three years, the authors have been involved in the design of a carrier-class SIP network and services.

The topics in this book reflect the multiple design and implementation issues and also the decisions service providers have to make to provide SIP-based IP communication services. The authors have had the benefit of working with some of the leading experts on SIP from the IETF, WorldCom, and from many vendors in this emerging field.

Real time IP communications are by no means a closed chapter, so we had also to rely on concepts that are discussed in IETF working groups or have been proposed by various engineers, without having as yet been accepted as a standard, or even enjoy rough consensus.

Important lessons were learned from implementing SIP and not least after both authors installed SIP phones at home and in the office. Memorable evenings and weekends were spent discussing the protocol and the book on our flawless SIP phone connection over the public Internet (using cable modem and DSL Internet access), and also within the enterprise network and for overseas. Hopefully some of this "hands on" experience has found its way into the book.

# Acknowledgments

We have enjoyed the benefit of early and significant support from colleagues and management in WorldCom. Vint Cerf was, as mentioned, one of the early supporters, and so were Teresa Hastings, John Gallant, Bob Spry, and Robert Oliver who first took the responsibility to develop and deploy SIP in their respective engineering departments. John Truetken, Lance Lockhart, and many other engineers in WorldCom also had critical contributions to the implementation of SIP. Fred Briggs, Patrice Carroll, Barry Zip, and Leo Cyr from WorldCom helped with the challenge to develop marketable services based on SIP. We were fortunate to work jointly in the development and deployment of SIP services with Steve Donovan, Diana Rawlins, Dean Willis, Robert Sparks, Ben Campbell, Chris Cunningham, Kevin Summers, and many other engineers from WorldCom and elsewhere in the industry engaged in the development of SIP in the Internet Engineering Task Force (IETF). Chris Martin from WorldCom has been very helpful with the topics in Chapter 8, *Security, NATs, and Firewalls*.

Most ideas and inspirations driving SIP are due to Prof. Henning Schulzrinne from Columbia University and to Jonathan Rosenberg from DynamicSoft and are reflected in this book. Among the many industry contributors, we gratefully acknowledge discussions and guidance from Rohan Mahy from Cisco

Corporation, Gonzalo Camarillo and Adam Roach from L.M. Ericsson. Jiri Kuthan from GMD Focus, Berlin, was helpful with SIP tutorial charts and with discussions in transatlantic calls using SIP phones—again, calls of crystal clear clarity to our surprise. The authors are grateful to Richard Shockey from NeuStar, Inc. and Douglas Ranalli from NetNumber, Inc. for numerous discussions regarding ENUM. Theodore Havinis has contributed to the SIP-QoS-AAA aspect for mobile users.

We acknowledge countless helpful discussions and insight from many participants in the IETF and especially to Scott Bradner for holding the authors and others in the IETF SIP community in line to the true conceptual, technical, and procedural spirit of the Internet.

Jeff Pulver has played a special role in providing a platform and leading exhibition of products for what was initially an obscure and unknown protocol in the Voice ON the Net (VON) and other conferences held in America, Europe, and Asia.

Carrol Long, Gerry Fahey, and Adoabi Obi from John Wiley & Sons have been instrumental in editing this book.

# Internet Communications Using SIP

# Introduction

The telecommunications, television, and data network industries are driven by growth based on new services, more complete global coverage, and consolidation. In this chapter, we will explore some of the problems and solutions for end users and service providers alike.

## Problem: Too Many Networks

Before the emergence of the Internet, users and service providers were generally accustomed to thinking in terms of three distinct network types: networks for data, networks for voice, and networks for television. Each of these dedicated network types could, in turn, be divided into many incompatible regional and even country-specific flavors with different protocol variants.

Thus, we find many types of telephony numbering plans, signaling, and audio encoding, several TV standards, and several types and flavors of what the telecom industry calls *data networks*—all of them incompatible and impossible to integrate into one single global network.

Data networks that originated in the telecom industry come in many forms, such as digital private lines, X.25, ISDN, SMDS, frame relay, and ATM networks. These so called data networks are mostly inspired by circuit-switched telephony concepts. Their name is derived from the fact that they were not designed to carry voice.

Voice networks are also used for data and fax due to their general availability. However, these networks have come to the end of their evolution, since they are fundamentally optimized for voice only. Finally, TV networks were designed and optimized for the distribution of entertainment video streams. The proliferation of various types of wireless mobile networks and pagers has increased network diversity even more.

Needless to say, all three network types have specific end-user devices that cannot be ported to other service providers or network types, and most often cannot be globally deployed.

# Network Consolidation

The Internet has benefited from a number of different fundamentals compared to legacy networks, such as the tremendous progress of computing technology and globalization. This progress can be attributed to the expertise of the research, academic, and engineering communities whose dedication to excellence and open collaboration on a global basis have surpassed the usual commercial pressure for time to market and competitive secrecy.

The result is an Internet that uses consistent protocols on a global basis and is equally well suited to carry data transactions, voice, and video.

## Voice on the Net

Although the Internet quickly established itself as the preeminent network for data, commercial transactions, and audio-video distribution, the use of voice over the Internet has been slower to develop. This has less to do with the capability of the Internet to carry voice with equal or higher quality than the telephone network, but rather the critical nature of signaling in voice services, as we will see in Chapter 5, *SIP Overview*.

There are various approaches for voice services over the Internet, based on different signaling and control design. Some examples include the following:

- Use *signaling* concepts from the telephone industry: H.323.
- Use *control* concepts from the telephone industry: Softswitches.
- Use the Internet-centric *protocol*: Session Initiation Protocol (SIP), the topic of this book.

The movement from such concepts as telephony call models to sessions between any processes on any platforms anywhere on the Internet is opening up completely new types of communication services.

The use of SIP for establishing voice, video, and data sessions places telephony as just another service on the Internet using similar addressing, data types, software, protocols, and security. A separate network for voice is no longer necessary.

Complete integration of voice with all other Internet services is probably the greatest opportunity for innovation. The open and distributed nature of this service and network model will empower many innovators, similar to what has happened on the Internet and the resulting new economy.

## SIP Is Not a Miracle Protocol

As discussed in Chapter 2, *IP Communications Enabled by SIP*, SIP is not a miracle protocol and is not designed to do more than discover remote users and establish interactive communication sessions. SIP is not meant to assure quality of service (QoS) all by itself or to transfer large amounts of data. It is not applicable for conference floor control. Neither is it meant to replace all known telephony features, many of which are due to the limitations of circuit switched voice or to the regulation of voice services. And such a list can go on.

In summary, various other Internet protocols are better suited for various features. As for telephony, not all telephone network features lend themselves to replication on the Internet.

## The Short History of SIP

By 1996, the Internet Engineering Task Force (IETF) had already developed the basics for multimedia on the Internet (see Chapter 4, *Internet Multimedia and Conferencing*) in the Multi-Party, Multimedia Working Group. Two proposals, the Session Initiation Protocol (SIP) by Mark Handley and the Simple Conference Invitation Protocol (SCIP) by Henning Schulzrinne, were announced and later merged to form Session Initiation Protocol. The new protocol also preserved the HTTP orientation from the initial SCIP proposal that later proved to be crucial to the merging of IP communications on the Internet.[1]

Henning Schulzrinne focused on the continuing development of SIP with the objective of "reengineering the telephone system from ground up," an "opportunity that appears only once after 100 years" as we heard him argue at a time when few believed this was practical.

---

[1] The authors would like to thank Professor Dr. Jörg Ott, co-chair of the SIP WG and early contributor to the MMUSIC WG for helping with data on SIP history.

SIP was approved as RFC 2543 in the IETF in March 1999. Due to the tremendous interest and the increasing number of contributions to SIP, a separate SIP Working Group (WG) was formed in September 1999. The SIP for Instant Messaging and Presence Leveraging (SIMPLE) was formed in March 2001.

As of this writing, due to the overload of the SIP WG, another working group is being chartered, known as the Session Initiation Protocol Project INvestiGation (SIPPING) working group. The core task of this group is on moving SIP from Proposed Standard to Draft Standard. All protocol extensions will remain in the SIP WG, while SIPPING will concentrate on the frameworks, requirements, and practices related to SIP and its extensions.

## References in This Book

Due to the many developments on the Internet, SIP is continuing as a work in progress, as evidenced by its rapid growth. The IETF SIP WG has twice as many drafts from contributors as any other working group. This book reflects SIP developments up to and including the fiftieth IETF in 2001.

We have included, by necessity, many Internet drafts that are designated *work in progress*, since they are the only reference source for this particular information. Some of these drafts may become standards by the time the reader is ready to use them, some may be work in progress and have a higher version number, and still others may be found only in an archive for *expired drafts*.

The SIP WG drafts that are work in progress can be found online at the IETF Web site:

http://ietf.org/html.charters/sip-charter.html

Additional individual submissions and Internet drafts from other working groups can be found at:

http:// ietf.org/ID.html.

SIP-related drafts that have *expired* (older than 6 months) can be found at several archives. At the time of this writing, some of the sites are:

http://www.cs.columbia.edu/sip/drafts/

http://softarmor.com/sipwg/

http://iptel.org/info

Few books have been published on Internet multimedia, Voice over IP, and SIP as yet, and some are listed here. They focus mainly on how SIP works. This book is less about explaining how SIP works, but rather what it does and the new communications and services it enables.

We have reproduced some of the exciting services and features discussed in the IETF SIP WG and its offspring the SIPPING and SIMPLE Working Groups. Also included in our discussion are some drafts from Bird Of Feather (BOF) sessions that have not even made it to an accepted WG charter, such as the IPAC BOF (at IETF 50) on IP appliances.

Many of these expired proposals may not make it as an IETF standard for various reasons, but represent good work, often backed up by running code. The references to such expired Internet drafts are intended to make readers aware of these ideas that may otherwise remain buried in an archive. Such references are clearly marked as expired, so as to distinguish them from accepted work in progress items of IETF WGs that are on the path toward acceptance as standards.

## References for Telephony

We assume throughout this book some understanding of telephone services and of telecommunication protocols. There is a vast literature pool available on telephony and telecommunications. We refer the reader to *Newton's Telecommunications Dictionary* [4], to brush up on various terms used in the following chapters.

## References

[1] Jon Crowcroft, Mark Handley, and Ian Wakeman. *Internetworking Multimedia*, Morgan Kaufmann Publishers, London, New York, October 1999.

[2] Olivier Hersent, David Gurle, and Jean Pierre-Petit. *IP Telephony: Packet-Based Multimedia Communications Systems*, Addison-Wesley, Reading, MA, December 1999.

[3] Alan B. Johnston. *SIP: Understanding the Session Initiation Protocol*, Artech House, Boston, London, January 2001.

[4] Harry Newton. *Newton's Telecommunications Dictionary*, 17th ed., CMP Books, Manhasset, NY, March 2001.

[5] Gonzalo Camarillo. *SIP Demystified*, McGraw-Hill Professional Publishing, New York, August 2001.

# IP Communications Enabled by SIP

The Internet challenges and transforms the close to one-trillion-dollar-per-year business of telecommunications. A renaissance in communications is taking place on the Internet. At its source are new communication protocols that would be impractical on the centralized control systems of circuit-switched networks used in telecommunications. Internet communications can benefit from the packet nature of the Net, and from electronic messaging and its associated addressing and data representations. Users and Internet service providers (ISPs) will benefit from standards that allow problem-free interoperability with all connected parties on a global scale.

While we do not believe in forecasting technology and services, it is already apparent the Internet and Web technology have created an unprecedented toolkit for new services. However, these new services are hard to predict, just as presence and instant messaging were not predicted in the telecom world. What can be shown, however, are some of the capabilities of the technology that are presently well understood in already established services. New IP communication services may create new revenue opportunities for service providers and their suppliers of software and network elements.

In this chapter we will review which services can be delivered using SIP; how such services are delivered will be discussed in Chapters 5 through 17.

We refer to many telephony type services in this chapter. Please see reference to Newton [4] in Chapter 1, *Introduction*, for definitions of the telephony and telecom services mentioned here. Chapter 9 also discusses in detail many enhanced telephone services.

The overview of SIP services provided here reflects current thinking in the community of SIP service and technology developers. Not all of them have been actually tested and implemented. Some proposed Internet drafts on SIP will make it to the level of IETF standards, some will not. It also is likely that new technologies and services will emerge that have not been communicated or envisaged as of this writing.

# Internet Multimedia Protocols

Networks are defined by their protocols. The global telephone network uses its own signaling and communication protocols, as do other telecom networks such as X.25, ISDN, SMDS, frame relay, ATM, mobile circuit-switched networks, and the proposed ITU Next Generation Public Networks. Besides network protocols, there are also application level protocols, such as those used between fax machines.

Though started with much smaller resources than the previously dominant telecom and non-IP data networks (SNA, DECnet, Novell), the Internet's success is due to its architecture and well-engineered protocols. The architectural principles of the Internet (RFC 1958 covered in Chapter 3, *Architectural Principles of the Internet*) have made it the most effective network for any type of application, including real-time communications.

IP telephony and the wider family of IP communications are defined by several key application level protocols. The list of Internet protocols used for interactive communications is given in Table 2.1.

The nature of interactive communications and the type of service is determined by the signaling used for establishing the communication, hence the name *value of signaling*.

# The Value of Signaling

Signaling in telephone systems is the key mechanism by which telephone calls are set up and terminated. For example, signaling from a desktop phone tells the PBX to forward the call to another phone. In the public telephone network, signaling instructs the switching systems to forward an 800 call to a specific agent to answer the call.

Signaling defines the desired service for the user, such as point-to-point calls, multipoint conferencing, Centrex services, text, voice and video, etc.

**Table 2.1** Internet Multimedia Protocols

| PROTOCOL | OBJECTIVE |
|---|---|
| RFC 1889: Real Time Transfer Protocol (RTP) | To packetize various media streams, such as voice, text, and video and the associated RTP/AVP specifications. |
| RFC 1890: Real Time Transfer Protocol Audio Video Profiles (RTP/AVP) | To specify media encodings and other parameters. |
| RFC 2327: Session Description Protocol (SDP) | To convey the parameters for a session. |
| RFC 2543: Session Initiation Protocol (SIP) | To setup sessions between processes running on computers attached to the net, such as for telephony, video, chat, games, etc. |
| RFC 2326: Real Time Streaming Protocol (RTSP) | For remote media play-out control. |
| Presence and Instant Messaging for SIP | Work in progress in the SIMPLE Working Group. |
| Synchronized Multimedia Integration Language (SMIL) | To insert other media such as text, graphics and URLs in audio/video streams for synchronized display (w3c.org). |

An example of the value of signaling is the comparison between a telephone call between two residences and an 800-number call to a customer-support center. In the end, both phone calls sound the same, except that signaling has enabled an added value to the 800 number call for a possible business transaction.

Value-added telephony services based on signaling are shown in Table 2.2.

Signaling for IP communications is accomplished by SIP.

# Addressing

IP communications use SIP Uniform Resource Locators (URLs) for addressing similar to the Internet, where the form of the URL resembles an e-mail address in mailto:, such as user@host. A more detailed discussion of URLs is given in Chapter 14, *DNS and ENUM*.

SIP URLs can have various forms and include telephone numbers. For example,

sip:henrys@wcom.com

**Table 2.2**  Value-Added Telephony Services Based on Signaling

| |
|---|
| Intelligent Network (IN) services |
| PBX features |
| PSTN Class services |
| Mobile cellular roaming |
| Desktop call manager |
| Computer Telephony Integration (CTI) |
| Group calling |
| Click-to-connect |
| Internet call waiting |
| "Dialing" an e-mail address or URL |

refers to the PC of Henry S. in the domain wcom.com. (See Chapter 14 for more about domain names.)

sip:+1-972-555-1234@wcom.com; user=phone

is a phone number that can be reached via a gateway (note that visual separators within a telephone number, such as dashes and dots, are optional and ignored by the protocol);

sip:123-4567@wcom.com; user=phone; phone-context=VNET

is a phone number in the internal network "VNET" of WCOM; and

sip:guest314@wcom.com

is the address of the laptop of a guest plugged into the LAN of a conference room in the wcom.com domain.

The support of both telephony and Web-type addressing enables IP communications to bridge in a seamless way the telephone network and the Internet. Users on either network can reach any point on the PSTN or the Internet without giving up existing devices or the advantages of either. For example, a user of the telephone network can make a call to a device on the Internet or to any other device on any other network (mobile voice, paging, data networks) by just dialing a number, as will be explained further. This allows users to have a single URL or phone number, if they so prefer, on their business card for contact information.

## SIP Capabilities

SIP-enabled IP devices can call each other directly, if they know each other's URL. Thus, an IP phone call can be placed directly between two or more SIP phones or PCs. Small-sized conferences can be accomplished by several users connecting to one device acting as the conference bridge as shown in Figure 2.1, where one of the SIP phones can act as both conference participant and conference bridge.

Besides SIP devices such as phones, PCs, IP telephony gateways, and mobile devices, service providers also deploy SIP servers for a variety of additional services. Figure 2.2 shows an enterprise network connected to an Internet service provider (ISP) with SIP servers and various other SIP devices such as SIP phones and also the gateway to the Public Switched Telephone Network (PSTN). Firewalls and network address translators (NATs) are not shown here for simplicity, but are discussed in Chapter 8, *Security, NATs, and Firewalls*.

SIP servers placed in both public IP network domains of ISPs and in private enterprise networks can, however, perform many functions for end users, as shown in Table 2.3.

Figure 2.2 serves to illustrate how SIP servers perform a routing service that puts the caller in contact with the called party in a step-by-step fashion, taking into account the desired service and user preferences. We will show in the following sections that the SIP services model provides users all services known

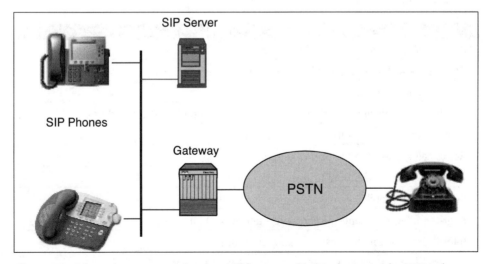

**Figure 2.1** Direct three-way conference call between IP SIP phones and a PSTN phone.

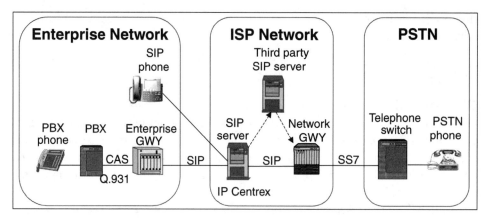

**Figure 2.2**  Voice signaling between an enterprise network and the PSTN using SIP.

from the circuit-switched telephone network, as well as new services that result from taking advantage of the Internet.

## Overview of Services Provided by SIP

Multimedia on the Internet was well developed by the research and academic community by 1997. This has been reflected in the explosion of commercial ventures for Internet multimedia during the past decade. Work started at the same time to extend the Internet multimedia architecture for use in telephony. Due to the enormous complexity and richness of services on the PSTN, this

**Table 2.3**  Functions Performed by SIP Servers

| |
|---|
| Register IP phones and other SIP devices |
| Register individual end users for access to their services |
| Register end-user preferences |
| Perform Authentication, Authorization, and Accounting (AAA) for end users |
| Look up the address of the other endpoint |
| Route call requests to the appropriate server |
| Route to devices according to user preferences |
| Support user mobility across networks and devices |
| Register, filter, and publish information about presence |
| Inform users of call progress, success, or failure |
| Communicate requests for QoS to other network elements |

work has taken much longer to develop and only recently, at the end of 2000, has reached a critical mass where true reengineering of the telephone system for the Internet is well understood.

In the history of science and technology, many new technologies have found applications that were not envisaged by their inventors. With this limitation in mind, we will provide here an overview of services that can be provided by SIP. In the following we provide a list, mapped mostly to published work.

## Intelligent Network Services Using SIP: ITU Services CS-1 and CS-2

The extensive capabilities provided by the existing PSTN Intelligent Network services can be supported by SIP. Authors from Columbia University and Lucent Bell Labs have published a detailed paper on Intelligent Network services that can be provided by SIP [1]. The capabilities also include mobile telephony features.

Service Examples for PBX and Centrex-style IP Systems are given in Table 2.4.

PBX systems have additional features that we do not list here for brevity and also for other reasons: Most people do not make use of them and such features are mostly proprietary.

**Table 2.4** IP PBX and Centrex Service Examples Using SIP

| |
|---|
| Call Hold |
| Consultation Hold |
| Unattended Transfer |
| Call Forwarding, Unconditional |
| Call Forwarding on Busy |
| Call Forwarding on No Answer |
| Three-Way Conference |
| Single Line Extension |
| Find-Me |
| Incoming Call Screening |
| Outgoing Call Screening |
| Secondary Number - In |
| Secondary Number - Out |
| Do Not Disturb |
| Call Waiting |

## *User Preferences*

Caller preference allows a user to specify how a call should be handled in the network, for example, if the call should be queued or forked to several destinations, and what features should be supported, such as media types, language, and mobility. Additional preferences are also supported, for example, avoiding disturbing someone at their residential number.

Called party preferences include such as accepting or rejecting calls (from unlisted numbers), depending on time of day, location of the called party, and origin of the call and other criteria.

SIP caller preferences and called party capabilities reveal unprecedented service capabilities under control of the service provider, the caller, and the called parties. Services can be customized with ease on a dynamic basis, depending on a large set of criteria such as presence, time of day, caller or called party identity, call urgency, personal caller preferences, network status, and the content of external databases [2]. User preferences are presented in more detail in Chapter 7, *User Preferences.*

## *Conferencing*

Conferencing allows users from different locations to participate in a conference call.

As previously mentioned, SIP was initially developed for multimedia conferencing on the Internet. The use of SIP for various conferencing features has been investigated and applied. There are a number of models and applications for conferencing, such as:

- Multimedia conferencing,
- Multipoint conferencing,
- Call control for conferencing.

Conferencing will be discussed in more detail in Chapter 4, *Internet Multimedia and Conferencing* and Chapter 12, *SIP Conferencing.*

## *Mobility in the Wider Concept*

### Local Number Portability

Local number portability allows telephone subscribers to keep their phone number when changing service providers in the same local calling area. Local number portability poses an implementation challenge on the PSTN but is a trivial application for SIP services if the user has a domain name and address such as firstname@lastname.net. With their own domain name, users can actually have service portability by choosing any service provider, for example, when on relocation, to host their service. The caller may always use the same address, phone number (using ENUM; see page 21), or URL in the personal domain of the called party, but will be redirected transparently to the network, location, or device of choice of the called party.

### Mobility at Higher Levels Than Mobile Phone Networks

One can make the distinction between:

- Terminal mobility—terminal moves between subnets
- Personal mobility—different terminals, same address
- Service mobility—keep same services while mobile

SIP has been chosen for call control for the third-generation (3G) wireless networks by the Third-Generation wireless mobile Partnership Program (3GPP) initiative.

Mobility for IP has been defined in the IETF by RFC 2002 with the basic concept that a mobile host maintains its IP address while changing the point of attachment to the IP network. Mobile IP is therefore valid for any application, be it file transfer, Web browsing, or communications. For example, mobile IP is a useful feature when moving with a wireless-connected laptop to another office in the same building or campus.

Though there is no agreement yet in the IETF about application level mobility, many SIP developers feel that terminal mobility, personal mobility, and service mobility—where users can change devices, networks, and the IP address used for communications—is a valid extension of the more limited notion of mobile IP. SIP mobility will allow users to communicate while on the move, but an uninterrupted file transfer or Web browsing would not be possible with changing IP addresses.

Mobile IP and SIP mobility are therefore complementary capabilities with different areas of applications.

We believe SIP mobility is a wide-open field where many interesting developments are possible. SIP mobility is presented in Chapter 15, *SIP Mobility*.

## Presence and Instant Communications

*Presence services* are a new form of communication [3]. Presence is possible due to the datagram nature of the Internet. As shown in Table 2.5, presence can provide information about various attributes.

Presence also can be signaled for various services as shown in Table 2.6.

Presence and its applications are discussed in more detail in Chapter 11, *Presence and Instant Communications*.

**Table 2.5** Attributes of Presence

| |
|---|
| Presence on the Net (which parties are available) |
| Location: office, home, visit, travel |
| Call state: ready, on another call (ID) |
| Willingness: available, in meeting |
| Preferred medium: text, voice, video, e-mail |
| Personal preferences |

## Instant Messaging and Instant Communications

Instant messaging [4] allows users to exchange short text messages in real time, in contrast to e-mail that is a store and forward communication, well suited for large messages and attachments. While some e-mail may take considerable time to reach the destination, instant messages are transferred in real time and are well suited for interactive communication. Text chat and voice chat have proven to be widely popular forms of communication offered by many emerging application service providers (ASPs).

The advantage of using SIP for presence and instant messaging (IM) lies in the common infrastructure with many other communication services. Presence and IM come virtually at no extra cost in a SIP environment. Instant communications are presented in Chapter 11, *Presence and Instant Communications.*

## Integrating Presence with Multimedia Communications

Telecom conferences are a key service for the business environment. They are, at present, usually rigorously scheduled events. Presence and instant communications may change this in many instances, since a conference can happen in a spontaneous fashion, if the parties are available. Presence provides the availability and willingness information of the other parties to communicate.

**Table 2.6** Services Enabled by Presence

| |
|---|
| Hop-on to an existing call—instant conference |
| Mobile phone state: online, can use camp-on |
| Location-based screening: home/work |
| Intercom telephony: between trading desks |
| Presence for any type of communications |

Conference behaviors with SIP can actually range from rigorously scheduled, as in commercial telephony conferencing services, to spontaneous conferences enabled by presence.

The presence information can be used by the conference application for various types of media and applications as shown in Table 2.7.

Besides convenience, SIP-based conferencing also can be used with any devices, fixed and mobile.

Presence and instant communication clients can have a small graphic user interface (GUI) that fits on PC displays and also on display phones, palm computers, and other devices. It is possible that future communication interfaces will resemble an instant messaging GUI rather than the present telephone keypad.

## Desktop Communication Management

SIP-based communications can be deployed easily for new applications based on third-party call control. Rich interaction between the applications on a desktop PC and a desktop phone can be implemented using SIP third-party control [5] as an open standard interface between a SIP PC client and a SIP phone. Applications include dialing from the address book on the PC and automatic accounting for the time spent for certain phone calls.

Agents for customer support can have specific applications developed for their workplace in Web-based customer support centers. The whole industry for Computer Telephony Integration (CTI) soon may be completely reengineered based on SIP, as we discuss in the following section on CRM.

## e-Commerce: Customer Relations Management

Traditional voice call centers for customer support are migrating to Web-based support centers where the focus is shifting from pure voice (800 numbers) to

**Table 2.7** Conferencing Services Enabled by Presence

| |
|---|
| Text chat, often used for quasi-permanent sessions |
| Voice chat (chat rooms for groups) |
| Games (can be considered as a form of personal communication) |
| Multimedia conferencing |
| Document sharing |
| Web page sharing (useful for customer support services) |
| File swapping for work or entertainment (peer-to-peer exchanges of work documents, music, or other files) |

email support, text chat, and voice with click-to-connect service. Besides the shift in functionality, the voice call center part also can be re-architected from ground up, as shown in Table 2.8.

Integration of all of these in an IP-Web-centric manner is possible with email support, text chat with Web page push, and file transfer.

Though discussed at the VON Europe 2000 conference (http://pulver.com), we believe this to be another area where minimal work has been published. It is the authors' opinion that customer relations management (CRM) is a bigger near-term business opportunity than long-distance telephony and international PSTN bypass based on arbitrage of PSTN telephony rates.

## *Call Control Services*

Call control services [6], [7] enable advanced telephony features, such as:

- Call Transfer, both Attended and Unattended
- Call Park/Un-Park
- Multi-Stage Dialing
- Operator Services
- Conference Call Management
- Call Mobility
- Call Pickup

Complex call control services are usually available on PBXs but only as proprietary implementations. By contrast, SIP call control is entirely based on proposed public Internet standards and works across any media or device.

Standard messages allow rich visual (icons), text, or audio interfaces to make use of complex features. Here is a summary of various reported work on call control services:

**Table 2.8** Call Center Redesign Opportunities Using SIP

| |
|---|
| Call center switch—replace with voice over IP (VoIP) |
| Interactive Voice Response (IVR)—replace with media server and SIP signaling |
| Automatic Call Distributor (ACD)—replace with script-based application (use Call Processing Language [CPL]) |
| Agent workstation—replace with SIP PC client and SIP phone (interworking using SIP third-party call control) |
| Applications and data bases—replace with Web-centric applications |
| Customer and other data pop-up for the agent can include Web search engines. |

- SIP call control services
- Third-party call control
- Transporting user call control information
- Conference control

Call control service and third-party call control are presented in Chapter 9, *SIP Telephony*.

### Miscellaneous Services

The telephone system has various other services, some of which are critical for safety or for certain user groups that can be implemented using SIP. These are listed in Table 2.9.

## Service Creation

The wide range of possibilities for new services is matched by the ease of service creation and deployment [8]. Simple services can even be developed by end users.

**Call Processing Language (CPL)** [9] is mainly intended for nontrusted end users to upload their services on SIP servers. XML scripts created by end users can be uploaded to SIP servers for call setup in a secure execution environment. CPL is described in more detail in Chapter 6.

**SIP Common Gateway Interface (CGI)** [10] is analogous to the common gateway interface (CGI) used for Web server access to databases. Complex services can be programmed under control of network administrators using SIP CGI.

**Table 2.9** Miscellaneous SIP Services

| |
|---|
| SIP for the Hearing Impaired. |
| Emergency services (known as 911 or E911 in the United States). This is an area still under active research. |
| Precedence signaling services, such as for the military. |
| Message waiting using SIP and an implementation for call waiting. |
| Call control for voice mail functions for unified messaging. |
| Programming Internet Telephony Services by users; see also the section on "Service Creation" in this chapter |

**SIP Servlets** [11]. SIP Java Servlets are a powerful tool for extending the functionality of a SIP client by allowing it to pass received messages to SIP servlets. SIP servlets can then process the message and even interact with the SIP client to generate new messages (if the security settings allow it).

SIP services can be created and hosted in both: (1) SIP end devices, as for any Internet host and (2) in SIP servers. This is shown in Figure 2.3.

The potential to easily create services by third parties and end users (within limits) may enable a Web-like creativity for new services. Also, special SIP servers can be built for services that are difficult to implement with CPL, CGI, or SIP Java Servlets.

SIP service creation is discussed in more detail with examples in Chapter 6.

## Mixed Internet-PSTN Services

There are a wide range of interworking modes between the PSTN- and SIP-based IP communication networks.

### PSTN and INTerworking (PINT)

*PSTN and Internet INT*erworking (PINT) [13] is a service where an action from the Internet, such as a click on a Web page, invokes a PSTN service, such as setting up a call between two phones (RFC 2848) or between two fax machines, or connects a fax machine to an information service that can send a fax on demand. Applications are click-to-connect, click-to-fax, click for information, and various others. PINT-based services are discussed in Chapter 13, *Mixed PSTN and Internet Telephony Services*.

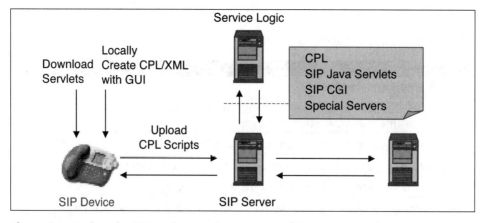

**Figure 2.3** Options for SIP service creation.

### SPIRITS

*Servers in the **P**STN **I**nitiating **R**equests to **I**n**T**ernet **S**ervers* (SPIRITS) [14] is the name of a family of IN services on the PSTN that can be implemented using SIP. It also applies to such services as Internet call waiting, where an event (calling a busy phone line) on the PSTN can generate an action on the Internet (call waiting pop-up panel on the PC that is using the called line for Internet access). SPIRITS-style services are discussed in Chapter 13, *Mixed PSTN and Internet Telephony Services.*

### TRIP

The *Telephony **R**outing over **IP*** (TRIP) protocol [15] is designed to find the desired gateway to terminate a call on the PSTN. Given the increasing number of IP telephony gateways, it may not be practical to maintain huge SIP routing tables. It also may be desirable to route calls to gateways that meet certain criteria. The Telephony Routing Protocol is modeled after the IP Border Gateway Protocol (BGP) routing protocol and inherits its scalability.

## ENUM

*ENUM* stands for **E**.164 addressing plan-based **NUM**bers and is a service that allows users to have only one single phone number on their business card. The ENUM user may have multiple PSTNs, mobile and PBX phone and fax numbers, both at home, at work, and in vehicles and also several IP devices such as PCs, laptops, and palm computers, as well as pagers. ENUM can use the domain name system (DNS) in combination with SIP user preferences, so if someone uses the single number on the business card, the call, page, voice mail, or email can be directed to the device of preference of the called party.

Using a single telephone number to be reached anywhere is a valid concept at present, since most phone calls originate on circuit-switched networks, using PSTN or PBX-type telephones. However, telephone numbers need not be the preferred contact address everywhere and for all times. As communications over the Internet gain user acceptance, the single contact address in the form of a URL, like an e-mail address, may become the more practical choice.

Figure 2.4 shows the overall idea how ENUM allows callers from circuit-switched networks that are predominant at present can reach any device on either a circuit-switched network or an IP network. ENUM service with SIP is described in Chapter 14, *DNS and ENUM.*

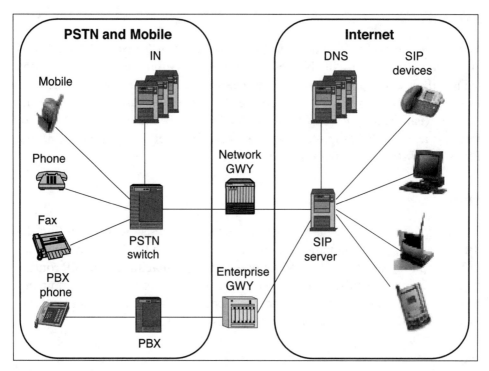

**Figure 2.4** ENUM service enables "dialing" any user device using one single phone number.

## SIP Security

Signaling information by itself can reveal sensitive data that is of prime privacy concern to users such as traffic history, patterns, and location of the user. SIP Security (RFC 2543) has a variety of procedures to ensure security for signaling, authentication, and privacy.

How SIP interacts with existing security measures on the Internet, such as firewalls and Network Address Translators (NATs), [16] is still work in progress. A security task group is associated with the IETF SIP WG for SIP security.

SIP security is presented in more detail in Chapter 8, *Security, NATs, and Firewalls*.

## SIP Orphans

The overload of work of the IETF SIP WG and other IP communications-related IETF working groups has made it impractical at this point to address all proposed applications, leaving many ideas without a home in a working group for follow-up work. Other proposals have been discarded on technical grounds. We will mention here some of the work that has not yet found a home in an IETF working group. The newly chartered SIPPING WG may adopt some of these proposals as work items. The ideas presented here may or may not prove to be successful in the marketplace, but are worth mentioning to show other possible uses of SIP.

**SIP for Control of Home Appliances** [17]. Though the phone is the most common networked home appliance, it could make sense to use SIP-based call routing, security, and application to control home appliances as varied as "dumb slave" appliances via a controller to intelligent appliances such as audio/video entertainment electronics.

**SIP for Hearing and Speech Disabled Persons** [18]. People with hearing or speech disabilities can use SIP capabilities such as caller preferences and called party preferences to signal the preferred mode of communication, such as text and/or video for manual communication and also if a relay service should be inserted between the impaired user and other communication parties. SIP is thus a most powerful technology for impaired users.

**The Internet Printing Protocol** [19]. The Internet Printing Protocol combined with SIP may allow, for example, routing of fax calls or various print jobs to remote IP-enabled printers, without knowing exactly what printers the called party may have, and also without knowing the required printer drivers. The print options of the called party can be part of the SIP contacts and user preferences.

**Using SIP for Multi-Protocol Label Switching (MPLS) based QoS.** Other work points to the usefulness of SIP in recording the route taken by SIP signaling messages. This property may be used for optimal choosing of paths across an MPLS network [20] or for choosing a service provider for certain calls. Use of SIP for the reservation of QoS guaranteed paths also has been proposed.

### Mobility Management in a SIP Environment

A large segment of SIP-related work is being addressed in other organizations not directly related to the Internet, such as the International Telecommunications Union (ITU-T), the European Telecommunications Standards Institute (ETSI), and the Third-Generation Partnership Project (3GPP) for wireless [21] technology. SIP mobility is presented in Chapter 15, *SIP Mobility*.

## SIP Interworking with ITU-T Protocols

Much work has been dedicated by the IETF, ITU-T, and ETSI for interworking of SIP with other protocols, such as those shown in Table 2.10.

**Table 2.10** SIP Interworking with ITU-T Protocols

| |
|---|
| ENUM: E.164 [22] to IP address mapping using DNS |
| SIP-H.323 [23] Interworking |
| Accessing IN services from SIP networks [24] |
| SIP-IN Applications (INAP) Interworking [25] |
| SIP and QSIG for circuit-switched PBX interworking by transport of QSIG signaling [26] |
| SIP for Telephony, for transport of telephony signaling across IP [27] |
| Telecommunications and Internet Harmonization (TIPHON) [28] |

In addition to the preceding protocols interworking with ITU-style networks, interworking with or making use of new protocols also is being investigated. See, for example, SIP and SOAP [29].

## What SIP Does Not Do

The preceding list of communications services that can be provided by SIP should not leave the impression that SIP is a "miracle protocol" that can solve all communications problems [30].

As will be discussed in Chapter 5, *SIP Overview*, SIP is a very powerful, yet simple and general protocol for establishing interactive communication sessions across the Internet. SIP is a protocol for initiating, modifying, and terminating interactive sessions. This process involves the discovery of a user, wherever he or she may be located, so that a description of the session can be delivered to the user. There are quite a number of features and services that SIP was *not* designed to support, such as:

1. SIP is not a resource reservation or prioritization protocol, so it cannot assure QoS, but can only interwork with other protocols designed to support QoS as will be discussed in Chapter 16, *AAA and QoS for SIP*.

2. SIP is not a transfer protocol such as HTTP, designed to carry large amounts of data. It is designed to transport only small amounts of data required to set up interactive communications. Small amounts of data not related to call setup, such as short text messages for instant messages, are well suited for SIP, as will be shown in Chapter 11, *Presence and Instant Communications*, but large amounts of general data are not suited for carrying by SIP.

3. SIP is not designed to manage interactive sessions, once sessions are established. For example, it is not designed to exercise floor control in

conference sessions, as in ISDN conferencing, where speakers are given access to transmit media only in a controlled manner.

4. We believe SIP is especially not meant to replace all known telephony features and services from circuit-switched networks with identical services. There are many telephony services that have their rationale due to the limitations of circuit-switched technology and in telecommunications regulation, rather than in objective needs for communication. Many Class 5 features make no sense on the Internet. Local telephone number portability is another example of a service that makes no sense on the Internet. While SIP can support local number portability, on the Internet such a service is not required in the first place, since URIs have no geographic significance. Caller ID is another "service" that makes no sense for SIP, since just like in e-mail, the To: and From: headers are always there.

## Overview of SIP Services by Market Segment

The Internet has dramatically changed business models, as demonstrated by the advent of e-commerce. The same will probably happen with telecommunications and entertainment, so any analysis can be only within the present context of these industries, a context that will probably change considerably. The following is a breakdown within the existing ("legacy") context. The authors would like to thank the discussion group of the SIP Forum (http://www .sipforum.org) for these ideas.

### 1. Service Categories Involving Voice Transport

The opportunities for new services enabled by SIP are detailed here by the type of service for various market segments (see Tables 2.11 through 2.14). This list is not comprehensive, and as mentioned, innovation is hard to predict. The list is also formulated in terms of present telecommunications and Internet services as perceived by users and these terms may change with the developing market for IP communications.

### 2. Overlay SIP Services Potentially Offered by Application Service Providers

Table 2.15 is a view for voice services from the perspective of service providers for SIP based services. Service providers are focused on added value that can be provided from the IP network. As can be seen there is a rich and consistent portfolio of services that can be provided over the Internet and private IP net-

**Table 2.11**  Residential Services over Broadband (Cable, DSL, Fixed Wireless)

| |
|---|
| SIP adapters and phones for residential broadband access |
| Consumer telephony (PC to PC and PC to phone) |
| Consumer communication devices (SIP cordless phone, IP Centrex for second residential line) |

**Table 2.12**  Business and Enterprise Applications

| |
|---|
| Customer relations management (CRM) for Web call centers |
| Virtual LAN PBX (SIP server from service provider) |
| Small-office communication services using SIP phones (IP Centrex) |
| Remotely managed business network services for IP PBXs |

**Table 2.13**  Carrier Centric Services

| |
|---|
| PBX trunking for business/enterprise |
| Toll-switch bypass |
| Calling card services |
| Wholesale backbone and PSTN access services |
| SIP clearinghouse |
| Prepaid services |

**Table 2.14**  Wireless

| |
|---|
| Multimedia messaging service based on the SIP message method |
| SIP registrars making use of the positioning information available in wireless networks and services related to it |
| SIP services and roaming in 3G networks |
| SIP for optional call control in circuit-switched wireless networks (GPRS) |
| SIP transport over the wireless protocol stacks |
| Third-generation wireless clients and access infrastructure |

works. Such a complete portfolio of a mix of voice and Web services is difficult or impossible to provide over circuit switched telecom networks such as PSTN

**Table 2.15** SIP for Application Service Providers

| |
|---|
| Unified messaging |
| IM and presence |
| Call routing services related to presence (find me / follow me / page me...) |
| e-commerce (CRM) |
| Web call routing, virtual interactive voice response systems (IVRs) using SIP-based voice browsing and virtual automatic call distributors (ACDs) |
| Virtual (service provider) Web call center |
| Auto attendant work place |
| Information / content services with voice browsing (411, tell me services) |
| Call setup as trigger for other media (video games, Web page sharing) |
| Third-party call control |
| Conferencing |
| Third-party Internet hosted PSTN services enabled by SIP (personal call manager) |

or ATM. Some IP-based PBX may also provide such services as well, but in a proprietary manner by contrast to SIP and SIP-based PBXs.

## Commercial SIP Products

The growing list of vendors offering SIP products is shown at the Pulver Web page on SIP Products (http://pulver.com/sip/products.html). A number of U.S. and European startup companies have made SIP their main or only business focus.

Many companies have developed SIP devices ranging from simple adaptors for PSTN and PBX phones to highly intelligent phones (http://www .pingtel.com). Figure 2.5 shows an intelligent SIP phone that can support appli-

**Figure 2.5** Intelligent SIP phone that can deliver features without a central office switch.

cations such as personal information managers (PIM) or any other download-able applications such as call management, conferencing, etc.

### Service Providers Using SIP

Early thinking and presentations on SIP focused on the idea of reengineering the telephone system. It soon became clear, however, that the incentive to do so for service providers was the potential of new services. Several service providers have published Internet drafts and presentations on SIP-based services. We indicate here only some that have been published, though we believe much work remains unpublished for competitive reasons. More detailed references can be found in publications by their respective service providers. We list the service providers as of April 2001 in alphabetical order:

- 3GPP: Mobile service providers in the Third Generation wireless Partnership Program (3GPP) have adopted SIP for call control of IP multimedia-based services.
- Cablelabs/AT&T: the Distributed Call Signaling Architecture, co-authored by numerous network and telecom equipment vendors.
- Level 3.
- Telia.
- WorldCom.

Presentations on SIP from an increased number of other service providers at various conferences indicates the popularity of SIP with companies interested in providing new value-added communication services.

## More Work Ahead

We believe there are other fields critical to the success of Internet communications such as quality of service, security, and payment systems.

### Quality of Service

It has been experienced that IP networks with ample bandwidth can provide adequate QoS as required for voice, but some implementations of mixed data and voice IP networks may require network-wide QoS that we believe is still not too common, since current routing is optimized for data only. Significant upgrades of existing IP networks may be required for voice QoS.

Global commercial quality voice will happen after Internet transit networks implement QoS, such as with Differentiated Services (RFC 2475). QoS issues are discussed in detail in Chapter 16, *AAA and QoS for SIP*.

### AAA Mechanisms for SIP and QoS

Implementing QoS for IP communications requires considerable resources for enterprise network managers, ISPs, and transit network service providers. QoS-enabled communications require, therefore, adequate standardized tools for authentication, authorization, and accounting of usage [31]. A new SIP open settlement protocol (OSP) token authorization header [32] has been proposed for interdomain QoS call setup with support from a clearinghouse. This is also work still in progress.

### Conclusions and Future Directions

SIP has all the marks of a thoroughly disruptive technology. It may fundamentally change communication services as we know them today and also the communication habits of users. The complete integration of communications with the Web and email has thus started, and much innovation and the resulting new services are still ahead as shown in the preceding section on SIP orphans. SIP and its related protocols may prove to be the enabling ingredients for new communications much like its model protocol HTTP 1.1 was to the World Wide Web. Chapter 18 summarizes the information on future work and current directions for IP communications.

# References

[1] J. Lennox, H. Schulzrinne, and T. F. La Porta. "Implementing Intelligent Network Services with the Session Initiation Protocol," Technical Report, 1999, http://www.cs.columbia.edu/~hgs/papers/cucs-002-99.pdf.

[2] J. Rosenberg and H. Schulzrinne. "SIP Caller Preferences and Callee Capabilities," Internet draft, IETF, October 1999, work in progress.

[3] J. Rosenberg, D. Willis, R. Sparks, H. Schulzrinne, J. Lennox, B. Aboba, C. Huitema, D. Gurle, and D. Oran. "SIP Extensions for Presence," Internet draft, IETF, June 2000, work in progress.

[4] J. Rosenberg, D. Willis, R. Sparks, H. Schulzrinne, J. Lennox, B. Aboba, C. Huitema, D. Gurle, and D. Oran. "SIP Extensions for Instant Messaging," Internet draft, IETF, June 2000, work in progress.

[5] J. Rosenberg, J. Peterson, and H. Schulzrinne. "Third Party Call Control in SIP," Internet draft, IETF, September 2000, work in progress.

[6] H. Schulzrinne and J. Rosenberg. "SIP Call Control Services," Internet draft, IETF, June 1999, work in progress.

[7] R. Dean and B. Biggs. "SIP Call Control: Call Handoff," Internet Draft, work in progress, IETF, January 2001.

[8] J. Rosenberg, J. Lennox, and H. Schulzrinne. "Programming Internet Telephony Services," Columbia University Tech/Report CUCS-010-99, 1999.

[9] J. Lennox and H. Schulzrinne. RFC 2824: Call Processing Language Framework and Requirements, IETF, May 2000.

[10] J. Rosenberg. "Programming IP Telephony Services with CPL and SIP CGI," Open Sig '99 Conference, Lucent Technologies, Bell Labs.

[11] A. Kristensen and A. Byttner. "The SIP Servlet API," expired IETF Internet draft, September 1999.

[12] A. Brown and Greg Vaudreil. "ENUM Service Specific Provisioning: Principles of Operation," IETF Internet draft, July 13, 2000, work in progress.

[13] S. Petrack and L. Conroy. RFC 2848: "The PINT Service Protocol: Extensions to SIP and SDP for IP Access to Telephone Call Services," IETF Internet draft, June 2000, work in progress.

[14] I. Faynberg, H. Lu, and L. Slutsman. "Toward Definition of the Protocol for PSTN-initiated Services Supported by PSTN/Internet Interworking," IETF Internet draft, March 2000, work in progress.

[15] J. Rosenberg and H. Schulzrinne. "A Framework for Telephony Routing over IP," IETF Internet draft, June 2000, work in progress.

[16] Frederick Thernelius, Ericsson, and the Royal Swedish Technical Institute. "SIP, NAT and Firewalls," Master's Thesis, May 2000.

[17] S. Moyer, et al. "Framework Draft for Networked Appliances Using the Session Initiation Protocol," IETF Internet draft, July 2000, work in progress.

[18] A. van Wijk, J. Rosenberg, K. Gearhart, H. Sinnreich, H. Schulzrinne. "SIP Support for Hearing and Speech Impaired Users," Internet draft, work in progress, IETF, July 2001.

[19] T. Hastings and C. Manros. RFC 2639: "Internet Printing Protocol/1.0: Implementer's Guide," IETF, July 1999.

[20] M. Gibson. "The Management of MPLS LSPs for Scalable QoS Service Provision," IETF Internet draft, March 2000, work in progress.

[21] F. Vakil, A. Dutta, J.-C. Chen, S. Baba, and H. Schulzrinne. "Mobility Management in a SIP Environment," IETF Internet draft, August 2000, work in progress.

[22] P. Fälström. "E.164 Number and DNS," IETF Internet draft, August 2000, work in progress.

[23] K. Singh and H. Schulzrinne. "Interworking Between SIP/SDP and H.323," IETF Internet draft, January 2000, work in progress.

[24] V. Gurbani. "Accessing IN Services from SIP Networks," IETF Internet draft, November 2000, work in progress.

[25] H. Schulzrinne, L. Slutsman, I. Faynberg, and H. Lu. "Interworking between SIP and INAP," IETF Internet draft, June 2000, work in progress.

[26] E. Zimmerer, A. Vemuri, L. Ong, M. Zonoum, and M. Watson. "MIME Media Types for ISUP and QSIG Objects," IETF Internet draft, June 2000, work in progress.

[27] A. Vemuri and J. Peterson. "SIP for Telephones (SIP-T): Context and Architectures," IETF Internet draft, July 2000, work in progress.

[28] P. Sijben. "Telecommunications and Internet Protocol Harmonization Over Networks (TIPHON); TIPHON Release 3; Network Architecture and Reference Configurations," IETF Internet draft, July 2000, work in progress.

[29] N. Deason. "SIP and SOAP," IETF Internet draft, June 2000, work in progress.

[30] J. Rosenberg and H. Schulzrinne."Guidelines for Authors of SIP Extensions," IETF Internet draft, September 2000, work in progress.

[31] H. Sinnreich, D. Rawlins, A. Johnston, S. Donovan, and S. Thomas. "AAA Usage for IP Telephony with QoS," expired Internet draft, IETF, July 2000.

[32] A. Johnston, D. Rawlins, and H. Sinnreich. "OSP Authorization Token Header for SIP," IETF Internet draft, July 2000, work in progress.

CHAPTER

3

# Architectural Principles of the Internet

After the overview on SIP-based IP communication services in Chapter 2, we will provide here a brief summary of the Internet architecture, with emphasis on the control part, by contrasting it to the telecom-style circuit-switched networks. This review will facilitate an understanding of the following chapters.

## Telecom Architecture

We refer readers to the numerous references available on ITU-T telecommunications networks. The complete, original, and up-to-date documents are available from the ITU-T at the following address: http://itu.int/home/index .html.

Other relevant documents, such as for ATM networks, can be obtained at no cost at the following address: http://www.atmforum.com.

Figure 3.1 shows the architecture of all ITU-T-style circuit-switched networks. The main features of this architecture are:

- Central control, such as the Intelligent Network (IN) in each network for setting up the paths across each of the respective networks.

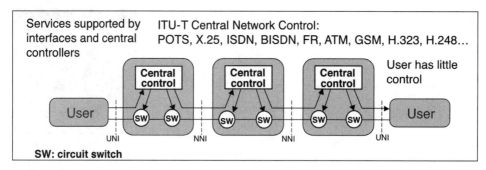

**Figure 3.1**  Circuit-switched network architecture.

■ Telecom standards are focused on interfaces. The most common inter-faces are standard user-to-network interfaces (UNI) and network-to-net-work interfaces (NNI).

■ Services  must be supported by the features in all NNIs, UNIs, and in all the central control units.

■ New services require new standards support in all UNIs, NNIs, and cen-tral controllers.

No service intelligence is presumed in the user devices.

Users have no control over the applications or the choice of services, except to the services made available by subscription by the access service provider, such as the local telephone company.

The previous features are of critical importance for the richness and time to market for new services, as well as for user choice of services. Experience has shown that this type of network is not favorable to innovation, since developers cannot get easy access to the central control units, or change the interface standards in a timely manner. Other features that are more of an engineering concern and are also reflected in the high cost of service are dis-cussed next.

The circuit-switch nature requires the keeping of state for a connection or call in every switch, and in several switch subsystems in every switch, as well as in every central control unit. State requires expensive processing and mem-ory in all network elements and components where state is kept.

There are single points of failure. Protection against network failures require carrier grade equipment, stand-by equipment, and entire stand-by network paths.

Network standards are not global; regional standards and various options are permitted. As a consequence, interoperability of telecom networks is a hard problem and is usually achieved only for the least common denominator of standard features.

In spite of these comments made in hindsight, the global telecom networks amount to close a trillion-dollar industry that is still growing. Most of the Internet traffic also is still carried on telecom-type transmission systems. The growth of telecom transmission systems in developed countries is, however, predominantly due to the Internet, and this points, in our opinion, to the probable end of the life cycle for most telecom networks, except for mobile phone networks. The end of the life cycle for telecom networks can probably be argued by the absence of new services that has been observed for some time.

# Internet Architecture

The engineering of Internet communications differs in many ways from telecommunications engineering. We will quote the relevant passages from RFC 1958, "Architectural Principles of the Internet," [1] by Brian Carpenter and reproduce some paragraphs, since we find it impossible to articulate the issues in any better way:

> The end-to-end argument is discussed in depth in Saltzer [2]. The basic argument is that, as a first principle, certain required end-to-end functions can only be performed correctly by the end systems themselves. A specific case is that any network, however carefully designed, will be subject to failures of transmission at some statistically determined rate. The best way to cope with this is to accept it, and give responsibility for the integrity of communication to the end systems. Another specific case is end-to-end security.
>
> To quote from Saltzer [2]:
>
> The function in question can completely and correctly be implemented only with the knowledge and help of the application standing at the endpoints of the communication system. Therefore, providing that questioned function as a feature of the communication system itself is not possible. (Sometimes an incomplete version of the function provided by the communication system may be useful as a performance enhancement.)
>
> This principle has important consequences if we require applications to survive partial network failures. An end-to-end protocol design should not rely on the maintenance of state (i.e., information about the state of the end-to-end communication) inside the network. Such state should be maintained only in the endpoints, in such a way that the state can only be destroyed when the endpoint itself breaks (known as fate-sharing). An immediate consequence of this is that datagrams are better than classical virtual circuits. The network's job is to transmit datagrams as efficiently and flexibly as possible. Everything else should be done at the fringes.
>
> To perform its services, the network maintains some state information: routes, QoS guarantees that it makes, session information where that is used in

header compression, compression histories for data compression, and the like. This state must be self-healing; adaptive procedures or protocols must exist to derive and maintain that state, and change it when the topology or activity of the network changes. The volume of this state must be minimized, and the loss of the state must not result in more than a temporary denial of service given that connectivity exists. Manually configured state must be kept to an absolute minimum.

Fortunately, nobody owns the Internet, there is no centralized control, and nobody can turn it off.

We hope not to quote out of context with the above extract. The document on the architectural principles of the Internet deals with many other issues, such as focus on the network layer protocol, scalability, heterogeneity, security, simplicity, internationalization, standards proven by interoperable implementations, etc. Those issues are, however, beyond the scope of this book, and we recommend reading this important document separately.

Figure 3.2 is a summary graphic representation of the end-to-end control architecture of the Internet. The Internet is characterized mainly by:

- No single point of failure.
- Connectionless.
- Soft state or no session state in the network.
- End-to-end control.
- Users have complete control over the applications and selection of services.

Internet standards are focused on protocols and not on interfaces, specifying only how the devices communicate across the Net.

The end-to-end control design of the Internet cannot be always maintained, due to various developments such as firewalls and other devices. This problem is discussed in RFC 2775 [3].

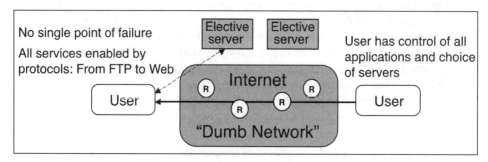

**Figure 3.2** Internet architecture.

## The Internet Standards Process

The Internet architecture has a vibrant vitality due to the Internet standards creation process [4] and the open participation structure of the Internet Engineering Task Force (IETF).

The IETF is a large, open international community of network designers, operators, vendors, and researchers concerned with the evolution of the Internet architecture and the smooth operation of the Internet.

To become a participant in the IETF, one merely becomes active in one or more working groups by asking to be added to the WG's mailing list. It is open to any interested individual. No membership fee is required from individuals interested in contributing to the work of the IETF.

Technical excellence is the top requirement for Internet standards. At each stage of the standardization process, a specification is repeatedly discussed and its merits debated in open meetings and/or public electronic mailing lists, and it is made available for review via worldwide online directories.

A candidate specification must be implemented and tested for correct operation and interoperability by multiple independent parties and utilized in increasingly demanding environments, before it can be adopted as an Internet standard.

This Internet standards process [4] has made the IETF probably the most effective standards organization in the areas of computing, networks, and communications.

## Protocols and Application Programming Interfaces

The reliance on protocols in Internet engineering is another significant difference from the practice in the telecom industry to use application programming interfaces (APIs).

*Internet protocols* specify only how processes running on different computing devices on the Internet communicate "across the wire" and do not impose any restriction on how the protocol machines are implemented—(this is best left to the creativity and competitiveness of the software developers).

*Application programming interfaces* are commonly used to program most telecommunication equipments by developers and users. APIs are, however, most often owned and under the control of the equipment vendor. In addition, they are often written for a specific operating system only.

Users and developers of telecommunication equipment are informed of the "open APIs" for the equipment so as to develop or customize services. One must remember, however, that "open APIs" introduce a certain level of dependency on the equipment vendor and the operating system vendor as they both have intellectual property rights and change control.

Protocols are preferred on the Internet for these reasons, since any Internet standard or practice has to be completely vendor independent. Moreover, a core design principle for the Internet and the World Wide Web is that the various parts should be designed and implemented independently of each other.

## References

[1] Brian Carpenter and the Internet Architecture Board (IAB). RFC 1958: "Architectural Principles of the Internet," June 1996, ftp://ftp.isi.edu/in-notes/rfc1958.txt.

[2] J.H. Saltzer, D.P. Reed, and D.D. Clark. "End-to-End Arguments in System Design," *ACM TOCS*, Vol. 2, No. 4, ACM, November 1984, pp. 277–288.

[3] Brian Carpenter and the IAB. RFC 2775: "Internet Transparency," IETF, February 2000, ftp://ftp.isi.edu/in-notes/rfc2775.txt.

[4] Scott Bradner and the IETF. RFC 2026: "The Internet Standards Process," IETF, October 1996.

# Internet Multimedia and Conferencing

This chapter provides an overview of the Internet multimedia architecture. Other key Internet transport and multimedia protocols besides SIP, such as IP unicast and multicast transport protocols, RTP/RTCP, SDP, and RTSP are briefly introduced.

## Introduction

Though the Internet was not created primarily for real-type communications, and its present growth has been driven mainly by e-mail, data, and information services, multimedia on the Internet has also seen tremendous growth for various applications, including but not limited to telephony. Indeed, many online magazines routinely carry links to streaming audio or streaming audio/video news clips, movie trailers, or online tutorials and presentations. There is an ever increasing number of radio and video stations worldwide on the Internet, rivaling the number of stations on short-wave radio. The Internet has shown its capability of:

- Consolidating all types of media and data on one single network.
- Integrating all services at the application layer for information, communications, entertainment, and transactions.

- Scaling from point-to-point "calls" to conferences and network broadcasts encompassing millions of users.

- Empowering end users to choose both applications and services on a global basis that best suits their needs.

- Revolutionizing the software industry in forcing the redevelopment of practically all software applications to become Internet-centric and provide newer office productivity applications to be communication aware.

For any type of communications and media, these features of the Internet are leading to "democratization" of both the: (1) telecommunication services such as telephony and (2) broadcast services such as TV and radio. We share the belief found in the Internet community that the Internet will lead to services and social structures that do not exist today, similar to e-commerce that has recently emerged with profound implications for all commerce.

Such an impact, however, does not come without a price, and very appropriate for the Internet, the price is not primarily in a new physical infrastructure (huge in itself by any measure), but what we believe to be in a large and ever-expanding mandatory knowledge base and skill set. We will attempt to provide here a short overview of the main protocols required for Internet multimedia and conferencing.

An overview of the Internet protocol stack for multimedia [1] is shown in Figure 4.1.

## Freshening Up on IP

Though most readers are fairly familiar with IP, those interested in boning up on it may want to review RFC 791, published in 1981 [1]. In this RFC, Jon Postel

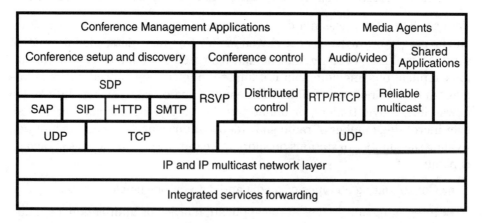

**Figure 4.1** Internet multimedia protocol stack.

expresses, in standard form, the concepts of *interworking and IP*, first introduced by Vint Cerf in 1978 [2] and others.

An excellent summary of recent items of interest for IP, most notably IP address allocation, is provided in RFC 2002 [3].

IP multicast has always played a large part in the Internet concepts on conferencing and multimedia, though its deployment has been rather sparse up to the present. Source Specific Multicast (SSM) [4] reflects current IETF work on IP multicast.

The relevant protocols for Internet multimedia and conferencing are summarized in Table 4.1. We will provide in the following a short list of the main topics for Internet multimedia and conferencing [5] and refer the reader to Table 4.1 for the applicable protocols. The cross-headers in Table 4.1 refer to the protocols grouped under the respective cross-header.

# Internet Multimedia Protocols

The following sections discuss in greater detail some of the protocols listed in Table 4.1. The discussion is limited to the generic groups listed under the cross-headers in the table.

## Multicast Protocols

IP multicast is not yet implemented in most public IP networks, but is an important concept to discuss with regard to Internet multimedia. The Internet multimedia conferencing architecture was initially developed on experimental Internet multicast networks in the early 1990s.

IP multicast is the most efficient procedure to distribute data and multimedia to large groups of users by locating the distribution function in the IP network layer and thus making it available to any type of application. IP multicast also absolves applications from establishing any type of communications between senders and receivers, since joining a multicast group is all that is required. The IP multicast address is the unique identifier for senders and receivers to join a multicast session. Multicast is also highly scalable, since the data replication is delegated to the edge of the network as required by traffic patterns.

### Multicast Address Allocation

Multicast addresses are allocated from a pool of class D IP addresses that are reserved for multicast. Most multicast address allocations are implemented at present in a static manner with manual configuration. However, work is in progress to dynamically allocate multicast group addresses and to provide directory services for multicast groups.

### IP UNICAST AND MULTICAST

In unicast IP packet forwarding a single packet is delivered to a single destination. Multicast IP delivers a single packet to a set of destinations. Note that this is different from packet broadcast which can be done on an Ethernet LAN. Packet broadcast delivers the packet to *every* destination on the LAN. As a result, packet broadcast does not scale outside the LAN, as it can generate huge traffic loads. Multicast IP is different in that an endpoint must join a multicast group before any of the multicast packets will be forwarded by routers serving that user. This multicast group is identified by a multicast IP address, described in the next section. This scalable architecture limits the distribution of multicast packets to users that are participating in the session.

IP multicast is generally not enabled on the public Internet. However, it is available using an overlay network called the MBONE (Multicast Backbone). For example, some video and audio of IETF conference sessions are distributed over the MBONE using multicast.

**Table 4.1**  Network Protocols for Internet Multimedia and Conferencing

| NAME | DOCUMENT | SUBJECT | |
|---|---|---|---|
| **IP Unicast** | | | |
| Internet Protocol | RFC 791 | DARPA Internet Protocol Specification | |
| IP Policies | RFC 2008 | IP Address Allocation | |
| **Multicast Protocols** | | | |
| SSM | Internet Draft | Source Specific Multicast | |
| IP Multicast | RFC 1112, 2236 | Host extensions for IP Multicast | |
| DVRMP | RFC 1075 | Dense mode multicast | Intradomain multicast routing protocols |
| PIM-SIM | RFC 2362 | Sparse mode multicast | |
| PIM-DM | Internet Draft | Dense mode multicast | |
| CBT | RFC 2189 | Sparse mode multicast | |
| **Multicast Address Allocation** | | | |
| MADCAP | Internet Draft | DCHP-like for multicast address allocation | |
| AAP | Internet Draft | Intradomain multicast address allocation | |
| MASC | Internet Draft | Interdomain multicast address allocation | |
| BGMP | Internet Draft | Interdomain multicast routing | |
| **Internet Services (*See* Figure 4.2)** | | | |
| IP | RFC 791 | Internet Protocol | |
| **Resource Reservation** | | | |
| RSVP | RFC 2205 | Resource Reservation Protocol (RSVP) | |

| NAME | DOCUMENT | SUBJECT |
|------|----------|---------|
| Controlled load | RFC 2211 | Controlled load service model for RSVP |
| Guaranteed | RFC 2212 | Guaranteed service model for RSVP |
| **Differentiated Services** | | |
| DiffServ | RFC 2474 | Differentiated services field in IP header |
| DiffServ | RFC 2475 | Differentiated services architecture |
| **Data and Formats** | | |
| XML | | Extensible Markup Language |
| VoiceXML | | XML-style customized for voice markup |
| **Presentation of Synchronized Multimedia** | | |
| SMIL | | Synchronized Multimedia Integration Language |
| **Media Transport and Codecs** | | |
| RTP, RTCP | RFC 1889 | Packet format for real-time traffic |
| RTP AV Profile | RFC 1890 | RTP profile for audio/video traffic |
| Payloads | RFC 2032, 2035, etc. for many types of payloads. | RTP payloads for specific codecs |
| **Multimedia Server Playback Control** | | |
| RTSP | RFC 2326 | Real-Time Streaming Protocol for audio / visual playback and recording |
| **Session Description** | | |
| SDP | RFC 2327 | Session description format |
| **Session Directory** | | |
| SAP | Internet Draft | Multicast Session Announcement Protocol |
| **Session Invitation** | | |
| SIP | RFC 2543 | Session Initiation Protocol |
| **Authentication and Key Distribution** | | |
| PGP | RFC 1991 | Public key cryptography |
| X.509 | ITU recommendation | Directory-based authentication |

The RFCs quoted here are available online at http://ietf.org/rfc.html.

We refer the reader to the very informative Web pages of the IP Multicast Initiative at http://ipmulticast.com/ for more information on IP multicast technology, services, and events.

## Transport Protocols

Media streams, such as voice and video for real-time communications, use UDP packet transport, since it makes no sense to delay the reception for retransmitted packets that were lost, as done using TCP. Lost media packets are discarded in favor of getting the shortest delivery time possible. Media delivery using UDP over IP is sensitive to packet delay and packet loss. Quality of IP service is therefore an important part for real-time Internet multimedia communications.

## Internet Services

Though the terms "Internet service" or "IP service" have many marketing connotations, IP-level services in the technical sense really refer to the level of quality of service (QoS) provided. Figure 4.2 shows the spectrum of IP services.

Most Internet and IP users are familiar only with the best effort-type of service. Best effort service is shown at the far left of the spectrum in Figure 4.2. Best effort service can provide adequate QoS for interactive communications as long as there is no traffic congestion on any of the links between the respective endpoints. Best effort IP service, however, cannot provide assurance that QoS will be maintained at all times during a session, since congestion may affect packet delay and packet loss in an unpredictable manner for media packets.

Readers should not assume that best effort service might not be adequate for IP communications. Daily use of SIP telephones on the public Internet by the authors have convinced us that with adequate access, such as cable or DSL for home use, best effort service provides quality telephony equal or better than that on the PSTN, though no guarantees can be provided.

### *Resource Reservation*

At the other end of the IP services spectrum from best effort service is the guaranteed-by-per-flow reservation service based on the Resource Reservation Protocol (RSVP) [6], shown at the right in Figure 4.2. RSVP resembles the bandwidth and delay qualities of TDM circuits, either for guaranteed service or to the degree to which TDM circuit properties can be emulated over an unloaded

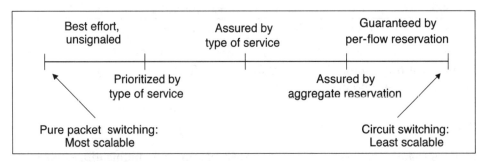

**Figure 4.2** Range of IP and Internet services.

IP network. RSVP reserves the resources across the IP network associated with individual flows. The IP addresses and port number of the IP endpoints, and also the transport layer protocol, such as UDP or TCP, characterize an IP packet flow. RSVP is a form of virtual circuit setup over a packet switched network.

The main properties of RSVP are:

- Applications in endpoints can communicate their requirements for QoS to the network directly and in a flexible manner.

- The ownership of the RSVP-supported QoS flows can be clearly distinguished. This allows accounting for the use of network resources by individual users.

- Routers in the network have to keep state for each RSVP reservation, and, as a consequence, RSVP is not scalable to large networks. The use of RSVP is restricted to the access part, in the periphery of the network.

Two types of services have been standardized for RSVP: *Controlled load,* which offers service with QoS equal to that of the unloaded network, and *Guaranteed* with hard QoS limits.

An industrywide effort in the Integrated Services over Specific Link Layers (ISSLL) working group of the IETF has produced detailed specifications on how to map IP QoS in the integrated services architecture onto most link layer technologies, such as slow links, PPP, Ethernet 802.3-style LANs, frame relay, and ATM.

## Differentiated Services

The *Differentiated Services* [7] model is the complementary approach to RSVP, in the sense that only certain classes of service are defined in the network. The main properties of differentiated services are therefore:

- Applications can be fit only within certain classes of service.

- The network is not aware of the individual IP packet streams, but only of classes of service. Accounting for individual users is therefore not possible.

- Differentiated services are highly scalable and therefore well suited to be used in the core of the IP network.

## Integrated Services and DiffServ Networks

Using RSVP at the edge of the network in the access portion, and differentiated services in the core is a good match of two QoS approaches [8]. Edge routers in access networks can aggregate all the outgoing RSVP flows into corresponding differentiated service classes. RSVP-enabled flows can transverse transit networks that support differentiated services. In other words, differentiated services transport represents just another media for RSVP, similar to all the other layer 2 media types.

Several intermediate QoS models are possible between the extremes of RSVP and differentiated services, as shown in Figure 4.2. For example, so-called RSVP aggregators can have another, aggregated RSVP as the output, or certain classes of services can be associated with guaranteed delivery. The latter raises the intriguing possibility of a standard class of service for voice across the Internet and private IP networks. Since voice seems to require only a small part of the overall bandwidth, compared to data, setting a standard guaranteed QoS for telephony might simplify considerably IP network design.

## Media and Data Formats

The predominant media types for conferencing are audio and video, though other real-time media such as games may also be part of a conference. Various types of data also are exchanged during a conference, such as Web pages, and desktop applications. The protocol for media transport is the Real-Time Transport Protocol (RTP). In addition, during a conference, presentations are made. The protocol for synchronizing various media and data types during a presentation is the Synchronized Multimedia Integration Language (SMIL). Finally, recorded media streams of complete presentations can be uploaded, downloaded, and replayed using Real-Time Streaming Protocol (RTSP).

### Media Transport Using RTP

The Real-Time Transport Protocol (RTP) document, RFC 1889 [9] consists of:

- RTP for media packet transport.
- The RTP Control Protocol (RTCP) to monitor the quality of service and generate reports to the network.

A complete treatment of RTP would require a book by itself. We will provide here in a nutshell only the most relevant aspects required to understand the environment for SIP. We refer readers to the Web site of the IETF AVT WG at http://ietf.org/html.charters/avt-charter.html for more information. RTP uses UDP for transport over IP.

Audio and video packets are encapsulated in RTP packets that provide the following information carried in the RTP header:

- **Packet sequence number.** Allows the user to reorder packets on arrival and to detect the loss of packets.

- **Timestamps.** Allows jitter to be detected (that is, packet arrival time variations across the network).

- **Synchronization (media) source.** Allows the identification of the sources of the packet streams.

It is important to realize that RTP is an application layer protocol and does not provide any QoS guarantees at all. However, it does allow various types of impairments such as packet loss or jitter to be detected.

RTCP uses the preceding data at the receiver to convey back to applications in the network that monitor quality of service, perform fault diagnosis, and report long-term statistic data. Information conveyed by RTCP includes:

- Network Time Protocol (NTP) timestamps that can be used to assess absolute round-trip delay

- RTP timestamps that can be used in conjunction with NTP timestamps and also can be used to assess the local RTP clock rate

- Synchronization (media) source identifier (SSRC)

- Packet and byte counts

- Lost packets reported as a fraction of the total and as a cumulative number

- Highest sequence number received

- Inter-arrival jitter and other parameters

Listening-only participants will send Receiver Reports (RR) to applications that monitor the quality of service, while speaking participants will also send Sender Reports (SR).

A special Source Description RTCP packet (SDES) conveys information about the user:

- Canonical Name (CNAME) to identify the participants in the conference

- User name, such "John Doe, Bit Recycler, Megacorp"

- Phone number

- Geographic user location

- Application or tool name

- NOTE: Such as "on the phone, can't talk"

RTP also uses protocol-specific devices such as translators and mixers.

An *RTP translator* connects two different transport networks, such as IP v.4 and IP v.6 networks. Translators also may change the media encoding as required, allowing two endpoints that have no common codecs to be able to communicate.

An *RTP mixer* receives media streams from several sources, combines them, and forwards the combined stream. An RTP mixer will add its own SSRC identifier to the existing identifiers in the component streams.

### RTP Payloads and Payload Format Specifications

The Audio/Visual Profile (AVP) for RTP [9] specifies payloads registered with the Internet Assigned Numbers Authority (IANA) and specifies such items as the name, clock rate, or frame size of audio codecs and encoding independent parameters, such as the audio left, right, center, surround, front, and rear.

RTP payloads are grouped for specific applications, such as for audio/video conferencing. Payload types specify specific codecs, such as for MPEG-4 streams, DV format video, or Enhanced Variable Rate Codec (EVRC) Speech [10] (EVRC is of special interest for VoIP and mobile services).

The highly structured and open approach of the RTP payload and format specifications has led to a rich portfolio of standard payloads for the most used audio and video codecs.

RTP also allows dynamic payloads, which are defined at the initiation of a session.

## Multimedia Server Recording/Playback Control

The Real-Time Streaming Protocol [11] is an application level protocol for the control of the delivery of data with real-time properties, such as audio/visual media using RTP. Readers may think of recording video sessions and replaying them over the Internet with playback controls, such as found in popular Internet sound and video players. The protocol is similar in syntax and operation to HTTP/1.1, so that extension mechanisms to HTTP also can be added, in most cases, to RTSP. However, RTSP differs in a number of aspects, such as:

- RTSP introduces new methods.
- RTSP servers maintain state, contrary to Web servers.
- Data is carried out-of-band, such as in RTP packets.
- RTSP has the notion of the request URI pointing to the desired service.

RTSP is similar in many ways to SIP in its approach to protocol design. Also in common with SIP, RTSP uses Web security mechanisms and can use different transport mechanisms such as UDP and TCP.

## Session Description

The Session Description Protocol (SDP) [12] is rather a session description format than a protocol. The description of the session parameters are used by SIP for session initiation. SDP will be covered in more detail in Chapter 5, *SIP Overview.*

## Session Announcements

The Session Announcement Protocol (SAP) [13] is a multicast session announcement protocol. SAP advertises multicast sessions by stating the specific multicast address and time information, and it carries a payload that describes the session. In some ways, SAP is analogous to the TV Guide where information about the channel, time, and program is provided.

## Session Invitation

The Session Initiation Protocol (SIP) is the object of this entire book.

## Authentication and Key Distribution

Messages used by the protocols in the Internet multimedia conferencing architecture can be signed and encrypted using the "Pretty Good Privacy" data formats specified in Atkins, et al. [14].

The Key Exchange Algorithm (KEA) for X.509-type certificates over the Internet, used with PGP, are specified in the Internet X.509 Public Key Infrastructure [15].

# Summary

The architecture and protocols of the Internet multimedia conferencing architecture have been discussed in this chapter. IP multimedia makes use of various network and transport layer protocols, such as IP multicast and protocols for quality of service. The family of Internet application layer protocols: RTP/RTCP, SAP, SDP, SIP, and others were developed for multimedia in this architecture. Internet multimedia leverages the entire suite of protocols in designing the complete network and applications for multimedia.

# References

[1] "Internetworking Multimedia" by Jon Crowcroft, Mark Handley, Ian Wakeman. Morgan Kaufmann Publishers; ISBN: 1558605843, London, New York, 1999.

[2] V. Cerf. "The Catenet Model for Internetworking," Information Processing Techniques Office, Defense Advanced Research Projects Agency, IEN 48, July 1978.

[3] Y. Rekhter and T. Li. RFC 2002: "Implications of Various Address Allocation Policies for Internet Routing," IETF, October 1996.

[4] H. Holbrook and B. Cain. "Source Specific Multicast," IETF Internet draft, 2001, work in progress,.

[5] M. Handley, et al. "The Internet Multimedia Conferencing Architecture," expired Internet draft, IETF, 2000.

[6] R. Braden, L. Zhang, S. Berson, and S. Herzog. RFC 2205: "Resource Reservation Protocol (RSVP)," IETF, 1997.

[7] S. Blake, D. Black, E. Davies, Z. Wang, and W. Weiss. RFC 2475: "An Architecture for Differentiated Services," IETF, 1998.

[8] Y. Bernet, et al. RFC 2998: "A Framework for Integrated Services Operation over Diffserv Networks," IETF, 2000.

[9] H. Schulzrinne, S. Casner, R. Frederick, and V. Jacobson. RFC 1889: "RTP: A Transport Protocol for Real-Time Applications," IETF, 1996.

[10] A. H. Li. "An RTP Payload Format for EVRC Speech," IETF Internet draft, June 2001, work in progress.

[11] H. Schulzrinne, A. Rao, and R. Lanphier. RFC 2326: "Real-Time Streaming Protocol (RTSP)," IETF, 1998.

[12] M. Handley and V. Jacobson. RFC 2327: "SDP: Session Description Protocol," IETF, April 1998.

[13] M. Handley, C. Perkins, and E. Wheelan. RFC 2974: "Session Announcement Protocol," IETF, October 2000.

[14] D. Atkins, W. Stallings, and P. Zimmermann. RFC 1991: "PGP Message Exchange Formats," IETF, August 1996.

[15] R. Housley and W. Polk. RFC 2528: "Internet X.509 Public Key Infrastructure," IETF, March 1999.

CHAPTER 5

# SIP Overview

In this chapter, an overview of the operation of the SIP protocol will be given, followed by a discussion of its basic functions. We start the overview with the topic on what makes SIP special and what the properties of a SIP enabled network are. A tutorial section explaining how SIP works, to complement the rest of the book focused on what SIP does, follows this. Call-flow diagrams are used as examples throughout to illustrate the protocol.

## What Makes SIP Special

We will try here to provide a summary for readers who have no special interest in protocols of why SIP has the capabilities to redefine communications, as they migrate from the telephone network to the Internet. As we will see, SIP combines the features of the Advanced Intelligent Network (AIN) from the telecom world for fixed and mobile telephony, with Internet features for email, Web, transactions, and entertainment. To illustrate SIP concepts, we will introduce the notion of a SIP-enabled IP network.

## SIP-Enabled Network

Figure 5.1 shows the elements of a SIP-enabled IP communication network. The network is composed of:

- **SIP endpoints.** SIP endpoints such as phones, gateways, and various types of computers. A SIP endpoint is a computer that understands the SIP protocol. These can be general-purpose computers such as PCs, workstations, and handheld computers, or embedded devices such as IP telephones or other IP devices. SIP endpoints are fully qualified Internet hosts, as defined in RFCs 1122 and 1123. Internet hosts are very different from telecommunication devices, such as phones, fax machines, or mobile phones in the sense that: (1) they may use the services of any other host on the IP network, and (2) they may run any and all applications the user may desire. The user can direct communications via any service provider and can load any application, similar to other services on the Internet. Depending on the service and user preferences, most communication services can also be controlled end-to-end without support from the network for call setup. There are two types of SIP endpoints:

  - User devices such as phones and personal computers.

  - Gateways to other networks, especially IP telephony gateways that use CAS, Q.931, or SS7 signaling. Other gateways can connect to

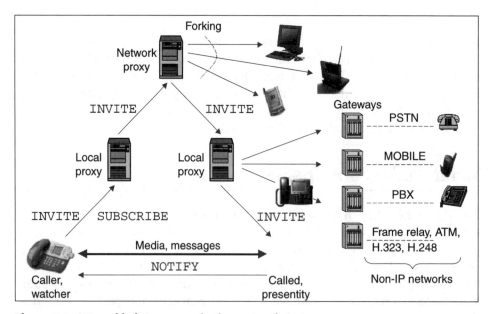

**Figure 5.1** SIP-enabled IP communication network.

voice over ATM or frame-relay networks to H.323 networks and device control networks, such as those found in certain IP PBXs and so called softswitches, using MGCP, MEGACO, or H.248 master/slave protocols.

- **SIP servers.** A SIP server is a computer in a network that performs special functions at the request of SIP endpoints. Servers typically act in response to SIP endpoint requests, but also can initiate functions on their own. The server can be under the management of an individual end user, corporate department, enterprise IT department, or service provider. There is no requirement that the SIP server be on the same network as the SIP endpoints that use it. The only requirement is that the server be reachable via an IP network.

Most users have no desire to understand the internal working and manage the services they use, and there are also security and technical reasons to place services on dedicated servers in the network, where they can be accessed from anywhere and used with various communications devices. SIP servers accomplish the functions found in the telecom AIN, in email systems, and in Web servers, as well as new functions specific to SIP. SIP servers can be stateless, similar to other Internet devices. This ensures very fast response time and avoids failures in the network to disable calls, since the call state is kept at the periphery of the network and not in the core. Users do not depend on any potential central points of failure in the network and can communicate as long as they have working end devices.

Using SIP, a caller can establish a session to the called party without knowing exactly where the other endpoint may be and the SIP servers will route the call to the destination. The route to the destination can be forked in the network so as to find the other endpoints. The same infrastructure also can serve for an instant message and presence service. A watcher can subscribe to a presentity and receive messages from the presentity. The watcher and presentity can exchange short text messages using SIP itself, or RTP packets for any other communications media such as audio, various data applications, video, or games, for instant communications.

Endpoints and servers benefit from a long list of protocol features of SIP:

- **Web-style and telephony-type addressing.** SIP devices can use URIs that are location independent and URLs that point to a specific domain host. Addresses can take the form of email addresses or telephone numbers, with clearly defined options for E.164 public telephone numbers and private numbering plans.

- **Registration.** Devices connected to the network are registered so as to route calls to and from the device. Users may register themselves using their ID to get access to their particular information and services, independent from the device registration. This is similar to email access from Web kiosks or Internet cafes. Such dynamic routing to and from the user is accomplished without needing "switch translations" or other static routing tables to be managed.

- **Security.** SIP is designed to use the Internet security mechanisms to protect sensitive signaling information from various types of attack. User location and traffic patterns can be kept confidential. SIP security can be quite complex and uses the advances of all generic IP security mechanisms.

- **Redirect.** A SIP server can redirect a request to another address, similar to the core function of the AIN.

- **Proxy.** SIP proxy servers will forward the request of the user to another server that can provide the requested service, such as voice mail, conferencing, or presence information.

- **Forking.** A request from a user can be forwarded in several directions simultaneously, such as when trying various locations where the called party may be found.

- **Rendezvous and presence.** The active form of rendezvous consists of routing a request for call setup to another server or endpoint where the desired service may be performed, such as communication with an individual, or with a machine. The passive form of rendezvous consists of presence information; that is, letting someone know that a party of interest is connected to the network and its communication state, such as available or busy.

- **Mobility.** Users may have many communication devices such as phones, fax machines, computers, palm computers, and pagers—at home, at work, and while traveling. User devices can be attached to various types of networks if proper gateways are provided: IP, PSTN, mobile telephony, wireless mobile data, or paging. SIP call setup can proceed without regard to the type of network or type of device the parties may use at a certain instance.

- **User preferences.** Callers can specify how servers and the network should handle their requests and also specify what type of service is desired or acceptable, who they would like to reach, and who they would like to avoid, for example, to avoid making calls to busy lines or to speak to machines. Called parties can specify how to handle incoming calls, depending on a very large set of criteria such as who the caller is, where the call is coming from, time of day, and the preferred communication device.

■ **Routing control.** The route taken by SIP messages can be specified and recorded for various services.

Some, but not all of the preceding features are known from the AIN and others from email and the Web. It is the combination of all these features that makes SIP unique. Last but not least, SIP has unique features of interest to developers and service providers that are not available in telecommunication networks:

■ The similarity of SIP to HTTP facilitates easy service creation by a very large community of software developers that may be familiar with Web site development.

■ SIP is text based and easy to debug without using specialized test equipment. SIP messages are seen on standard data analyzers in the very form shown in this introduction.

## Watching How Sausages Are Being Made

We believe the style in which SIP has been developed is another feature that is equal in importance to what gets actually written in the standard.

### Open Standards Development Process

SIP is a product of the Internet Engineering Task Force (IETF), a loosely organized group of individual developers, service providers, and researchers dedicated to the evolution of the Internet and its protocols. The development of SIP in the IETF mirrors many other developments that have contributed to the success of the Internet. The SIP protocol development is a completely open process where everybody, from anywhere, can follow the online postings and discussions and make technical contributions. There are no fees for participating, except a moderate attendance fee to cover the cost of IETF meeting logistics. The conference fees also provide funding for the IETF secretariat who edits and publishes the Requests For Comments (RFCs) document series. Nothing in SIP involves intellectual property rights claimed by organizations or individuals, and free code and testing facilities are available on the Internet in addition to the ample technical information.

### Contributors

Technical discussions conducted by email and concluded in face-to-face IETF meetings are moderated by some of the most recognized academics and industry experts in the field, regardless of the size or origin of the organization from which they come. The authors of the base SIP protocol standard and its extensions are clearly identified and can be contacted by anyone for discussions regarding their contributions. The SIP discussion mail is mostly populated by hands-on developers exchanging notes on issues with running code on their machines.

### Surge of Creativity

The completely open and collaborative environment for SIP has generated the largest number of technical contributions experienced in any other area of Internet technology, from many individuals, working for various organizations, small and large, from all over the world. The top problem facing the chairs of the IETF SIP Working Group (WG) is managing the very large number of technical contributions. Various subgroups have been created within the SIP WG to cope with this problem.

### The SIP Standard Is Based on Running Code

Contributors to the SIP WG bring to the table experience from building SIP products and SIP services. Numerous interoperability tests are conducted on a regular basis as SIP matures, so that features are proven before declaring them part of the standard.

The abundance of SIP implementations across the industry is the result of this working style in the development of SIP.

## What SIP Is Not

The virtual explosion in proposals to extend the SIP protocol to solve various problems has resulted in much discussion about whether a particular application is well suited to SIP or not. Some of the results of this discussion are summarized here. A more detailed discussion of this topic can be found in the SIP extension guidelines document [1].

SIP is a protocol for initiating, modifying, and terminating interactive sessions. SIP is not a protocol for device control or remote procedure calls (RPC). It is not a transport protocol—it can carry small message body attachments, but not large chunks or streams of data. SIP is not a resource reservation protocol, since the path of SIP messages generally does not reflect the path of the resulting media. SIP also is not a PSTN replacement protocol—its approach is very different from telecommunications call models and telecommunication signaling protocols. SIP can interwork with the PSTN through gateways, but this is not the primary function of SIP. In addition, SIP is not a session management protocol, but only a session setup protocol.

SIP is not a VoIP protocol, although VoIP is one possible service that can be implemented over a SIP-enabled network. SIP is purely a signaling protocol, and makes no specification on media types, descriptions, services, etc. This is in comparison to a VoIP umbrella protocol such as H.323, which specifies all aspects of signaling, media, features, services, and session control, similar to the other ISDN family of protocols from which it is derived.

# Introduction to SIP

SIP is a text-encoded protocol based on elements from the Hyper Text Transport Protocol (HTTP) [2], which is used for Web browsing, and also the Simple Mail Transport Protocol (SMTP) [3], which is used for e-mail on the Internet. SIP was developed by the IETF Multiparty Multimedia Session Control (MMUSIC) Working Group as part of the Internet Multimedia Conferencing Architecture [4], but has since gained its own SIP WG within the IETF, and has also spawned new related working groups: SIPPING and SIMPLE, besides PINT that also relies on SIP. As the name implies, the primary function of SIP is session initiation (setup), but it also has other important uses and functions, such as notifying for presence and short messaging. SIP is used for peer-to-peer communications—that is, both parties in the call are considered equals, there is no master or slave. However, SIP uses a client-server transaction model similar to HTTP, as described in the next section. A SIP client generates a SIP request. A SIP server responds to the request by generating a response. During a session, a SIP endpoint will typically switch between being a client and a server, depending on if it is initiating or responding to a request.

## Elements of a SIP Network

There are three main elements in a SIP network: User Agents, Servers, and Location servers.

### *User Agents*

User agents are the end devices in a SIP network. They originate SIP requests to establish media sessions and send and receive media. A user agent can be a SIP phone, or SIP client software running on a PC or palmtop. Alternatively, a user agent can be a gateway to another network, such as a Public Switched Telephone Network (PSTN) gateway, which allows a SIP phone to receive and make calls to the PSTN.

A User Agent Client (UAC) is the part of the user agent that initiates requests, while the User Agent Server (UAS) is the part of the user agent that generates responses to received requests. Every SIP user agent contains both a UAC and a UAS. During the course of a session, both parts are typically used.

This is different from most other client/server architectures, such as Web browsing. During a Web browsing session, a PC is always the HTTP client (Web browser software) and the Web server is always the HTTP server.

SIP user agents are usually assumed to be intelligent, in the sense they are part of a fully qualified Internet host, as defined in RFC 1121 and RFC 1122 [7],[8], and support many other basic Internet protocols, including DHCP, DNS, and IMCP.

## Servers

Servers are intermediary devices that are located within the SIP-enabled network and assist user agents in session establishment and other functions. There are three types of SIP servers defined in RFC 2543: Proxy, Redirect, and Registrar servers:

**SIP proxy.** A *SIP proxy* receives SIP requests from a user agent or another proxy and forwards or proxies the request to another location.

**Redirect server.** A *redirect server* receives a request from a user agent or proxy and returns a redirection response (3xx), indicating where the request should be retried.

**Registrar server.** A *registrar server* receives SIP registration requests and updates the user agent's information into a location server or other database.

---

**FINDING SIP SERVERS**

SIP servers can be found using a number of schemes. User agents are typically configured with IP addresses of a primary and secondary SIP proxy server, in much the same way that a Web browser has a default Web page that it loads on initialization. This proxy server is sometimes referred to as the outbound proxy since a user agent will route outgoing messages to that proxy.

Proxies can also be located using a DNS lookup, in which the domain name from a SIP URL is extracted and the IP address of the proxy server which supports that domain is found. This proxy is sometimes called an incoming proxy, since it is used to route incoming calls for that particular domain.

A SIP registrar server can be hand configured in the device or can be located using IP multicast. Registrar servers listen at the well-known SIP multicast address such as sip.mcast.net and can receive registrations. A SIP registrar server often can be located by sending a registration request to an outbound proxy, which then proxies the request to a registrar server. In this way, SIP servers can be located by sending requests to other SIP servers, as part of the address resolution process described for SIP in the next section.

SIP proxy, redirect, and registrar servers are purely signaling relay elements—they have no media capabilities and do not initiate requests except on behalf of a user agent.

### Location Servers

A location server is a general term used in RFC 2543 for a database. The database may contain information about users such as URLs, IP addresses, scripts, features, and other preferences. It also may contain routing information about the SIP-enabled network, including the locations of proxies, gateways, and other location servers. User agents generally do not interact directly with a location server, but go through a proxy, redirect, or registrar server. SIP servers use a non-SIP protocol to query, update, and retrieve records from the location server in the course of routing a SIP message.

The role of these elements will be discussed in terms of SIP functions in the next section.

## SIP Methods and Response Codes

The growing set of SIP request types, known as *methods*, are shown in Table 5.1. The first six methods are defined in RFC 2543 [5], the base SIP specifica-

**Table 5.1**  SIP Methods

| METHOD | DESCRIPTION |
| --- | --- |
| INVITE | Session setup |
| ACK | Acknowledgment of final response to INVITE |
| BYE | Session termination |
| CANCEL | Pending session cancellation |
| REGISTER | Registration of a user's URL |
| OPTIONS | Query of options and capabilities |
| INFO | Midcall signaling transport |
| PRACK | Provisional response acknowledgment |
| COMET | Preconditions met notification |
| REFER | Transfer user to a URL |
| SUBSCRIBE | Request notification of an event |
| UNSUBSCRIBE | Cancel notification of an event |
| NOTIFY | Transport of subscribed event notification |
| MESSAGE | Transport of an instant message body |

tion. The rest are extensions to SIP, and are defined in separate RFCs or Internet drafts that are working group items that will shortly become RFCs. New methods are continually being proposed to add additional functionality to the protocol. As of this writing, some extensions are proposed for the Third Generation wireless Partnership Project (3GPP).

Responses in SIP are numerical. Many response codes have been borrowed from HTTP in addition to the newly created ones. SIP response codes are divided into six classes, identified by the first digit of the code, as shown in Table 5.2.

The response codes are a good illustration of the resemblance of SIP to HTTP. The response code "404 Not Found" is similar to Web browser error codes.

SIP requests and responses are composed of either the request method or response code, followed by a list of fields called *headers*, which are similar to the headers in an e-mail message. In fact some, such as To, From, Subject, and Date, have an identical meaning.

An example SIP Request message is shown in Table 5.3 along with the minimum required set of headers and a line by line description.

The details of SIP headers will be discussed as needed in the explanations that follow. For a full description and examples of all SIP headers see [5].

# SIP Functions

The SIP protocol will be introduced in terms of some of the basic functions of a communications network: address resolution, session-related functions (including session setup, media negotiation, session modification, session termination and cancellation, mid-call signaling, call control, QoS call setup), and non-session-related functions such as mobility, message transport, event sub-

**Table 5.2** SIP Response Code Classes

| CLASS | DESCRIPTION |
|-------|-------------|
| 1xx | Provisional or Informational: Request is progressing but not yet complete |
| 2xx | Success: Request has completed successfully |
| 3xx | Redirection: Request should be tried at another location |
| 4xx | Client Error: Request was not completed due to error in request, can be retried when corrected |
| 5xx | Server Error: Request was not completed due to error in recipient, can be retried at another location |
| 6xx | Global Failure: Request has failed and should not be retried again |

**Table 5.3** SIP Example with Line by Line Description

| LINE | DESCRIPTION |
|---|---|
| INVITE sip: UserB@there.com SIP/2.0 | The first line of a SIP request does not contain headers, but starts with the name of the method (INVITE), followed by a space, the **Request-URI,** in this case **sip:UserB@there.com,** which is the destination address of the request, a space, then the current version of SIP (2.0). Each line ends with a CRLF (Carriage Return and Line Feed). |
| Via: SIP/2.0/UDP 4.3.2.1:5060 | The Via header contains the version of SIP (2.0) and the transport protocol (UDP) followed by the IP Address (4.3.2.1) or host name of the originator of the request and the port number (5060, the well-known SIP port number). Any server that forwards the request adds a Via header with its own address to the message and the port number at which it wants to receive responses. |
| To: User B <sip:UserB@there.com> | The To header contains a display name (User B) followed by the URL of the destination enclosed in angle brackets < > (sip:UserB@there.com). |
| From: User A <sip:UserA@here.com> | The From header contains a display name (User A) followed by the URL of the request recipient originator in < > (sip:UserA@here.com). |
| Call-ID: 4598998103413 @4.3.2.1 | The Call-ID header contains a unique identifier for this call (session). It is made up here of a locally unique random identifier followed by @ and the globally unique hostname or IP Address, making the entire string unique. All requests and responses during the call will contain this same Call-ID. Unique Call-ID strings can be generated in many other ways. |
| CSeq: 1 INVITE | CSeq is the Command Sequence number, which contains an integer (1) a space, then the request method (INVITE). Each successive request (command) during the call will have a higher CSeq number. The caller and called parties each maintain their own separate CSeq counts. |
| Contact: <sip:UserA@4.3.2.1> | Contact contains one or more SIP URLs which provide information for the other party in the session to contact User A. |
| Content-Length: 126 | Content-Length is the octet (byte) count of the message body (126) which follows the list of SIP headers and is separated from the headers by a single CRLF. A Content-Length of 0 indicates no message body. |

scription and notification, authentication, and extensibility. Each of these will be discussed and explained in turn.

## Address Resolution

Address resolution is one of the most important functions of the SIP protocol. The SIP address resolution process usually begins with a Uniform Resource Indicator (URI) and ends with a username at an IP address. This resolution from a general name to an actual user at a host is extremely powerful in that various types of mobility and portability are automatically implemented. Address resolution can be performed by both user agents and servers.

The address resolution process can involve the following steps:

- DNS SRV [9] lookup (see Chapter 14, *DNS and ENUM*),
- ENUM [10] lookup (see Chapter 14, *DNS and ENUM*),
- Location server lookup, as described in RFC 2543.

While it is possible that a SIP user agent may have access to a location server, this lookup is usually performed by a proxy or redirect server on behalf of a user agent.

In general, the address resolution process involves multiple steps and multiple SIP message hops. This allows user agents and proxies to perform request routing on a hop-by-hop basis. Each proxy consults a location server and modifies the Request-URI accordingly, then forwards the request to the next hop. This process continues until the request is delivered to the destination. Note that routing of the responses in SIP does not involve address resolution—all responses route back through the same set of proxies as the request. This is possible due to the `Via` header chain in the request message.

Consider the request routing example of Figure 5.2. This example does not show outgoing and incoming proxy servers, but just one proxy server in the middle. Such a simple network configuration may apply for routing calls within a small private IP network. The SIP user agent A wishes to send a general SIP request to another user agent B identified by the SIP URL `sip:UserB@there.com`. The SIP telephone A first performs a DNS SRV query to locate the proxy server for the there.com domain, which is `sipproxy.there.com` in steps 1 and 2. The SIP request 3 is then sent to the IP address of `sipproxy.there.com`. This proxy then consults a location service in step 5, which locates the current registration URL for user B, which is `tel:+65123456789`. The proxy then sends an ENUM DNS query (described in detail in Chapter 14, *DNS and ENUM*) in step 7 to DNS to find the corresponding IP address, which is returned and used as `sip:UserB@100.101.102.103` in step 9. The request is then routed to user B at that IP address, who returns a successful SIP response `200 OK` in step 10 to the proxy server. The proxy server forwards the success response `200 OK` in step 11 back to caller A.

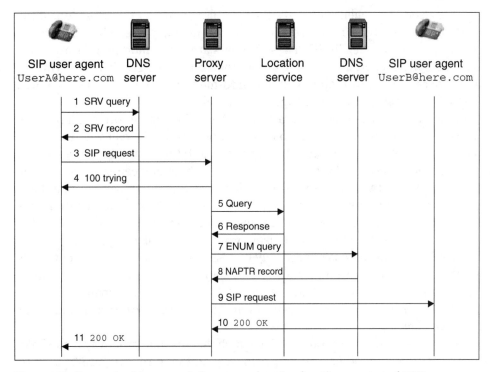

**Figure 5.2** Request address resolution example using location server and DNS.

The address resolution process in SIP is dynamic. A proxy can use *any* header present in a request and many other factors in routing decisions, including time of day, `From` header, and various request header fields for load-sharing or ACD applications.

Usually, this process of address resolution only occurs once at the start of a session. The results of the initial address resolution are cached and used in future requests between user agents.

## Session-Related Functions

Most SIP functions involve setting up sessions or occur during an established session. Although some applications of SIP do not make any use of session-related functions, most useful applications of SIP make use of these powerful functions.

### Session Setup

As the name of the protocol implies, session setup is the primary function of SIP. Being a polite protocol, SIP uses an `INVITE` request to set up a session between two user agents. The `INVITE` message usually contains a message body that describes the type of session the user agent wishes to establish.

A SIP user agent client initializes the To, From, and Call-ID headers at the start of the session. These are then used to uniquely identify this session, referred to as a call leg in SIP. These headers are never modified during a session, with the exception of adding tags to the To and/or From headers. This set of headers, plus any required media information represents the minimum amount of call state that a user agent must maintain.

In the event of a user agent "crash" or reboot, the state information must be recovered somehow for the call to continue; otherwise, the call will have to be re-initiated. Note here that in harmony with the Internet architecture, the call state can be maintained in the SIP endpoints, without any call state kept in the servers in the networks, if so desired. However, SIP proxy servers may keep transaction state during the call setup phase. Keeping the state in SIP endpoints makes the call setup independent of transient failures in the network, since the endpoints can use the state to retransmit messages for call setup.

The SIP session setup is a three-way handshake—the user agent client sends an INVITE request, receives a 200 OK response, then sends an ACK request (this will be written in shorthand as an INVITE/200/ACK exchange).

A session setup failure will result in an INVITE/4xx or 5xx or 6xx/ACK message exchange.

INVITE is the only method in SIP in which there is this three-way handshake involving ACK. All other SIP requests are of the form REQUEST/200 or REQUEST/4xx or 5xx or 6xx for a failure.

Figure 5.3 shows a successful session setup between two SIP phones involving an INVITE, two provisional responses (100 Trying and 180 Ringing), and a final response (200 OK), which receives an ACK. Zero or more provisional (1xx) responses can be sent prior to a final response.

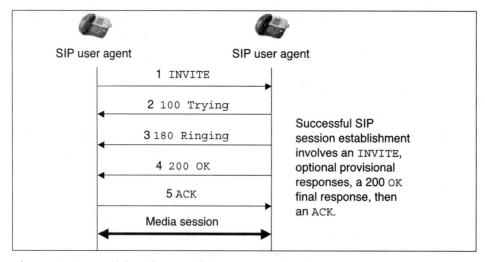

**Figure 5.3** Successful session establishment example using INVITE.

## TRANSPORT OF SIP MESSAGES OVER IP

SIP messages can be carried by any transport layer IP protocol, including Transmission Control Protocol (TCP) or User Datagram Protocol (UDP).

SIP has built-in reliability mechanisms so that it can use a "best effort" unreliable transport protocol such as UDP. When UDP is used, one SIP message is carried per UDP datagram. When TCP is used, a TCP connection is first opened between the user agent and the next hop (which could be directly to the other user agent or to a server). SIP messages are then sent over the connection.  If the connection closes during a pending transaction, the connection will need to be reopened. After the transaction has completed, the TCP connection can be closed. A new TCP connection would then have to be opened to send a re-INVITE or a BYE to close the session.

Note that a SIP message path with multiple hops can use UDP for some hops and TCP for other hops. The transport protocol used for a hop is recorded in the Via header along with the IP address and port number for sending responses. SIP messages can also be carried using other transport protocols such as Stream Control Transport Control (SCTP) developed by the IETF SIG-TRAN Working Group [11]. SCTP provides a reliable connection and additional functionality such as multihoming.

The choice of transport protocol is determined by the application.  Most simple SIP user agents, such as SIP phones and PC clients, use UDP for transport due to the simplicity of managing a UDP session compared to other transport protocols. Also, there is no setup delay in opening up a connection (like with TCP transport) before the SIP message exchange can begin. TCP is sometimes used between proxies, or in other applications where a more permanent SIP connection is useful. SCTP has been proposed in connections between proxies or between proxies and large PSTN gateways where a high throughput and low latency connection is needed.

Once established, a media session continues indefinitely without requiring further SIP signaling message exchange. If one party of the session wishes to modify or terminate the session, a new exchange of SIP signaling messages ensues.

This three-way handshake allows for forking, a parallel search initiated by a proxy, in which multiple successful responses can be returned for a single INVITE in a reliable way. Forking is supported with SIP to allow multiple destinations to be tried at the same time. This behavior is supported in the base SIP specification.

## *Media Negotiation*

Media negotiation is part of the INVITE/200/ACK sequence to establish a SIP session between two endpoints. SIP itself does not provide the media negotiation, but it enables media negotiation to occur between the user agents using the Session Description Protocol (SDP). SDP is not a true protocol, but is rather a text-based description language, which is defined by RFC 2327 [12]. It has both required and optional fields. Some of the required fields are included in a SIP message body but are not used, as will be shown next.

SDP was initially developed in the framework of the Internet multimedia architecture, together with SAP, as a sort of "TV Guide" for multicast multimedia sessions over the Internet. Some of the capabilities of SDP are therefore not used in SIP, such as advertising the origin of the session advertisement, the subject of the session, and the scheduling function based on starting and end time, with repeat features (the t=... line shown in the SDP Offer example). There have been recent proposals in the SIP WG discussion list to use XML instead, but the idea was rejected mainly due to the advantage of simplicity and fast processing of SDP.

The negotiation is an offer-response model in which one user agent proposes one or more media types, and the other user agent either accepts or declines each media session in a response. Referring again to Figure 5.2, the offer is usually made in the initial `INVITE` by the caller, and the response is carried in the `200 OK`. However, the caller can allow the called party to select the media session type by not sending SDP in the `INVITE`. In this case, the called party makes the offer in the `200 OK` and the caller responds in the `ACK`. In the SDP body attached to the SIP header, the user agents specify the media type, codec, IP address, and port number for each media stream. More than one codec can be specified for each media type. Once a user agent offers a codec, it must be prepared to receive media with that codec for the duration of the session.

## SDP Offer Example

The example SDP offer shown here and in Table 5.4 contains two media lines, one for video and one for audio. Each media line has two possible alternative codecs that the calling user agent supports.

```
v=0
o=
s=
c=IN IP4 128.2.3.1
t=
m=video 4004 RTP/AVP 14 26
a=rtpmap:14 MPA/90000
a=rtpmap:26 JBEG/90000
m=audio 4006 RTP/AVP 0 4
a=rtpmap:0 PCMU/8000
a=rtpmap:4 GSM/8000
```

**Table 5.4** SDP Offer Example with Line by Line Description

| LINE | DESCRIPTION |
|---|---|
| v=0 | Version - Current version number of SDP (0) - Not used by SIP |
| o=- | Origin - Not used by SIP |
| s=- | Subject - Not used by SIP |
| c=IN IP4 128.2.3.1 | Connection - network (IN for Internet), address  type (IP4 for IP Version 4) and address (128.2.3.1) |
| t=- | Time - start and stop time - not used by SIP |
| m=video 4004 RTP/ AVP 14 26 | Media - media type (video), port number (4004), type (RTP/AVP Profile), and number (Profiles 14 or 26) |
| a=rtpmap:14 MPA/ 90000 | Attribute - rtpmap lists attributes of RTP/AVP video profile 14 including codec (MPA) and sampling rate (90000 Hz). |
| a=rtpmap:26 JBEG/ 90000 | Attribute - rtpmap lists attributes of RTP/AVP video profile 26 including codec (JBEG) and sampling rate (90000 Hz). |
| m=audio 4006 RTP/ AVP 0 4 | Media - second media type (audio), port number (4006), type (RTP/AVP Profile), and number (Profiles 0 or 4) |
| a=rtpmap:0 PCMU/8000 | Attribute - rtpmap lists attributes of RTP/AVP audio profile 0 including codec (PCMU - PCM μ-Law) and sampling rate (8000 Hz). |
| a=rtpmap:4 GSM/8000 | Attribute - rtpmap lists attributes of RTP/AVP audio profile 4 including codec (GSM) and sampling rate (8000 Hz). |

In the response to this offer, shown here and in Table 5.5, the other party declines the video media session by setting the port number to 0, and accepts the audio session by selecting the GSM codec and returning a nonzero port number, as shown in the following SDP example.

```
v=0
o=
s=
c=IN IP4 16.22.3.1
t=
m=video 0 RTP/AVP 14
m=audio 6002 RTP/AVP 4
a=rtpmap:4 GSM/8000
```

Further negotiation and changes to the media can be accomplished using a re-INVITE once the session is established, as described in the next section on session modification.

This type of limited media negotiation capability is supported by SDP and hence in SIP. Work currently is underway to develop a successor to SDP, ten-

**Table 5.5** SDP Response Example with Line by Line Description

| LINE | DESCRIPTION |
|------|-------------|
| v=0 | Version - Current version number of SDP (0) - not used by SIP |
| o=- | Origin - not used by SIP |
| s=- | Subject - not used by SIP |
| c=IN IP4 16.22.3.1 | Connection - network (IN for Internet), address type (IP4 for IP version 4) and address (16.22.3.1) |
| t=- | Time - start and stop time - not used by SIP |
| m=video 0 RTP/AVP 14 | Media - media type (video), port number is set to zero, which indicates that the video session has been declined. |
| m=audio 62002 RTP/ AVP 4 | Media - media type (audio), port number (62002), type (RTP/AVP profile), and number (profile 4). By specifying a non-zero port number, the audio session has been accepted. |
| a=rtpmap:4 GSM/8000 | Attribute - rtpmap lists attributes of RTP/AVP audio profile 4 including codec (GSM) and sampling rate (8000 Hz). |

tatively called *SDPng* for Next Generation [13]. This new protocol will have more advanced media negotiation and description capabilities. It is likely that support of SDP will remain in the base SIP specification, with successors to SDP being optional to support.

## Session Modification

Once a session has been established using the INVITE/200/ACK sequence, it can be modified by another INVITE/200/ACK sequence, sometimes referred to as a re-INVITE. Since there only can be one pending SIP request of each type at a time, a re-INVITE cannot be sent until the initial INVITE has been completed with an ACK. The re-INVITE can be done by either party and uses the same To, From (including tags), and Call-ID as the INVITE. However, the SDP in the re-INVITE is assumed to replace the initial INVITE SDP, if the re-INVITE is successful. If the re-INVITE fails in any way or is refused, the original SDP and the original media session will continue until a BYE is sent by either party.

In the example of Figure 5.4, a call is set up between two user agents using the media description *sdp1*, carried in the initial INVITE and 200 OK response. The called party tries to change the session parameters by sending another INVITE with a new message body *sdp2'*. However, this is not acceptable to the other party, and the re-INVITE fails with a 405 Not Acceptable response. The media session continues using the initial media parameters. The called party tries one more time and this time the re-INVITE succeeds, and the old

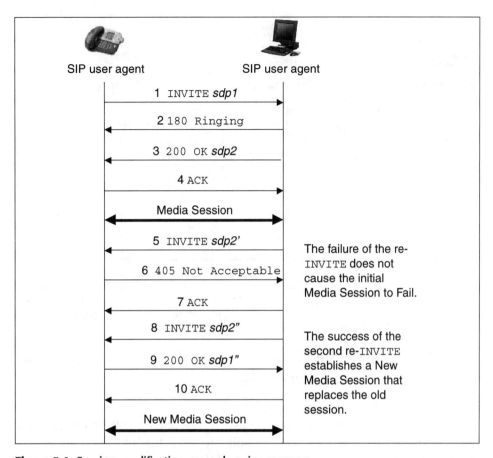

**Figure 5.4** Session modification example using INVITE.

media session is terminated and a new one using *sdp2"* and *sdp1"* is established. Note that the re-INVITEs do not usually generate provisional responses (such as 180 Ringing), since the two parties are already communicating with each other.

Note that a re-INVITE may change any of the media characteristics, including the session type, codec used, and even the source IP addresses and port number.

## Session Termination and Cancellation

Session termination and cancellation are two separate operations in SIP, but are often confused. Session termination occurs when either user agent sends a BYE referencing an existing call leg, that is, a session successfully established using the INVITE/200/ACK exchange. This is shown in the example of Figure 5.5.

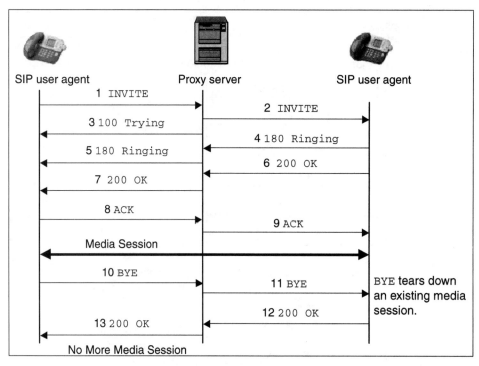

**Figure 5.5**  Session termination example using BYE.

Session cancellation occurs when a user agent ends a call before the call setup is complete and established. A similar action is that of the "stop" button on the browser. In this scenario, a user agent that has sent an INVITE, but has not yet received a final response (2xx, 3xx, 4xx, 5xx, or 6xx), sends a CANCEL request. A CANCEL can also be originated by a proxy to cancel individual legs in a forking proxy or parallel search.

While INVITE and BYE are end-to-end methods, CANCEL is an example of a SIP request that is a hop-by-hop request. A proxy receiving a CANCEL request immediately responds with a 200 OK response, then proxies the CANCEL on to the same set of destinations to which the original INVITE was sent.

A user agent receiving a CANCEL replies with a 200 OK if a final response has not yet been sent, or a 481 Transaction Unknown response if a final response has been sent. The latter corresponds to the "race" condition, where the CANCEL and final response "cross on the wire." In this condition, the user agent may have to send a BYE to cancel the call [6].

In the example of Figure 5.6, a user agent sends an INVITE request, then a CANCEL request. The INVITE is forwarded through two proxies to reach the destination user agent. Notice that the CANCEL request sent to the first proxy results in a 200 OK response to the CANCEL, and the CANCEL is forwarded to

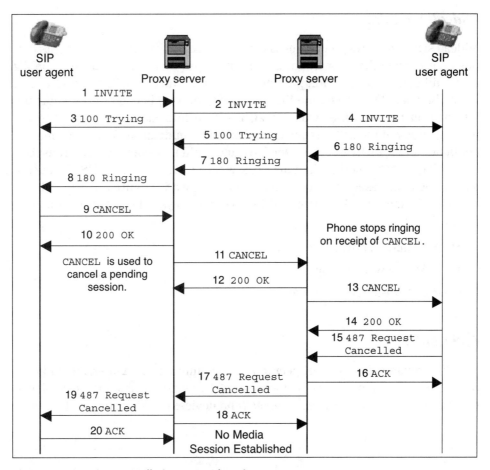

**Figure 5.6** Session cancellation example using CANCEL.

the next proxy. The second proxy immediately sends a 200 OK to the first proxy and forwards the CANCEL to the destination user agent. Finally, the user agent responds with a 200 OK to the CANCEL and a 487 Request Terminated response to the INVITE. The 487 response is acknowledged by the second proxy with an ACK, and is then forwarded to the first proxy, which is eventually received by the calling user agent, which then knows that the pending session was successfully cancelled. (Unsuccessful final responses such as 3xx, 4xx, 5xx, or 6xx, are always acknowledged on a hop-by-hop basis. Only a 200 OK receives an end-to-end ACK.) The user agent then has completed two transactions: a CANCEL/200 and an INVITE/487/ACK transaction.

Since it is possible that a CANCEL may be sent at the same time as a 200 OK response, the user agent must be prepared to send an ACK and a BYE to the 200 OK even after sending the CANCEL.

## Midcall Signaling

Midcall signaling is a signaling message exchange between two user agents that does not change the session parameters between them. If a midcall signaling event did change the session parameters (that is, the SDP), then a re-INVITE would be used. Otherwise, the SIP INFO method [14] is used to transport the information between the two user agents. The information is carried in the message body of the INFO request. For example, midcall signaling information contained in an ISDN User-to-User Message (USR) message can be transported using the INFO method in a network where ISDN User Part (ISUP) encapsulation is being used. An example of this is shown in Figure 5.7, where basic SIP-to-ISUP mapping is performed by two gateways. The ISUP messages in Figure 5.7 are:

- **IAM.** Initial address message
- **ANM.** Answer message
- **USR.** User-to-user message.

## Call Control

The SIP architecture is one of peer-to-peer communication and end-to-end control. For example, a proxy may not issue a BYE request terminating a call—it can only be issued by one of the user agents (end devices) participating in the call.

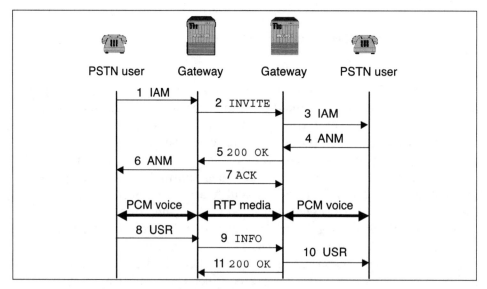

**Figure 5.7** Midcall signaling example using INFO.

However, the ability for a third party to direct or control a call between two other parties can be extremely useful in various service implementations. For example, an embedded SIP URL in a Web page, when selected, could cause a desktop SIP phone to place a call to the desired URL. Or, third-party call control can be used to implement a Web call center or Automatic Call Distribution (ACD) feature, useful for handling calls to customer service numbers, where the controller receives the call and routes it based on a number of factors such as available agents and time of day.

There are two ways of implementing third-party control. The first uses a controller that receives the SIP INVITE request, answers it, then proxies the INVITE to a third party. The controller then stays in the signaling path, swapping SDP from one leg to another, and transparently controlling the call. The second way uses the REFER method [15] to initiate the third-party control.

In the example of Figure 5.8, user A and user B establish a session. A then refers B to initiate a session, with user C using a REFER request. A then terminates the session with B, while B establishes a new session with C.

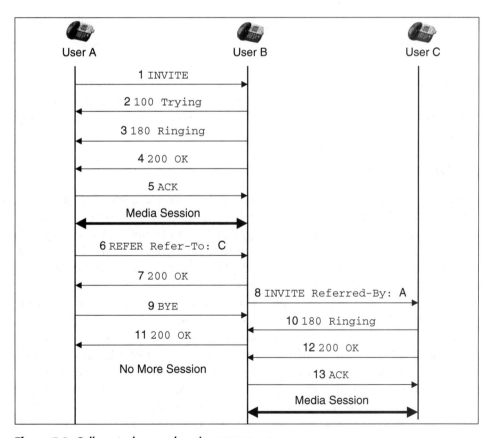

**Figure 5.8** Call control example using REFER.

The REFER request has the following form:

```
REFER sip:UserB@there.com SIP/2.0
Via: SIP/2.0/UDP 4.3.2.1:5060
To: User B <sip:UserB@there.com>
From: User A <sip:UserA@here.com>
Call-ID: a5-32-43-12-77@4.3.2.1
CSeq: 2 REFER
Refer-To: <sip:UserC@anywhere.com>
Referred-By: <sip:UserA@here.com>;ref=<sip:UserC@anywhere.com>
Contact: <sip:UserA@4.3.2.1>
Content-Length: 0
```

The resulting INVITE message (message 8 in Figure 5.8) would then have the form:

```
INVITE sip:UserC@anywhere.com SIP/2.0
Via: SIP/2.0/UDP 100.101.102.103:5060
To: <sip:UserC@anywhere.com>
From: User B <sip:UserB@there.com>
Call-ID: 383874109476@there.com
CSeq: 67 INVITE
Contact: <sip:UserB@100.101.102.103>
Referred-By: <sip:UserA@here.com>;ref=<sip:UserC@anywhere.com>
Content-Length: ...
```

The Refer-To header in the REFER contains the URL to whom A is referring, while the Referred-By header identifies A as the referrer, and is passed to C in the INVITE so that C knows that B has been referred by A in initiating this session.

## Quality of Service Setup

Another important area in communications is the setting up of a Quality of Service (QoS) for the connection. QoS is supported in the network layer (IP layer 3) and in the link layer below (layer 2). QoS in IP networks is independent of any specific application and therefore the network need not be aware of the specifics of the applications, be it telephony, multimedia, financial transactions, or games. SIP is orthogonal to QoS.

Setting up an application, such as a commercial grade phone call with QoS, requires the support of valuable network resources; for example, giving priority to a media flow having a data rate of 90 kb/s for 30 minutes over a distance of 5000 km. The authorization required to provide the network resources for the SIP-initiated session involves complex procedures for authentication, authorization, and accounting (AAA) that go beyond the topics discussed here [16],[17],[18]. We will therefore limit the discussion of QoS for SIP only for the simple case where the AAA issues can be ignored. AAA and QoS for SIP are presented in Chapter 16.

SIP enables user agents to establish sessions using the `INVITE/200/ACK` exchange. However, in order to establish an IP session with QoS, a more complicated message exchange is required. The Integrated Services QoS protocol assumed in these examples is the Resource Reservation Protocol (RSVP) [19]. However, the approach described here for SIP also will work with other QoS approaches such as setting the type of service (TOS) bits in the IP header used in DiffServ [20].

A simplified approach to QoS would be to first establish a "best effort" session between user agents, then use a re-`INVITE` to set up the new QoS session. However, since the SIP messaging is completely independent of the media, it is entirely possible to successfully set up a session using SIP, only to have the session fail due to lack of bandwidth for the media, in which case this approach will fail. Also, there was a desire to mimic the behavior in the PSTN where the called party's phone will not ring if there are not sufficient resources (that is, trunks) to complete the call if answered. The approach described here was developed by the PacketCable consortium [21] for the Voice over Cable Modem project. The call flow is shown in Figure 5.9.

This call flow makes use of three extensions to SIP. The first is Early Media [22], which allows SDP to be present in the provisional `183 Session Progress` response. This allows an additional media (SDP) handshake between the user agents necessary to establish the QoS prior to the call being answered. The second is the Reliable Provisional Responses extension to SIP, which allows a lost provisional response such as a `183` to be detected and retransmitted (see the sidebar *Message Retransmissions in SIP*). The receipt of the `183` response is indicated by the Provisional Response ACKnowledgment (`PRACK`) [23] message. The third extension is the use of the preCOnditions MET (`COMET`) [24] method, which allows the UAS to indicate that the QoS preconditions have been met and the user may now be alerted, and the `180 Ringing` response sent. The call then continues as normal. Note that the need for QoS was indicated in the last line of the SDP of the initial `INVITE` request, as shown here with the attribute `qos: mandatory`.

```
     INVITE with mandatory QoS request
INVITE sip:UserB@there.com SIP/2.0
Via: SIP/2.0/UDP 100.101.102.103:5060
To: <sip:UserB@there.com>
From: User A <sip:UserA@here.com>
Call-ID: 5448kewl13981304oierek
CSeq: 1 INVITE
Contact: <sip:UserA@100.101.102.103>Content-Length: ...

v=0
c=IN IP4 100.101.102.102
m=audio 47172 RTP/AVP 0
```

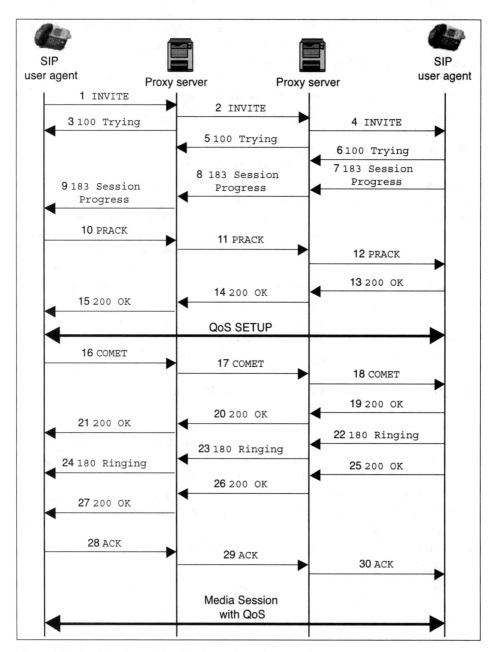

**Figure 5.9** Quality of service call setup using **PRACK** and **COMET**.

```
a=rtpmap:0 PCMU/8000
a=qos:mandatory
```

## Non-Session-Related Functions

Some SIP functions do not relate directly to session setup. These functions can occur outside of a session established using SIP.

### *Mobility*

The registration function of SIP is very similar to registration in cell phones. In a registration message, a user sends a proxy server the URL for which it wishes to receive calls. This built-in support of mobility is an extremely useful feature of SIP, and is one of the most cited benefits of the protocol over others. It is also this support of mobility that has lead to the application of the protocol in many new applications and its proposed use for call control in third-generation wireless networks. Note that as this work is ongoing, there are likely to be some additional SIP extensions developed for this application.

---

**MESSAGE RETRANSMISSIONS IN SIP**

The base SIP specification allows almost any lost request or response method to be automatically retransmitted. The sender of a SIP request using unreliable transport starts a timer, called T1 (default value is 500 ms). If a response is not received before the expiration of the timer, the request is retransmitted. If a provisional (1xx) response is received, the sender switches to a second, longer timer, called T2 (default value is 4 seconds). If the request itself is lost, the recipient will not have received it and will never generate a response. After the expiration of T1, the sender will resend the request. If the response to the request is lost, the sender will again resend the request. The recipient will recognize the request as a retransmission and retransmit its own response.

Handling of INVITE requests is slightly different than all other request types since it may take a long time for the call to be answered. The receipt of a provisional response to an INVITE does not switch to timer T2 but stops all retransmissions of the INVITE. A responder to an INVITE starts timer T1 when it sends a final response. If an ACK is not received, the responder resends the final response. This allows a lost INVITE, final response, or ACK to be detected and retransmitted.

The exceptions to this retransmission rule are provisional responses. Since provisional responses do not receive an ACK, there is no way for either party to know if one has been lost. The Reliable Provisional Response [23] extension to SIP was developed to allow a provisional response to be acknowledged with a PRACK, thus providing reliability for all requests and responses in SIP.

---

The SIP REGISTER request is used to accomplish this function. The request contains Contact headers which are the URLs being registered by the user. For example, a successful user agent registration is shown in Figure 5.10. The user initially registers his or her office SIP phone by sending a REGISTER message to the Registrar server. The Registrar updates the user's record in the location server and returns a 200 OK confirmation of the registration. Later in the day, the user leaves the office for home, where he or she cancels the office phone registration and registers the SIP home phone. (A mobile phone registration during the commute could also be envisaged.) Note that the protocol used to upload the registration to the location server or other database is not SIP. Incoming calls to the user's URL will now be routed to the IP address of the SIP home phone. Also note that the home phone need not be SIP for this precall mobility. The user could also register a PSTN phone using Web access, email or having the registration preprogrammed for certain times.

A user agent can be configured to automatically register upon initialization, at preset intervals, or whenever a new user signs on to the particular device.

Registration is not limited to a single URL. Multiple URLs can be used in a list of a number of alternative locations in a preferred order, or may list multiple possible services such as SIP, PSTN, and e-mail. For example, consider the following example REGISTER message:

```
SIP client to Registrar
REGISTER sip:registrar.wcom.com SIP/2.0
Via: SIP/2.0/UDP 4.3.2.1:5060
To: User A <sip:UserA@here.com>
From: User A <sip:UserA@here.com>
Call-ID: a5-32-43-12-77@4.3.2.1
```

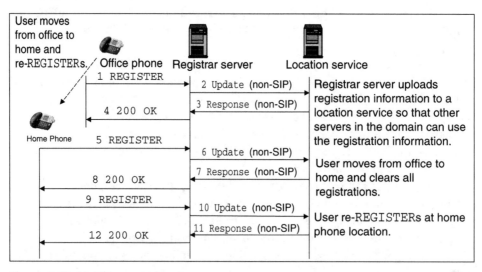

**Figure 5.10** Mobility example using **REGISTER**.

```
CSeq: 1 REGISTER
Contact: <sip:UserA@4.3.2.1>;class=personal
Contact: <sip:UserA-mesg-deposit@voicemail.provider.com>
 ;feature=voicemail
Contact: <sip:+3145551212@gateway.com;user=phone>;class=business
Contact: <sip:+3145553333@cellphone.com;user=phone>;mobility=mobile
Contact: <tel:+1-314-555-1212>
Contact: <mailto:UserA@here.com>
Content-Length: 0
```

**Registrar to SIP client**
```
SIP/2.0 200 OK
Via: SIP/2.0/UDP 4.3.2.1:5060
To: User A <sip:UserA@here.com>
From: User A <sip:UserA@here.com>
Call-ID: a5-32-43-12-77@4.3.2.1
CSeq: 1 REGISTER
Contact: <sip:UserA@4.3.2.1>;class=personal;expires=3600
Contact: <sip:UserA-mesg-deposit@voicemail.provider.com>
 ;feature=voicemail ;expires=3600
Contact: <sip:+3145551212@gateway.com;user=phone>;class=business
 ;expires=3600
Contact: <sip:+3145553333@cellphone.com;user=phone>;mobility=mobile
 ;expires=3600
Contact: <tel:+1-314-555-1212>
Contact: <mailto:UserA@here.com>
Content-Length: 0
```

The 200 OK response to a REGISTER echoes the six Contact URLs that have been successfully registered. In this case, a query to the Location server for the SIP URL sip:UserA@here.com would return the six Contact URLs that were registered. The first four are SIP URLs that can be used to reach user A. The last two URLs represent user A's telephone number, which could be reached via the PSTN (or through SIP and a gateway), and the e-mail address of user A.

The SIP URLs in this example contain parameter extensions to Contact, which are defined in the Caller Preferences document [25], which allow a user agent to identify information about the type of device identified by the URL. For example, the first URL is identified as a personal URL, the second as voice mail, the third business, and the fourth as a cell phone.

Normally, a SIP server would process a list of URLs by trying the first Contact header URI, then moving to the second, etc., assuming a sequential search. However, if the server received a request with an Accept-Contact: *;feature=voicemail header, the server would match the feature requested to the second Contact header, resulting in this URI being tried first. (The * is a wildcard that matches against any URI address part.) Or, a request with an Accept-Contact: *;class=buisness would result in the third URI being tried first.

The `Reject-Contact` header works in a similar way, but with the reverse result. In this way, SIP allows user preferences to be carried with a request message. For example, a SIP request sent to a user's URL could be routed to any number of devices, depending on where the user is currently registered and what features and scripts are activated in the called party's SIP network. A SIP request also could be sent containing a `Reject-Contact` [25] header indicating that the requestor does not want to reach voice mail, for example.

When a SIP message is processed by servers, it is usually up to the server whether to proxy or redirect the request and whether to invoke a serial or parallel search (forking). However, the use of the `Request-Disposition` header allows the requestor to have some input. For example, a request containing a `Request-Disposition: proxy, sequential` indicates that the requestor wishes the request to be proxied, instead of redirected, and to have a serial search as opposed to a parallel search. The Caller Preferences document [25] describes all the options. Note that a proxy that does not implement a particular feature may simply ignore the header. The Caller Preferences draft includes pseudo-code describing the exact URI and parameter matching, and the interaction of the preference values, if present.

Note that the use of the caller preferences defined `Contact` header extensions is useful in SIP common gateway interface (CGI) and call processing language (CPL) scripting for SIP service creation.

The use of the `Requires: prefs` header allows a user agent to require that a registrar support caller preferences and will act accordingly.

## Message Transport

The `MESSAGE` method [26] simply transports the message body to the destination URI within or outside an established session. For example, consider the following instant message (IM) transported using SIP:

```
SIP message
MESSAGE im:UserB@there.com SIP/2.0
Via: SIP/2.0/UDP 4.3.2.1
To: User B <im:UserB@there.com>
From: User A <im:UserA@here.com>
Call-ID: a5-32-43-12-77@4.3.2.1
CSeq: 1 MESSAGE
Content-Type: text/plain
Content-Length: 15

Hi, how are you?
```

Notice that the URIs in the example are IM URIs instead of SIP URIs. When user B receives the message, a `200 OK` response would be generated. Unlike the `INFO` method, which can only be sent when there is an established session between two user agents, a `MESSAGE` request can be sent at any time. SIP support for presence and instant messaging includes SIP messages, as in this example. The other methods in SIP to support instant communications are event subscription and notification for presence.

## Event Subscription and Notification

The ability to request and receive notification when a certain event occurs is supported in SIP by the SUBSCRIBE and NOTIFY request types [27],[28]. In addition, the UNSUBSCRIBE [28] request has been defined to cancel a subscription request. For example, the automatic callback feature in telephony can be used when the called party is busy (off the hook) and the caller wishes to be notified as soon as the called party is available [29]. In Figure 5.11, user A sends an INVITE request and receives a 486 Busy Here response from user B's user agent. User A then sends a SUBSCRIBE request to user B requesting notification when user B is available to establish a session. When user B

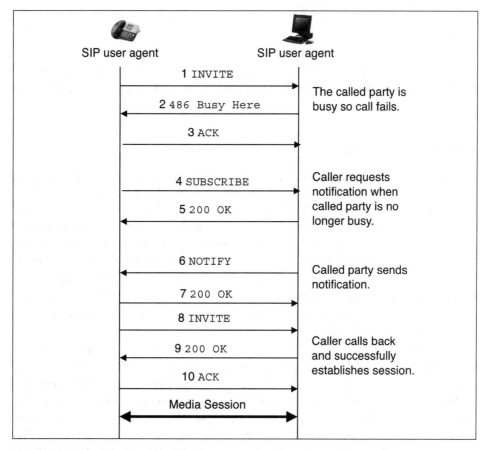

**Figure 5.11** Automatic callback feature example using **SUBSCRIBE** and **NOTIFY**.

sends a `NOTIFY` request indicating that the user is now available, user A immediately establishes the session.

The subscription request has the following form:

```
SUBSCRIBE sip:UserB@there.com SIP/2.0
Via: SIP/2.0/UDP 4.3.2.1
To: User B <sip:UserB@there.com>
From: User A <sip:UserA@here.com>
Call-ID: a5-32-43-12-77@4.3.2.1
CSeq: 1 SUBSCRIBE
Event: Available
Content-Length: 0
```

The notification request has the following form:

```
NOTIFY sip:UserA@here.com SIP/2.0
Via: SIP/2.0/UDP 129.5.3.2:5060
To: User A <sip:UserA@here.com>
From: User B <sip:UserB@there.com>
Call-ID: 52525213@129.5.3.2
CSeq: 5 NOTIFY
Event: Available
Content-Length: 0
```

The `Event` header indicates which event notification is being requested. If user B's user agent was not willing to provide the notification of this event, a `603 Decline` response could be sent.

## Authentication and Security

SIP supports two types of authentication: user agent-to-user agent, and user agent-to-server. It does not currently support server-to-server authentication, although this could be accomplished using a non-SIP scheme such as IP Security Protocol (IPSec) [30]. IPSec is an IP-layer security scheme that supports both encryption and signing of IP packets for secure transmission across the Internet. SIP supports a number of authentication schemes borrowed from HTTP. SIP digest authentication is the most commonly used scheme today, which relies on a challenge/response and a shared secret between the user agent requestor and the proxy or user agent requiring the authentication. Any SIP request can be challenged for authentication.

The shared secret usually will be an encrypted username and password. A typical authentication SIP message exchange between user agents has the form `INVITE/401 Authentication Required/ACK` in which the user agent discovers that the request requires authentication, and also learns the nature of the authentication challenge from the `401` response. Then, a new `INVITE` containing an `Authorization` header is resent. If it contains the correct credentials, the call will proceed as normal; otherwise another `401` response will be received.

A proxy server can also request authentication, using the 407  Proxy Authentication Required response. However, there is no support for one proxy to authenticate another proxy in SIP. Instead, a proxy can establish a secure connection to another proxy using IPSec.

An example SIP digest authentication exchange is shown in Figure 5.12. The initial INVITE message has no authorization credentials and has received a 407 Proxy Authorization Required response from the proxy, which contains a Proxy-Authorization header describing the nature of the challenge. After sending an ACK to the proxy, the user agent then resends the INVITE with an Authorization header containing the encrypted username and password of the user. The proxy then accepts the credentials, sends a 100 Trying response, and forwards the request to the destination user agent. The user agent then launches its own authentication challenge with a 401 Unauthorized response. This response is proxied back to the calling user agent. The SIP user agent then finally does the right thing and resends the INVITE request containing both the Proxy-Authorization with the credentials for the proxy and Authentication header with the credentials for the other user agent.

The details of message 11 in Figure 5.12, which contains both sets of credentials, is shown here:

```
INVITE sip:UserB@there.com SIP/2.0
Via: SIP/2.0/UDP 4.3.2.1:5060
To: User B <sip:UserB@there.com>
From: User A <sip:UserA@here.com>
Call-ID: a5-32-43-12-77@4.3.2.1
CSeq: 3 INVITE
Proxy-Authorization: Digest username="UserA",
 realm="SIP Telephone Company", nonce="814f12cec4341a34e6e5a35549"
 opaque="", uri="sip:proxy.sip.com", response="6131d1854834593984587ecc"
Authorization: Digest username="A", realm="UserB",
 nonce="e288df84f1cec4341ade6e5a359", opaque="",
 uri="sip:UserB@there.com", response="1d19580cd833064324a787ecc"
Contact: <sip:UserA@4.3.2.1>
Content-Length: ...
```

In this way, SIP supports both network (server) and user (user agent) authentication within a call.

## Extensibility

The SIP protocol was designed to be extensible. As a consequence, the protocol was designed so that user agents could implement new extensions using new headers and message bodies without requiring intermediate servers such as proxies to also support the extensions. By default, a proxy forwards unchanged unknown request types and headers. The use of the Supported header allows a requestor to inform the network and the other user agent of which extensions

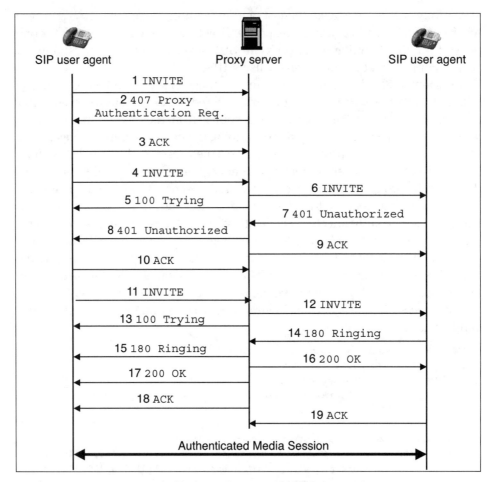

**Figure 5.12** Proxy and user authentication example using SIP digest.

and features it supports, allowing them the option of activating the feature. If it is required that the feature be understood or activated, there is a `Require` header [31] that is included in a request. A user agent receiving such a request must return an error if it does not understand or support the feature. There is also a `Proxy-Require` header that lists features that any proxies in the path must support. However, the use of this header is discouraged since its overuse will lead to call failures and interoperability problems.

# Summary

A SIP-enabled network has SIP endpoints and SIP servers with specific common functions such as using rich addressing formats, registration, and security. SIP servers can perform the functions for registration, proxy, redirect, and forking. A SIP-enabled network can support specific new types of services such as rendezvous, presence, mobility, user preferences, and message routing control.

SIP is result of and has benefited from the unique Internet standards creation process, but is not a miracle protocol.

SIP uses basic methods such as `INVITE` and `ACK` and also methods such as `SUBSCRIBE`, `NOTIFY`, and `MESSAGE` that allow a SIP-enabled network also to provide presence and instant messaging. These methods use the client server request and response approach. The standard SIP response codes are similar to those found in HTTP.

SIP session-related functions include address resolution, session setup, media negotiation, session modification, session termination, and cancellation of requests. SIP can support mid-call signaling and third-party call control. Non-session related features of SIP are mobility, message transport, event subscription and notification, and also authentication and security.

The following chapters will use these basic functions of SIP to build IP communication networks and implement services and features.

# References

[1] J. Rosenberg and H. Schulzrinne. "Guidelines for Authors of SIP Extensions," IETF Internet draft, work in progress, March 2001

[2] R. Fielding, et al. "Hypertext Transfer Protocol—HTTP/1.1," IETF RFC 2616, 1999.

[3] J. Postel. "Simple Mail Transfer Protocol," IETF RFC 821, 1982.

[4] M. Handley, J. Crowcroft, C. Borman, and J. Ott. "The Internet Multimedia Conferencing Architetcure," IETF Internet draft, work in progress, July 2000.

[5] M. Handley, et al. "SIP: Session Initiation Protocol," IETF RFC 2543, 1999.

[6] A. Johnston. *SIP: Understanding the Session Initiation Protocol,* Artech House: Boston, 2001.

[7] R. Braden. "Requirements for Internet Hosts—Communication Layers," IETF RFC 1121, 1989.

[8] R. Braden. "Requirements for Internet Hosts—Application and Support," IETF RFC 1122, 1989.

[9] A. Gulbrandsen. "A DNS RR for Specifying the Location of Services (DNS SRV)," IETF RFC 2782, 2000.

[10] P. Faltstrom. "E.164 Number and DNS," IETF RFC 2916, 2000.

[11] J. Rosenberg and H. Schulzrinne. "SCTP as a Transport for SIP," IETF Internet draft, work in progress, May 2001

[12] M. Handley and V. Jacobson. "SDP: Session Description Protocol," IETF RFC 2327, 1998.

[13] D. Kutscher et al. "Requirements for Session Description and Capability Negotiation," IETF Internet draft, work in progress, April 2001.

[14] S. Donovan. "The SIP INFO Method," IETF RFC 2976, 2000.

[15] R. Sparks. "SIP Call Control: REFER," IETF Internet draft, work in progress, 2001.

[16] H. Sinnreich, D. Rawlins, A. Johnston, S. Donovan, and S. Thomas. "AAA Usage for IP Telephony with QoS," IETF Internet draft, work in progress, 2000.

[17] A. Johnston, D. Rawlins, H. Sinnreich, and S. Thomas."OSP Authorization Token Header for SIP," IETF Internet draft, work in progress, 2000.

[18] G. Gross, H. Sinnreich, and D. Rawlins, "QoS and AAA Usage with SIP Based IP Communications," IETF Internet draft, work in progress, 2000.

[19] S. Herzog. "RSVP Extensions for Policy Control," IETF RFC 2750, 2000.

[20] S. Blake, D. Black, M. Carlson, E. Davies, Z. Wang, and W. Weiss, "An Architecture for Differentiated Services," IETF RFC 2475, 1998.

[21] Information about Packetcable is available at: http:// packetcable.com.

[22] S. Donovan, et al. "SIP 183 Session Progress Message," IETF Internet draft, work in progress, 1999.

[23] J. Rosenberg and H. Schulzrinne. "Reliability of Provisional Responses," IETF Internet draft, work in progress, 2001.

[24] W. Marshall, et al. "Architectural Considerations for Providing Carrier Class Telephony Services Utilizing SIP-based Distributed Call Control Mechanisms," IETF Internet draft, work in progress, 2001.

[25] H. Schulzrinne and J. Rosenberg. "SIP Caller Preferences and Callee Capabilities," IETF Internet draft, work in progress, 2001.

[26] J. Rosenberg, et al. "SIP Extensions for Instant Messaging," IETF Internet draft, work in progress, 2001.

[27] A. Roach. "Event Notification in SIP," IETF Internet draft, work in progress, 2001.

[28] S. Petrack and L. Conroy. "The PINT Service Protocol: Extensions to SIP and SDP for IP Access to Telephone Call Services," IETF RFC 2848, 2000.

[29] A. Roach. "Automatic Call Back Service in SIP," IETF Internet draft, work in progress, 2000.

[30] S. Kent and R. Atkinson. "Security Architecture for the Internet Protocol," IETF RFC 2401, 1998.

[31] J. Rosenberg and H. Schulzrinne. "The SIP Supported Header," IETF Internet draft, work in progress, 2001.

# SIP Service Creation

A major driver for many service providers adopting SIP is the advantages and flexibility of service creation using the protocol. Some of the typical approaches will be discussed in this chapter including server implementation, called user agent implementation, and calling user agent implementation. CPL and SIP CGI will also be introduced in this chapter. The various options for service creation, such as CPL, CGI, SIP Java Servlets, JAIN, and VoiceXML will also be discussed.

## Services in SIP

The basic functions of the SIP protocol involved in establishing sessions between two endpoints over the Internet were discussed in Chapter 5, *SIP Overview*. This chapter discusses implementations of additional functionality in relation to session establishment, henceforth referred to generically as "services." A classic example of a telephony service is call forwarding, which results in an endpoint being contacted that is different from the one that was dialed.

More advanced services can be implemented using SIP than can be implemented in the PSTN due to the increased amount of signaling information available during a call setup in SIP. Many of these advanced features and services will include integration with the World Wide Web or other databases of information. However, the first set of services implemented using SIP will be PSTN telephony features, which are used as examples throughout this chapter.

Services can reside in a number of locations in SIP. For example, many services can reside exclusively in user agents, requiring no support or servers in the network. Intelligent phones such as shown in Fig. 2.5 can well support a variety of SIP services. Other services can reside in proxy or redirect servers. The following simple example is used to illustrate the implementation options in SIP.

## Service Example

Consider a call-forward, no-answer service, in which a user wants an unanswered call to his or her SIP phone to automatically forward to a voice mail server after a certain period of time or a certain number of "rings." This service could be implemented in either a proxy server, called user agent, or calling user agent.

### Server Implementation

This service could be implemented in the proxy server that handles registrations for the called party. The resulting flow is shown in Figure 6.1. The proxy starts a timer when the INVITE is proxied to the latest registered address for the SIP phone. Since the call is not answered (no 200 OK is sent by the phone), the proxy sends a CANCEL to stop the phone from ringing, then forks the INVITE to the voice mail server, which answers, plays a prompt, and records a message.

If a SIP server wishes to provide services beyond the initial call setup (INVITE/200 OK/ACK exchange), the proxy must insert a Record-Route header into the INVITE request. This ensures that all future requests, such as re-INVITEs and other methods, will be routed through the proxy, giving the proxy an opportunity to invoke a service.

### Called User Agent Implementation

Figure 6.2 shows how the same feature can be implemented in the called SIP phone. In this case, the ring-no-answer timer is started in the called SIP user agent. When the timer expires, the phone sends a redirect 302 Moved Temporarily response containing a Contact: header with the URL of the voice mail server. This causes the calling SIP phone to generate a new INVITE directly to the voice mail server, which then answers, plays a prompt, and records a message.

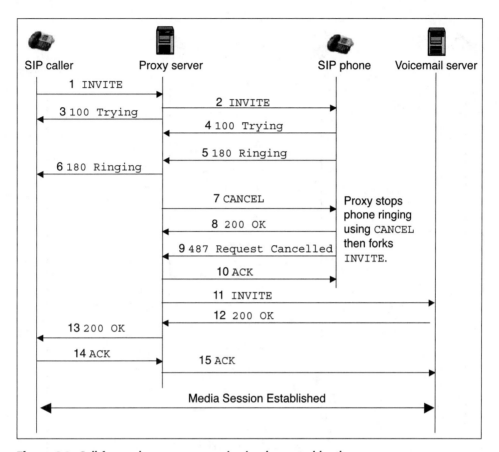

**Figure 6.1** Call-forward, no-answer service implemented by the proxy server.

## Calling User Agent Implementation

Finally, Figure 6.3 shows how this same feature can be implemented in the calling SIP phone. In this case, the SIP server redirects, instead of proxying the `INVITE`. The `302 Moved Temporarily` response contains two `Contact` headers:

```
Contact: <sip:alan@office51.example.com>
Contact: <sip:alan-msg-deposit-external@voicemail.example.com>
 ;feature=voicemail
```

The caller then sends an `INVITE` to the first URL. After the ring-no-answer timer expires in the calling user agent, the caller sends a `CANCEL`, then sends a new `INVITE` to the voice mail server. This second `Contact` header shows the use of caller preferences (covered in Chapter 7, *User Preferences*) in specifying that the URL is that of a voice mail server. This

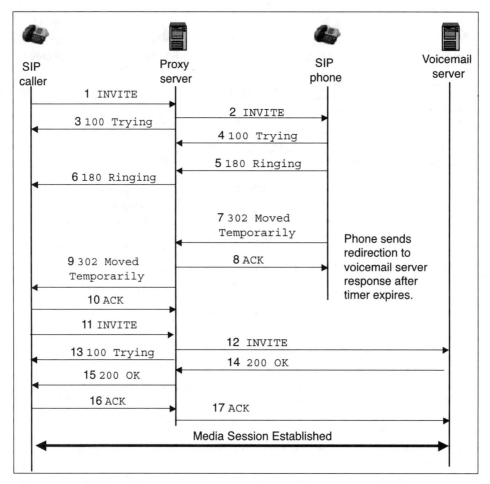

**Figure 6.2** Call-forward, no-answer service implemented by the called user agent.

URL also shows the method of using an "opaque" URI [1] to indicate to the voice mail server the intention of the INVITE. In this example, the user portion of the URL contains the username "alan" and also the keyword "msg-deposit-external," indicating that this is a message deposit session. This indicates to the voice mail server to play an external greeting and record a message. Another URL possibility would be "alan-msg-retrieval" which could indicate message retrieval. In this case, the voice mail server should challenge for appropriate credentials (username and password), then play back messages to the caller. Note that this same URL would have been used as the Request-URI of message 11 (INVITE from the proxy server to the voicemail server) of Figure 6.1, and also in the Contact header of message 7 of Figure 6.2 (302 Moved Temporarily).

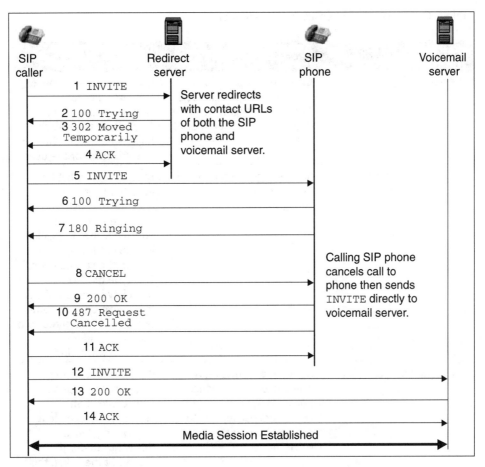

**Figure 6.3** Call-forward, no-answer service implemented by the calling user agent.

## Comparison

The advantages and disadvantages of these three implementations are summarized in Table 6.1. In summary, each implementation shifts the location of the service logic (such as the ring-no-answer timer and the recursive retries).

The implementation of a particular service will depend on many factors, and may be influenced by economies of scale.

In addition to these three common methods, there is a fourth method of service implementation that involves a Back-to-Back User Agent (B2BUA). This approach has been generalized to an architecture of special proxies that modify SIP messages (headers and message bodies), and generate and respond to requests. This is covered in detail in Chapter 17, *The Component Server Architecture*.

**Table 6.1**  Comparison of Service Implementation

| SERVICE IMPLEMENTATION | ADVANTAGES | DISADVANTAGES |
|---|---|---|
| Server | Called user agent does not need to be registered. Neither user agent requires any provisioning or special logic. | User must change proxy logic in order to change nature of service. As a result, the service logic is not under the direct control of the user. |
| Called User Agent | Service logic under control of user in phone configuration. | Feature logic must be in called user agent. User agent must be registered.  This means effectively that the called user agent must be "on" or else the service will fail. This type of "24x7" reliability is more difficult to achieve on a customer premise as compared to a service provider's centralized location. |
| Calling User Agent | No logic or provisioning in called user agent, which does not need to be registered.  Caller has the choice of connecting to voice mail. | Requires feature logic in calling user agent. Only works if SIP server redirects instead of proxying. Since this is not under the control of the caller, this service will not always work in a reliable way. |

# New Methods and Headers

New features and services can be implemented in SIP by defining new methods or headers. The basic set of methods and headers are defined in the SIP base specification, which covers basic session establishment and some features and services. New headers and methods can be proposed in the IETF through a process of writing and submitting an Internet draft document. If this document fits the chartered scope of the working group and gathers sufficient support, it may be adopted by the working group as an official work item. The status of the Internet draft is then tracked on the working group charter page as it is discussed and reviewed. Eventually, the document may become an RFC and an official extension to SIP. Nearly all the SIP extensions referenced in this book are official work items of the SIP, SIPPING, or SIMPLE working groups and are likely to become RFCs in the near future.

It is important to note that new methods or headers do not need support by SIP servers. For example, a SIP proxy receiving a request with an unknown method will proxy the request, treating it as if it were an OPTIONS request. A SIP proxy that receives a request with an unknown header will simply proxy the request, making no change to the header. Only the presence of a Proxy-Require header will force a proxy to understand and take action based on a particular header or method.

This allows new services to be created in user agents and deployed without any changes in the SIP network. Note that this is essentially what has happened with SIP-enabled telephony networks that can provide SIP instant message and presence transport without any changes to the SIP infrastructure.

Many new methods can be defined without having to use the Supported header. For example, a user agent sending an INFO request to a user agent that does not support this extension to SIP will receive a 405 Method Not Allowed (if it recognizes the method but does not support it) or a 500 Bad Request (if it does not recognize the method) response with an Allow header listing supported methods. However, other extensions, such as reliable provisional responses, need the Require header that lists required features of the UAS. If the UAS does not support the feature, the request should be rejected with a 420 Bad Extension response.

Any extension to SIP that can be referenced using the Require or Supported header must be fully documented in an RFC, even if it is an Informational and not a standards track document. This should prevent vendor proprietary headers and methods from causing interoperability problems in the SIP protocol. The use of headers and methods in SIP that have not been standardized by the IETF is extremely dangerous to interoperability, as these extensions may not be fully documented and may have been rejected by the working group for good reasons. All standardized extensions to SIP must describe how the extensions interact with elements that do not understand the extension.

The next section will describe how the service or feature logic can be scripted or programmed into SIP devices.

## Service Creation Options

Just as there are a number of options where service logic can reside in a SIP network, there are many options for the form of the service logic. These scripting and programming options include Call Processing Language (CPL), SIP Common Gateway Interface (CGI), and SIP Servlets.

# Call Processing Language

Call Processing Language (CPL) [2] was developed to allow nontrusted end users to upload their services to SIP servers. CPL will be briefly introduced in the following sections, which include some examples of services created using CPL.

## Introduction to CPL

CPL was developed by the IETF IP telephony (IPTEL) working group (WG) as executable code to be run on a SIP proxy server to implement services. CPL is an official work item of the IPTEL WG. CPL is based on Extensible Markup Language (XML) [3], which is a form of Standard Generalized Markup Language (SGML) [4] developed by the W3C.

Readers familiar with Hypertext Markup Language (HTML) [5], used to format Web documents, will recognize a similar structure. XML tags have the form `<tag>`, which opens the tag, and then `</tag>`, which closes the tag. There are, however, some important differences between XML and HTML. In XML, there are strict parsing rules that are defined by the document type definition (DTD) (in this case `"cpl.dtd"`) defined in the `<!DOCTYPE>` header. Any discrepancies between the script and the schema must produce an error. In HTML, parsing rules are forgiving. Unknown tags may be silently ignored, while missing required tags may be added. In HTML, some tags do not need to be closed, while in XML every opened tag must be closed.

CPL defines behavior for SIP URLs, tel URLs, and also H.323 URLs. Each action has a specific result for each of these signaling protocols. CPL, like SIP, is a text-based protocol.

Some tags have attributes, in which case they are written as `<tag attribute="value">`. Tags also can have multiple attributes. Tags without any attributes, or nested tags, can be opened and closed in a single tag using `<tag/>`, which is equivalent to `<tag></tag>`.

An example CPL script from the RFC to screen calls from anonymous callers is shown here:

```
<?xml version="1.0" ?>
<!DOCTYPE cpl PUBLIC "-//IETF//DTD RFCxxxx CPL 1.0//EN" "cpl.dtd">

<cpl>
  <incoming>
    <address-switch field="origin" subfield="user">
      <address is="anonymous">
        <reject status="reject"
                reason="I don't accept anonymous calls" />
      </address>
    </address-switch>
  </incoming>
</cpl>
```

In this example, the first line indicates the version of CPL. The second line lists the document type (cpl) and defines the DTD, which supplies the parsing rules for the document. The next line begins the CPL script with the <cpl> tag. Everything until the </cpl> tag is the CPL script itself. The next tag <incoming> indicates that this defines behavior for incoming calls, not outgoing. The next tag is <address-switch>, which is a type of switch or decision point. This switch specifies that the username part of the origin address (From header) is the value being tested. The <address> tag with the attribute is="anonymous" means that the username portion is anonymous. The <reject> tag with the attributes *status* and *reason* indicates that a call that matches this switch (user = "anonymous") should be rejected by the server. The rest of the tags simply close the opened tags. The complete set of CPL tags is listed in Table 6.2.

**Table 6.2** CPL Tag Summary

| TAG | DESCRIPTION |
| --- | --- |
| cpl | Begins the CPL script |
| incoming | Defines server operation for an incoming call |
| outgoing | Defines server operation for an outgoing call |
| location | Defines a URL location |
| lookup | Defines action based on result of lookup |
| remove-location | Removes a URL location from a set |
| proxy | Causes call to be forwarded (proxied) to the set of locations specified |
| redirect | Causes call to be redirected to the set of locations specified |
| reject | Causes call to be rejected |
| mail | Causes an e-mail notification to be sent to the specified e-mail address |
| log | Causes the server to log the specified information about the call |
| subaction | Defines a subaction, which can then be referenced in the script using the sub tag |
| sub | Causes server to execute the defined subaction script |
| address-switch | Choices or decision points based on address (From header) |
| string-switch | Choices or decision points based on a string |
| time-switch | Choices or decision points based on time of day |
| priority-switch | Choices or decision points based on priority of request (Priority header) |
| ancillary | Unused—available for future extensions |

CPL has switches defined for address, string, time, and priority. Each of these has a number of attributes, including fields and subfields. The matching rules include `is`, `contains`, and `subdomain-of`. The complete set of switches listing the matching conditions, fields, and subfields is shown in Table 6.3.

## Example of CPL Scripts

The following example from the CPL RFC shows a CPL script implementing a call-forward, no-answer and busy to voice mail.

```
<?xml version="1.0" ?>
<!DOCTYPE cpl PUBLIC "-//IETF//DTD RFCxxxx CPL 1.0//EN"
"cpl.dtd">

<cpl>
  <subaction id="voicemail int">
    <location url="sip:alan-msg-deposit-
                    internal@voicemail.example.com">
```

**Table 6.3** CPL Switch Types

| SWITCH TYPE | MATCHES | FIELDS | SUBFIELDS |
|---|---|---|---|
| address | is<br>contains<br>subdomain-of | origin<br>destination<br>original-<br>destination | address-type<br>user<br>host<br>port<br>display |
| string | is<br>contains | subject<br>organization<br>user-agent<br>language<br>display | |
| time | dtstart<br>dtend<br>duration<br>freq<br>interval<br>until<br>byday<br>bymonthday<br>byyearday<br>byweekno<br>bymonth<br>wkst | tzid<br>tzurl | |
| priority | less<br>greater<br>equal | | |

```
            <proxy />
          </location>
      </subaction>

  <subaction id="voicemail ext">
    <location url="sip:alan-msg-deposit-
                        external@voicemail.example.com">
            <proxy />
        </location>
  </subaction>

  <incoming>
      <address-switch field="origin" subfield="host">
        <address subdomain-of="example.com">
          <location url="sip:alan@office51.example.com">
            <proxy timeout="10">
              <busy> <sub ref="voicemail-int" /> </busy>
              <noanswer> <sub ref="voicemail-int" /> </noanswer>
              <failure> <sub ref="voicemail-int" /> </failure>
            </proxy>
          </location>
        </address>
        <otherwise>
          <sub ref="voicemail-ext" />
        </otherwise>
      </address-switch>
  </incoming>
</cpl>
```

In this script, two subactions are defined at the start. The first defines the voice mail-int subaction, in which the server proxies the call to the voice mail server with the Request-URI `sip:alan-msg-deposit-internal@voice-mail.example.com`. The second defines the voice mail-ext subaction, in which the server proxies the call to the voice mail server with a slightly different Request-URI. This allows the voice mail server to play different prompts for internal versus external callers.

The script operation begins with the `<incoming>` tag. The `<address-switch>` tag checks to see if the caller is part of the example.com domain or a different domain. If the caller is internal to the example.com domain, the call is proxied to the URL `sip:alan@example.com`. If the result of that proxy is busy, failure, or no answer, the call is then processed by the voice mail-internal subaction, which proxies the call to voice mail. For external callers, the call is immediately sent to voice mail.

Note that CPL also can be used for service creation for outgoing calls. Consider the following example, also taken from the CPL RFC.

```
<?xml version="1.0" ?>
<!DOCTYPE cpl PUBLIC "-//IETF//DTD RFCxxxx CPL 1.0//EN"
"cpl.dtd">

<cpl>
  <outgoing>
```

```
      <address-switch field="original-destination"
 subfield="tel">
      <address subdomain-of="1900">
        <reject status="reject"
              reason="Not allowed to make 1-900 calls." />
      </address>
    </address-switch>
  </outgoing>
</cpl>
```

In this example, any telephony URLs that begin with 1-900-... are rejected by the server as they might be 900-number toll calls.

## SIP Common Gateway Interface

The SIP CGI is analogous to HTTP CGI used for Web server service creation. SIP CGI is defined by an informational RFC [6], which means that it is not a standards track protocol. For example, Web page forms are usually implemented using HTTP CGI scripts. In a similar way, complex services can be programmed under control of network administrators using SIP CGI. SIP CGI runs on a SIP server that interacts with a program containing the service logic using the CGI interface. This arrangement is shown in Figure 6.4.

SIP CGI is an interface, not a programming language. It allows services to be developed in familiar languages such as Perl, C, TCL, etc. Due to the similarities, SIP CGI can reuse most HTTP CGI codes. Unlike HTTP CGI that deals exclusively with generating responses to requests, SIP CGI can be used to generate responses and also can cause the server to proxy requests to other locations. SIP CGI scripts are call-stateful, in that they can correlate multiple requests corresponding to the same SIP session. This allows a wide spectrum of SIP services to

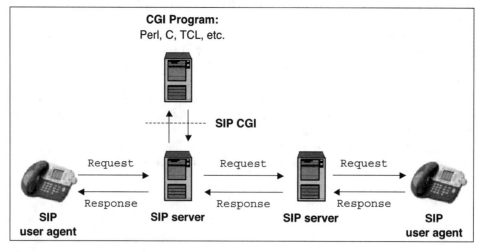

**Figure 6.4** SIP CGI model.

be developed using SIP CGI. So that the server does not have to execute the script for every SIP request, SIP CGI scripts allow the specification of a "default" action and the conditions under which this default action is executed.

RFC 3050 lists over 20 metavariables that can be used by the CGI script. In addition, the CGI script has complete access to the request SIP headers and message bodies.

For example, an INVITE request could generate the following SIP CGI response to the SIP server.

```
CGI-PROXY-REQUEST sip:j.customer@carrier.com SIP/2.0
Organization: MegaCarrier

SIP/2.0 100 Trying

CGI-SCRIPT-COOKIE hfkelwoeih SIP/2.0
```

The first line tells the server to proxy the request to the specified URL using the metavariable CGI-PROXY-REQUEST. The second line tells the proxy to insert the Organization header into the request. (The use of uppercase for SIP CGI metavariables allows them to be easily distinguished from SIP headers.) Note that the proxy knows to add a Via header and do the normal operations associated with proxying a SIP request—the script does not need to tell the server this. The third line tells the proxy to send a 100 Trying response back to the caller. The fourth line tells the SIP server to store a cookie associated with this call at the SIP server using the CGI-SCRIPT-COOKIE metavariable. If the script is reactivated for this call, this cookie would be returned to the CGI program, allowing it to operate statelessly, but still track the progress of the session.

## SIP Application Programming Interfaces

A number of SIP Application Programming Interfaces (APIs) have been developed, including SIP servlets and JAIN. The use of APIs offers the possibility of lower overhead compared to CPL and SIP CGI, since an external process does not need to be spawned each time. API capabilities for storing state and timers are also simpler than SIP CGI. However, a major disadvantage is that this approach is language dependent.

### SIP Servlets

SIP Java servlets [7], [8] are a powerful tool for extending the functionality of a SIP client by allowing it to pass received messages to SIP servlets. SIP servlets can then process the message and even interact with the SIP client to generate new messages (if the security settings allow it). This API can be used on both SIP servers and user agents. It is not a general-purpose SIP API, but rather an API for service extensions. SIP servlets are currently not a work item of any IETF working group, but may become an informational RFC in the future.

### JAIN

The Java Integrated Network (JAIN) SIP specification [9] is part of an effort to create a set of APIs for various telephony and Internet protocols for service development. The JAIN SIP specification provides a standard interface to proprietary vendor SIP stacks. JAIN is defined by various Java documents that are not related to the IETF in any way.

## SIP and VoiceXML

Voice Extensible Markup Language (VoiceXML) [10] has been developed to enable simple voice-enabled services and features to be developed. VoiceXML is defined by documents at the VoiceXML consortium, which is not related to the IETF. Like CPL, VoiceXML is based on XML and has a similar structure. VoiceXML scripts play prompts (either using prerecorded or synthesized speech), collect input (via DTMF tones or speech recognition), and take specified actions based on results. While VoiceXML does not relate directly to SIP, a VoiceXML script can be run in conjunction with a SIP CPL or CGI script to implement a complete interactive service. An example VoiceXML script to prompt a caller if he or she wishes to be connected to a voice mail server is shown here.

```
<vxml>
  <form id="message">
    <field name="choice">
      <prompt>
        <audio>Do you want to be connected to voicemail?
              Say yes or no.</audio>
      </prompt>
      <grammar>
      <![CDATA[
      [
        [yes] {<option "yes">}
        [no] {<option "no">}
      ]
      ]]>
      </grammar>
    </field>

<filled>
      <result name="yes">
```

```
        <goto next="#proxy_voicemail"/>
      </result>
      <result name="no">
        <goto next="#disconnect"/>
      </result>
    </filled>
  </form>
</vxml>
```

In this example, the system will play the audio prompt, "Do you want to leave a message? Say yes or no." The grammar is defined to be "yes" or "no," and this is used by the speech recognition system to make a decision. The SIP service logic will then perform the routing to the voice mail server or disconnect the call, depending on the outcome of the VoiceXML script.

## Summary

SIP provides an extremely flexible set of tools for service creation and implementation. The architectures and tools described in this chapter should allow the development of many different services in a SIP-enabled network. The large portfolio of available development tools and the open nature of these tools will enable the development of many domain-specific communication services by third-party developers. For example a courier or transportation company may develop a Presence-based communication application that allows tracking and contacting any of the fleet workforce according to certain criteria that are business specific for the company. Future development of SIP is discussed in Chapter 18.

## References

[1] B. Campbell. "Framework for SIP Call Control Extensions," IETF Internet draft, work in progress, March 2001.

[2] J. Lennox and H. Schulzrinne. "CPL: A Language for User Control of Internet Telephony Services," IETF Internet draft, 2001, work in progress.

[3] T. Bray, J. Paoli, and C.M. Sperberg-McQueen. "Extensible Markup Language (XML) 1.0 (second edition)," W3C Recommendation REC-xml-20001006, World Wide Web Consortium (W3C), October 2000.

[4] ISO (International Organization for Standardization), "Information Processing—Text and Office Systems—Standard Generalized Markup Language (SGML)," ISO Standard ISO 8879:1986(E), International Organization for Standardization, Geneva, Switzerland, Oct. 1986.

[5] HTML information is available at the W3C (World Wide Web Consortium) Web page at: http://w3.org/MarkUp/.

[6] J. Lennox, H. Schulzrinne, and J. Rosenberg. "Common Gateway Interface for SIP," IETF RFC 3050, 2001.

[7] A. Kristensen and A. Byttner. "The SIP Servlet API," Internet Draft, Internet Engineering Task Force, September 1999, expired.

[8] K. Peterbauer, et al. "SIP Servlet API Extensions," IETF Internet draft, 2000, work in progress.

[9] JSR-000032 JAIN(TM) SIP Specification is available at http://java.sun.com/products/jain/.

[10] VoiceXML information is available at the VoiceXML Forum Web page at: http://voicexml.org/.

# User Preferences

Any advanced network must be flexible enough to take into consideration the preferences and desires of users. In this chapter, we will show how SIP can use the preferences of both the caller and the called party in call routing, features, and services.

## Introduction

Telephony services based on the intelligent network architecture for public networks and private circuit-switched networks (PBXs) give the users, in general, little or no control over the preferences of how calls should be handled. Whatever call features are possible can be only subscribed to, but cannot be exercised as individual preferences on a call-by-call basis. There are many reasons, one of them being the frugal user interface of user devices, called *terminals* in ITU standards language, and the general concept of user devices not being the location for intelligence. Another reason is scalability: It is more difficult to store a page full of user preferences for millions of users in central servers of the IN in the PSTN and also have the data changed by users on a dynamic basis as compared to having such data and access to it be handled at the periphery of the network.

IP communications by contrast consider the intelligence, and control resides primarily in user devices and, as a consequence, dynamic user preferences can be fully enabled on a scalable basis, no matter how many users are on a network. User preferences are well documented for SIP [1].

Some examples of caller and called party preferences are:

- Call someone, but speak only to voice mail, so as to shorten the call as much as possible.

- Receive calls only from certain parties at certain times, such as accepting calls during lunch hour only from the spouse or the boss and sending all other calls to voice mail.

- Specify certain times/dates to be accessible only on the mobile phone or at hotel phone numbers when traveling.

- Specify instant text messaging only when in a meeting or at the theater.

There are three parties to user preferences, each having very different roles and using different technologies:

1. **Caller preferences**. Since the caller is the active party, it can express clearly the preferences for the call at call setup by three SIP headers, as will be shown later.

2. **Called party preferences**. The called party is passive, since it has to wait for incoming calls and it cannot anticipate all possible preferences of callers but can formulate clear rules how incoming calls should be handled. Such rules can be expressed in CPL scripts that reside either in the designated proxy server that handles the calls, or in the user agent.

3. **Server support for user preferences**. SIP servers can be designed to understand and process caller preferences and also to execute scripts with rules for incoming calls. SIP servers can, however, also enforce policy rules for communications on behalf of the network administrator.

## Preferences of Caller

The caller can request servers to proxy or redirect a call, and also how to search for the destination. The instructions are carried in the `Request-Disposition` header. For example:

```
Request-Disposition: proxy, parallel, queue
```

The instructions in the `Request-Disposition` header are explained here. The caller can request the server to:

- **Proxy.** Proxy or redirect the call.
- **Cancel.** Handle CANCEL requests on behalf of the caller or let the caller do it.
- **Fork.** Fork call requests to different URIs.
- **Recurse.** When receiving addresses to redirect the call to, the server should try the new addresses, or return them to the caller to make the decision to try again.
- **Parallel.** Try multiple addresses in parallel, or in sequential order, and wait for a response before trying the next address.
- **Queue.** Queue the call if the called party is busy and return the provisional response 182 Queued. Waiting in the queue can be terminated by CANCEL or BYE requests.

The caller can also express preferences how certain URIs should be handled by using the headers Contact, Accept-Contact, and Reject-Contact.

User preferences that relate to the same URI can have a range of classes to specify such preferences as:

- **Duplex.** To specify for certain types of lectures or conferences.
- **Feature.** To express preference for voice mail, for an agent, or for some other option.
- **Language.** To direct the call to someone speaking a specific language.
- **Media types.** Such as audio, video, text, or application. Text also can be "text/html."
- **Mobility.** To set preference for mobile phone or fixed phone.
- **Business or residential class**. So the caller can avoid calling someone at home.
- **Methods.** To specify the capabilities of the UA, such as voice or IM.

The following are examples of these classes.

## Example for Contact

The caller would specify in the REGISTER message or an INVITE message:

```
Contact: HenryS <sip:henrys@wcom.com>;lan="en,de,ro,fr"
    ;media"=audio,video,application/chat"
    ;duplex="full"
    ;priority="urgent"
```

This communicates the preference to be called at the specified URI in any of the following languages: English, German, Romanian, or French. The preferences include audio, video, and text chat in full duplex with a specification for urgency.

## Example for `Accept-Contact`

The caller would like to speak to someone, but not to anyone from the sales department, prefer to use the desk phone, and has a lower preference for using the mobile phone or video. The degree of preference is indicated by the weight factor q.

```
Accept-Contact: sip:sales@company.com ;q=0,
   ;media="!video" ;q=0.1,
   ;mobility="fixed" ;q=0.6,
   ;mobility="!fixed" ;q=0.3
```

The exclamation point serves to distinguish between two mobility preferences, so they effectively appear as two different parameters.

An important use for `Accept-Contact` has been identified in attended transfer [2]. In this call flow, shown in Figure 7.1, user B, in an established session with user A, wishes to perform an attended transfer of A to C. Note that for clarity this call flow shows a single arrow for the `INVITE`, `200 OK`, and `ACK` message exchange. First, user B places user A on hold, then calls the transfer target, user C. The transfer target is then placed on hold, and the `REFER` method is used to complete the transfer between A and C. However, it is extremely important in this example that the referred `INVITE` (message 7) reaches exactly the same user agent that the transferor reached. (For example, user C's proxy server may apply different call routing logic to an `INVITE` from B than it does to an `INVITE` from C. This could result in the `INVITE` from B getting redirected to voice mail.) The way this is accomplished is by using an `Accept-Contact` header in message 7 containing the `Contact` URL obtained from the `200 OK` of message 3.

The `Accept-Contact` header is passed as an escaped header in the `REFER` of message 5. An example would be:

```
Accept-Contact: sip:joe@65.64.32.32;only=true
```

The `only=true` parameter tells any servers to proxy only this request to this particular `Contact` URL.

## Example for `Reject-Contact`

The caller would not like to communicate with anyone in the sales department:

```
Reject-Contact: sip:sales@company.com
```

The `Reject-Contact` field can contain a list of URIs with which no call setup is desired.

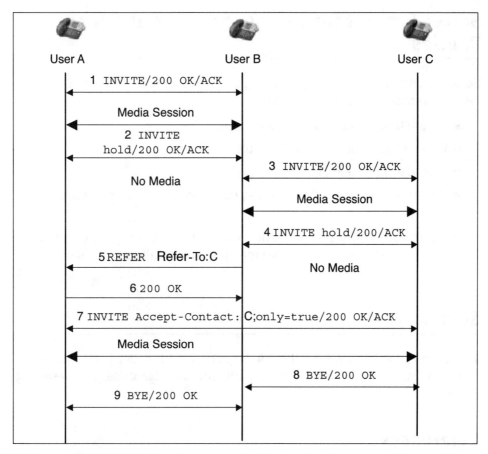

**Figure 7.1** Attended transfer using `Accept-Contact` header.

# Preferences of the Called Party

The preferences of the called party are generally invoked by an incoming proxy server that handles incoming calls for the called party. For example, calls to `sip:henrys@wcom.com` will route through the SIP proxy server specified in the DNS SRV records for the wcom.com domain.

Since this server will be making decisions on the called party's behalf, a mechanism has been developed in SIP for a user to upload their preferences and services into a SIP proxy server. This mechanism is the `REGISTER` message. It is the means for specifying preferences and services using Call Processing Language (CPL) [3], as introduced in Chapter 6, *SIP Service Creation*.

Many of the switches in CPL use the Caller Preferences parameters in the `Contact` headers of the caller's `INVITE` and the called party's `REGISTER`.

## Server Support for User Preferences and for Policies

Servers can use the Contact, Accept-Contact, and Reject-Contact headers to make the following decisions:

- Should it proxy or redirect the request?
- Which URIs to proxy or redirect to?
- Should it fork the request?
- How to search; recursively or not, or to search in parallel or sequentially.

Administrative policies also can be exercised at the server to exclude, for example, certain URIs or to exclude video for certain callers to conserve bandwidth.

## Summary

This chapter has shown how the combination of SIP caller preferences and CPL scripting provides a powerful capability for processing calls and designing services.

## References

[1] H. Schulzrinne and J. Rosenberg. "SIP Caller Preferences and Callee Capabilities," IETF Internet draft, work in progress, June 2001.
[2] A. Johnston et al. "SIP Service Examples," IETF Internet draft, work in progress, June 2001.
[3] J. Lennox and H. Schulzrinne. "CPL: A Language for User Control of Internet Telephony Services," IETF Internet draft, work in progress, May 2001.

# CHAPTER 8

# Security, NATs, and Firewalls

This chapter covers the basics of SIP security and the security mechanisms and functions utilized within a SIP-enabled network. The methods used to provide privacy in establishing SIP sessions also will be discussed.

SIP security is a complex topic and can be split into two categories: (1) how to insure security for SIP call setup and (2) how security devices such as firewalls and Network Address Translators (NATs) can complicate SIP call setup signaling and the flow of RTP media packets. NATs are used to create private IP networks that use internal IP addresses that are not part of the public Internet address space and are not routed over the Internet [1]. Network administrators use NATs either because they may not have enough public IP v.4 addresses or to avoid reconfiguring all their IP devices when they change service providers. However, this has quite a number of undesired consequences, as discussed in Hain [2]. The overall negative implications of firewalls and NATs on Internet transparency are discussed in Carpenter [3]. Since SIP signaling carries rich information, it can reveal valuable personal data of the calling and called parties such as IP addresses (location), contact lists, and traffic patterns. SIP security also involves designing networks that are protected from denial of service (DOS) attacks.

Firewalls and NATs greatly complicate calls for users in enterprise or home networks that use such devices. Several approaches are possible for firewall and NAT traversal for phone and multimedia communication calls, the most prominent being:

- Control of firewalls and NATs from a SIP proxy acting as an application level gateway (ALG)

- Modification of SIP signaling, without changing anything in existing firewalls and NATs

- Modifications to firewalls and NATs so as to make them SIP aware

# Basics of SIP Security

The SIP protocol includes three aspects of security: (1) authentication, (2) encryption, and (3) nonrepudiation with digital signatures. Many other elements of IP security are orthogonal to SIP and can be applied to a SIP network. The schemes discussed here are supported and contained within the SIP protocol specification.

## Authentication

Authentication in a SIP network is the process in which a user agent presents credentials to a SIP server or another user agent in order to establish a session or be granted access to some network features. For example, a SIP network may use a proxy authentication challenge to ensure that only authorized users may place calls to the PSTN through a SIP proxy to a PSTN gateway. Alternatively, a user agent may wish a caller to prove his or her identity by providing a credential.

SIP authentication applies a challenge/response mechanism utilizing a shared secret. The shared secret is encrypted and not passed in clear text. In addition, the challenge mechanism has a time/address sensitivity that precludes replay attacks using cached credentials. The mechanism is borrowed from HTTP [4], modified slightly, and is named SIP digest. This scheme was introduced in Chapter 5, *SIP Overview* and shown in Figure 5.12. A call request is challenged with a `401 Authentication Required` or `407 Proxy Authorization Required` response. The request is then retried containing the correct credentials.

SIP digest uses a nonce from the challenge as the key to perform a Message-Digest 5 (MD5) [5] hashing function on the secret, usually a username and password combination. The MD5 algorithm takes an arbitrarily large string and compresses it down to a 128-bit representation of the original. The resulting string is returned in the retried response.

Table 8.1 illustrates the fields in a WWW-Authenticate or Proxy-Authenticate header.

Table 8.2 illustrates the fields in an Authorization or Proxy-Authorization header.

One item to note about MD5 is that it is not considered one of the "strongest" cryptographic algorithms available. This does not exclude it from being an adequate method of encryption as it does provide a reasonable level of security in terms of associated cost in defeating it. The information being protected will be useless by the time a security compromise will be successful, if at all. Many initial SIP deployments currently use SIP digest authentication, using a username and password manually stored in the SIP phone or client.

This challenge/response mechanism can be used between user agents or between a proxy and a user agent. SIP does not support proxy-to-proxy authentication or the authentication of responses.

Note that authentication does not guarantee that the SIP message has not been modified or tampered with in any way. Encryption and digital signatures provide this functionality.

In the future, SIP authentication will likely be performed using certificates, which will eliminate the need for credential challenges in the SIP messaging.

## Encryption

The encryption of SIP headers and message bodies can prevent a third party from obtaining sensitive information about a user agent, such as IP addresses,

**Table 8.1** WWW-Authenticate or Proxy-Authenticate Header Fields

| | |
|---|---|
| Digest | Digest is the schema name |
| realm="UserB" | The realm is a string that can be displayed to a user to indicate which username/password should be provided. |
| domain="sip:proxy.com" | The domain is a URI that defines the protection space. |
| nonce="e288df84f1 cec4341ade6e5a359" | The nonce is a data string that typically is generated uniquely for each challenge using a timestamp and the server's private encryption key. |
| opaque="63632f41" | The opaque string should be returned in the response unchanged, allowing the challenging server to operate stateless. |
| stale=FALSE | The stale flag set to TRUE indicates that the previous response was rejected due to the nonce being stale (out of date). The response then can be retried with the new nonce supplied. |
| algorithm=MD5 | The algorithm string indicates the algorithm to be used to produce the digest. |

**Table 8.2** `Authorization` or `Proxy-Authorization` Header Fields

| | |
|---|---|
| `Digest` | Digest is the schema name |
| `username="A"` | The username is the user's name as specified in the credentials. |
| `realm="sip:proxy.com"` | The realm is copied from the challenge. |
| `nonce="e288df84f1cec 4341ade6e5a359"` | The nonce is copied from the challenge. |
| `opaque="63632f41"` | The opaque is copied from the challenge. |
| `uri="sip:UserB@there.com"` | URI is from the Request-URI of the request. |
| `response="1d19580cd 833064324a787ecc"` | The response is the message digest computed using the user's credentials and the nonce. |

port numbers, etc. In addition, encryption can mask the details of a session being established, for instance, if A calls B and establishes a session at a certain time on a certain day. Encryption has two forms: hop-by-hop or end-to-end. In hop-by-hop encryption, the entire SIP message could be encrypted allowing no information to be available to a third party. This is essentially what happens if IP Security Protocol (IPSec) [6] or Transmission Transport Layer Security (TLS) [7] is used between two SIP elements. No support in the SIP protocol is necessary for this type of encryption.

The use of IPSec "tunnels" between trusted network elements can allow a network to be designed such that authentication can be pushed to the edge of the service provider's network, with no further challenges needed for services and features after the first proxy challenge.

However, SIP also supports the partial encryption of a SIP message. For example, the message body of an `INVITE`, which describes the type of session to be established, could be encrypted. This will work in an end-to-end manner since proxies do not parse the message body. Alternatively, certain SIP headers could be encrypted to hide sensitive information. However, for end-to-end encryption of SIP headers to work without the support of every proxy in the path, only SIP headers not vital to request routing can by encrypted. For example, `Via`, `To`, `From`, `Call-ID`, and `CSeq` cannot normally be encrypted since they are used by proxies to route the request.

For example, the following SIP request uses encryption. The request has been encrypted using Pretty Good Privacy (PGP) [8], using the public key of the recipient so that only the recipient can decipher the request. The encrypted headers and message body are shown in italics. The `Content-Type: message/sip` would be replaced with the `Content-Type`, which is encrypted along with the message body.

```
INVITE sip:UserB@there.com SIP/2.0
Via: SIP/2.0/UDP 4.3.2.1:5060
To: User B <sip:UserB@there.com>
From: User A <sip:UserA@here.com>
Encryption: PGP version=5.0
Call-ID: 4598998103413565463443656
CSeq: 1 INVITE
Content-Type: message/sip
Content-Length: ...

Subject: Contract Discussion
Response-Key: PGP version="5.0", encoding="ascii",
 key="dAEDA3L7QvAdK2utY05fwmQBtAzNW5rNYAAAEgDAL7QvAdK2utY05wuUG+"
Content-Type: application/sdp

v=0
o=UserA 2114513523452 2114513523452 IN IP4 client.here.com
s=Session SDP
c=IN IP4 4.3.2.1
t=0 0
m=audio 5002 RTP/AVP 0
a=rtpmap: 0 PCMU/8000
```

The encryption in this example hides the Subject header, the PGP key to be used for encrypting the response to this request, and the nature of the connection established between the two user agents.

## Digital Signatures

SIP also supports the signing of all or part of the SIP message. This can be used to verify that the SIP request has not been modified or tampered with by a third party. Certificates also serve to provide nonrepudiation (under the assumption that only the sender knows his or her private key) guaranteeing that the user cannot deny that the message originated from the sender.

# Network Address Translators

Network Address Translators (NATs) are devices that modify the IP address and port numbers, in the case of network address and port translators (NAPT), of IP packets as they are forwarded from one network to another. NATs are commonly used when a local network utilizes IP addresses that are not globally unique. When an IP packet that originated from this network needs to traverse the public Internet, the use of NATs is required to replace the local addresses with globally routable addresses. The reason the private address space is not routable is that numerous entities on the public network utilize these addresses on their own internal networks. If these addresses were propagated on the public network, core routers would not know which direction to send the response due to the large number of locations that may utilize the same address space. NATs also are used sometimes as security mechanisms to hide the internal structure of a local network from users outside the network. For example, internal network topology can be hidden with a NAT by making all internal users appear to be one external, globally unique IP address to the rest of the world. NATs typically operate transparently to the application layer, modifying network layer fields as required to provide this transparency.

Many routers designed for home and small office use incorporate NAT functionality along with a Dynamic Host Configuration Protocol (DHCP) server often bundled with an Ethernet hub in the same device. As devices are plugged into the hub, they are assigned a local IP address (typically assigned from one of the private network address ranges such as 192.168.x.x), which allows them to communicate with other devices on the Local Area Network (LAN). When the packets leave the router, the NAT functionality allows multiple internal PCs or devices to share a single external, globally unique IP address. When used in this fashion, these routers are sometimes called *Internet sharing hubs*.

Some network administrators also use private numbering schemes to avoid having to renumber their network if they ever have to change Internet service providers (ISPs). Without a NAT, every IP device would need to be readdressed. With a NAT-enabled device, only the NAT device needs to be reconfigured with a new pool of IP addresses.

Since SIP was developed, guidelines for protocol design to make protocols more NAT "friendly" have been developed by the IETF [9]. Unfortunately, SIP violates most of these newer guidelines. For example, one of the major recommendations of this document is that application layer protocols should not transport IP addresses and port numbers. The next example shows why this is a major problem for routing SIP and resulting real-time protocol (RTP) sessions through a NAT. In this INVITE generated from behind a NAT, the fields in **bold** represent IP addresses that cannot be routed across a globally addressed network such as the Internet.

```
INVITE sip:UserB@there.com SIP/2.0
Via: SIP/2.0/UDP 10.1.1.221:5060
From: TheBigGuy <sip:UserA@customer.com>
To: TheLittleGuy <sip:UserB@there.com>
Call-Id: 123456@10.1.1.221
CSeq: 1 INVITE
Subject: Wow! It Works...
Contact: sip:UserA@10.1.1.221
Content-Type: application/sdp
Content-Length: ...

v=0
o=UserA 2890844526 2890844526 IN IP4 UserA.customer.com
c=IN IP4 10.1.1.221
m=audio 49170 RTP/AVP 0
a=rtpmap:0 PCMU/8000
```

Due to the presence of the NAT:

- The response to this request could not be routed back to the originator due to the inability to route these private network address ranges defined for use on private internal networks (based on an incorrect `Via` header).

- Future requests during this session would be misrouted (based on an incorrect `Contact` header).

- RTP packets sent by user B would be misrouted (based on an incorrect connection IP address for the media in the SDP).

Note also that the two port numbers contained in this `INVITE`, port 5060 and port 49170, also may be changed by the NAT and may cause signaling or media exchange to fail.

If the NAT is being used for security purposes, the amount of topology leakage shown in this `INVITE` would not be acceptable to a network administrator.

Of these three problems identified, only this first one has a solution in SIP. A proxy or user agent receiving this request would compare the IP address in the `Via` header to the IP address from which the packet was received. If the two are different, as they would be if a NAT is present, the correct IP address is added to the `Via` header with a `received=` parameter listing the actual IP address. This IP address would be used to route the response successfully back to user A, provided the NAT maintains the same binding between the private IP address and public IP address. (This is not a problem if TCP is used as the transport. When a TCP connection is opened, the NAT creates the binding between the private IP address and port number and the assigned public IP address and port number. When the connection closes, the NAT removes the binding.) However, no easy solution exists for the other two problems.

The second problem could be solved by a persistent TCP connection for the duration of the session. This would mean that the `Contact` header would never be used to route future requests (such as a re-`INVITE` or `BYE`) since there would always be an open TCP connection.

A possible solution to the third problem has been proposed [10] which involves making RTP flows symmetric. For the case where only one endpoint is behind a NAT, RTP packet flow will be possible in at least one direction. This is because the Session Description Protocol (SDP) of the endpoint outside the NAT will contain a correct globally routable IP address and port number. The modification to SDP to describe a symmetric RTP flow [11] would make the recipient of the successful RTP stream use the received IP address and port number to send RTP, ignoring the IP address in the SDP (which is not routable). For the case of both endpoints behind NATs, an RTP proxy/mixer outside both NATs must be used.

In addition to these SIP and RTP issues, there is the issue of the disclosure of the private IP address, information that administrators like to see blocked by the NAT. Although not significant from a signaling or media perspective, the Call-ID also leaks the private IP address of the user agent. The complete solution to this problem will be discussed after the other major obstacle to SIP—firewalls—is discussed.

# Firewalls

A firewall is a device typically present where a private IP network intercon-nects with the public Internet. A firewall acts like a one-way gate, allowing requests to go from the private network into the Internet, and allowing *only* responses to those requests to return, but blocking most requests originating in the Internet destined for the private network.

Certain types of requests from the public Internet are typically allowed. For example, HTTP requests to the corporate public Web server will not be blocked by the firewall, nor SMTP e-mail transfers, nor are DNS queries for the public DNS server. These types of legitimate requests can be identified by the firewall by examination of the destination IP address in the IP header and the destina-tion port number in the UDP or TCP headers.

For example, a valid Web-browsing request will contain the destination IP address of the public Web server and port 80 (a well-known port number for HTTP). A particularly diligent firewall may even parse the packet to ensure that it contains a valid HTTP message.

The nature of the interaction between SIP and a firewall depends on the transport protocol. If the user agent uses UDP to initiate the session, the server outside the firewall will be able to receive the SIP messages, but responses sent using UDP will be blocked by the firewall, since they are not associated with an outgoing request, as they are over a TCP connection. Any resulting media stream also will be one-sided only. This scenario is shown in Figure 8.1.

If TCP is used, it is possible for a SIP user agent to establish a SIP session with a server on the outside of the firewall. This is because the SIP responses will be sent in the TCP connection opened by the user behind the firewall and will not be blocked. However, RTP media packets sent by the called party will be blocked by the firewall. The resulting media session will be only one way. This is shown in Figure 8.2.

If the a user agent outside the firewall attempts to establish a session with the user agent inside the firewall, all SIP and RTP packets will be blocked, regardless of transport, resulting in no session.

Note that it is possible to configure a firewall to allow SIP. However, doing so opens so many holes and weakens the protection provided by a firewall to

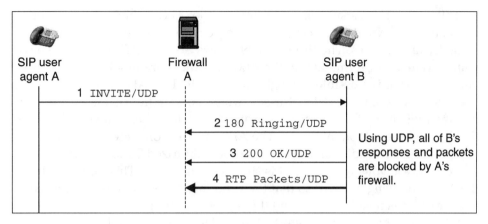

**Figure 8.1** Unsuccessful call through firewall using UDP.

such a degree that few network administrators would allow it. This is in contrast to NATs, which currently cannot be reconfigured to pass SIP and media.

Solutions to the firewall and NAT traversal problem will now be discussed.

## ALG, Firewall, and NAT Traversal

While there are a number of possible workarounds to trick a firewall into allowing a SIP session to be established, there is really only one permanent solution, commonly referred to as an Application Layer (or Level) Gateway (ALG). An ALG is a SIP and RTP proxy that is trusted by the firewall. That is,

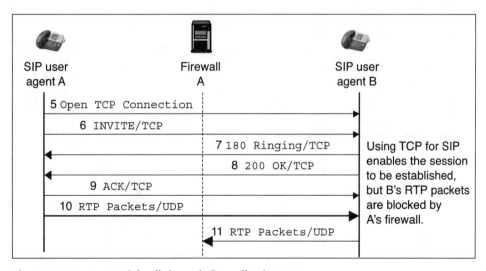

**Figure 8.2** Unsuccessful call through firewall using TCP.

all SIP and RTP packets are directed at the ALG, which then performs authentication, validation, etc., and enforces whatever policy the security administrator desires. The firewall only allows SIP and RTP packets to pass, which originate or terminate on the ALG; all others are blocked. In this way, communication is possible through the firewall. This ALG works with NAT operation as well, as the IP addresses, which contain internal addresses, are modified when the SIP message is proxied. A detailed call flow is shown in the SIP Call Flow Examples [12]. The ALG may be connected to the firewall in a secure subnet sometimes called the De-Militarized Zone (DMZ).

A call flow involving a SIP ALG is shown in Figure 8.3. This example shows the ALG modifying the SDP so that the resulting RTP session is established in two legs between user agent A and the ALG and user agent B and the ALG.

In this example, SIP messages 2, 4, 6, and 9, used to establish the session, are passed by the firewall since these packets were sent to or from the IP address of the SIP ALG at port number 5060. The resulting RTP media packets also are passed by the firewall since they originate or terminate at the IP address of the SIP ALG. In this way, the firewall needs only to open holes to allow SIP and RTP packets to the ALG. No dynamic changes in firewall policy are needed.

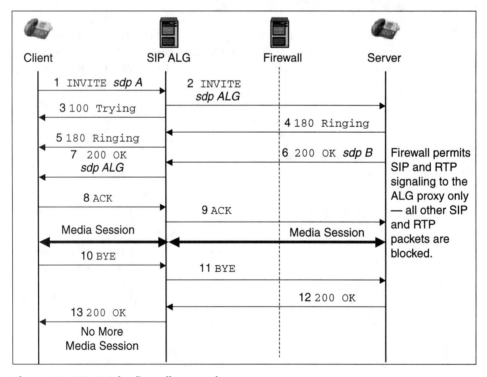

**Figure 8.3**  SIP ALG for firewall traversal.

The other alternative to an ALG, which proxies both the signaling and media, is to use a SIP firewall proxy that communicates with the firewall or NAT. The firewall proxy performs any authentication, authorization, etc., and then parses the SIP messages for the source and destination IP addresses and port numbers of the RTP packets. For example, the source and destination IP addresses and port numbers can be obtained from the SDP in the `INVITE` and `200 OK` messages. The firewall proxy then tells the firewall to open pin-holes to let only those RTP packets pass. The firewall proxy also maintains the NAT address binding, and modifies the SDP accordingly so that the RTP packets can be sent directly between the user agents. Upon session termination with a `BYE`, the firewall proxy tells the firewall to close the pin-holes and the NAT to remove the address binding. While there is currently no standard protocol for communication between the SIP proxy and the firewall/NAT, this is being developed in the IETF Middlebox Communication Working Group (MIDCOM WG) [13].

Figure 8.4 shows a call flow of a successful call through a firewall/NAT using a firewall proxy. Note that the messages between the proxy and the firewall/NAT are generic, as the MIDCOM protocol is still at the framework [14] stage as of IETF-50.

Note that this firewall proxy can be transparent in operation if no authentication is required. In this case, the transparent proxy can become part of the NAT or firewall, in which IP addresses and port numbers are modified in the SIP messages, and pin-holes are opened in the firewall and NAT address bindings are created for the duration of the call. However, the proxy need not add a `Via` header or perform any stateful proxy functions. In this way, neither party can tell that there is a proxy in the path. This approach is discussed in Martin and Johnston [15].

For these types of firewall traversal to work, the `Contact` header of the user agent behind the firewall either must be set by the user agent to resolve to the IP address of the ALG or firewall proxy or the ALG or firewall proxy must `Record-Route`. A proxy inserts a `Record-Route` header containing an entry that resolves back to the IP address of the proxy. This `Record-Route` header is forwarded with the request, stored by the user agent server, and included in the response sent back to the user agent client that originated the request. All future requests during the session must now include a `Route` header that forces the request to route through the proxy.

An example with one proxy that `Record-Routes` and another that does not is shown in Figure 8.5.

In this example, proxy A needs to be included in all future SIP messaging between the user agents, while proxy B does not. As a result, proxy A inserts a `Record-Route` header while proxy B does not add itself to the `Record-Route` header. As a result, the `ACK` and the `BYE` requests route through proxy A but bypass proxy B. Note that the `Route` header always contains information

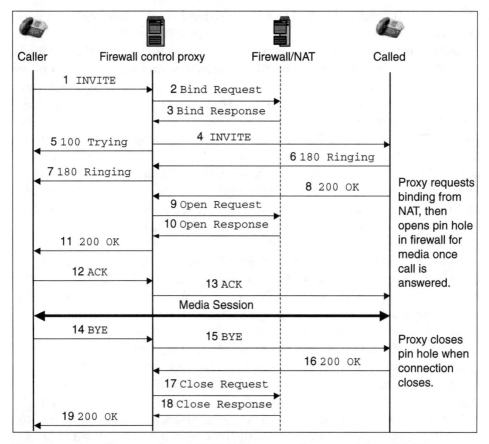

**Figure 8.4** Firewall proxy using a MIDCOM-like protocol to control firewall/NAT.

about the next hop, not the current hop. As a result, in this example, since the ACK of message 13 is sent to proxy A, the Route header does not contain the URL of proxy A, but instead contains the URL of the next hop, which is UA2. The same is true for the BYE of message 15. After the last URL in the Route header is used, the header is removed from the request, as it is in messages 14 and 16. Also note that the Route header is never present in responses, as they are always routed back through the same set of proxies taken by the request.

For this scenario to work, the user agent behind the firewall must have the ALG or firewall proxy set as the default outbound proxy for all outgoing requests.

## Privacy Considerations

Some aspects of privacy have been previously discussed in this chapter. However, these privacy aspects relate only to eavesdropping of a third party.

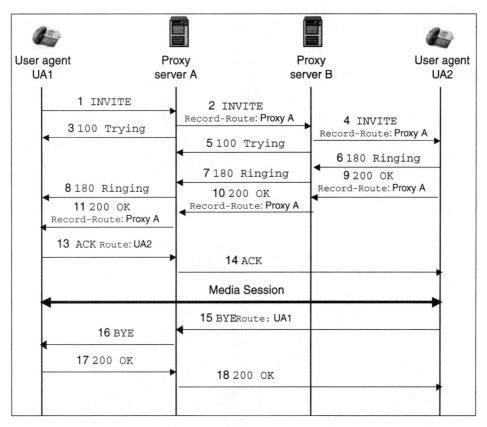

**Figure 8.5** SIP proxy `Record-Route` example.

Another issue is caller privacy. In the PSTN today, it is possible to block one's calling party number from display to the called party. It is also possible to place a phone call anonymously by using a payphone in which only the location but not the identity of the caller can be determined. In establishing a SIP session, the two parties must exchange significant information that might be considered private, including IP addresses, which can be traced to a particular subnet location or have a reverse DNS lookup performed to resolve the address back to a domain name.

In a session established directly between two user agents, there is no alternative to this information exchange. However, SIP network elements have been designed using a back-to-back user agent (B2BUA) to implement an "anonymizer" service in which a caller's IP address, URL, or other identifying information can be blocked from the called party. Figure 8.6 shows a B2BUA implementation of an anonymizer service. (In this example, only significant headers and messages are shown for clarity.) Notice that there are actually two completely separate sessions established, with the B2BUA proxying signaling

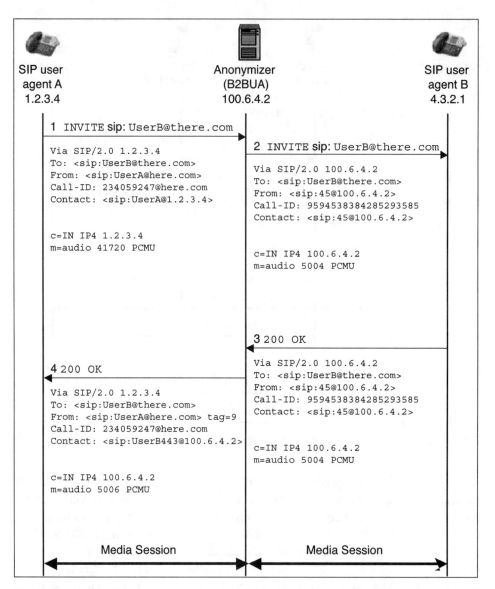

**Figure 8.6** Anonymizer service implemented using back-to-back user agent.

and media information from one call to the other. As a result, each party sends SIP and RTP packets to the B2BUA and not to each other. Once the call is over, the anonymizer service can erase any logs, flush all state, and the resulting call is essentially untraceable.

In the Distributed Call Signaling (DCS) architecture [16], a user agent can request a level of privacy by setting appropriate parameters in the Remote-

`Party-ID` header, which results in a proxy routing the call through the B2BUA for the desired level of privacy.

# Design of a Secure SIP Network

A secure SIP network for a service provider can be designed using the security tools and approaches described in this chapter. The elements of a secure SIP network are shown in Figure 8.7, which is based on Rosenberg [17]. A service provider's network is shown consisting of firewalls, different types of proxies, media servers, and gateways. A firewall is used to protect the network of proxies, media servers, and gateways from the public Internet. Only the edge proxies are accessible by users outside the firewall. The edge proxies can control the firewall to enable SIP and media sessions to be established between users outside the network and proxies and media servers within. Core proxies and service proxies provide routing within the SIP network and access to media servers and gateways.

Authentication challenges are performed by the edge proxies. Signaling between the edge proxies and other servers and gateways within the network

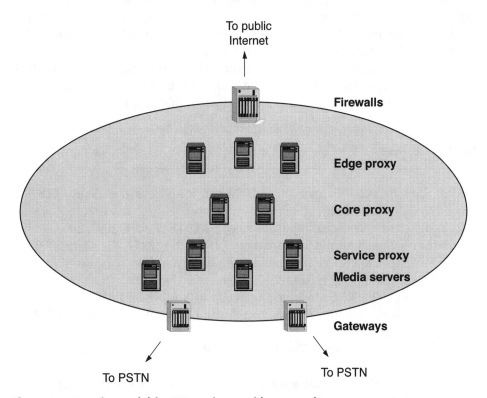

**Figure 8.7** Security model for SIP service provider network.

can be secured using IPSec or TLS. `Via` headers can be stripped by the edge proxies, thus hiding the internal topology of the service provider's network. The `branch` parameter inserted by the edge proxy can be used to look up the stripped `Via` headers which can then be reinserted for response routing within the service provider's network. Core proxies provide routing between proxies and gateways and media servers. Gateways provide the interworking between the SIP network and another network, such as the PSTN or an H.323 network. Service proxies perform third-party call control and other features and services, and handle routing to media servers.

The firewalls and edge proxies also help protect the entire network from denial of service (DOS) attacks, in which a client floods a network with requests. For example, an edge proxy can scan incoming SIP requests for malicious content such as viruses, or block frequent message transmissions.

## Summary

This chapter has introduced some basic security and privacy mechanisms in SIP: Authentication, encryption and digital signatures. Issues relating to existing security elements, such as firewalls and NATs, have also been covered, showing the problems faced in firewall and NAT transversal and various solutions available. Finally, privacy is also discussed.

It is important to note that security is an extremely complex and important topic; readers are advised to make a thorough investigation of this issue beyond the general guidelines and suggestions in this chapter.

## References

[1] K. Egevang and P. Francis. "The IP Network Address Translator," IETF RFC 1631, May 1994.

[2] T. Hain. "Architectural Implications of NAT," IETF RFC 2993, 2000.

[3] B. Carpenter. "Internet Transparency," IETF RFC 2277, February 2000.

[4] J. Franks, et al. "HTTP Authentication: Basic and Digest Access Authentication," IETF RFC 2617, 1999.

[5] R. Rivest. "The MD5 Message-Digest Algorithm," IETF RFC 1321, 1992.

[6] R. Atkinson. "Security Architecture for the Internet Protocol," IETF RFC 1825, 1995.

[7] T. Dierks and C. Allen. "The TLS Protocol Version 1.0," IETF RFC 2246, 1999.

[8] M. Elkins. "MIME Security with Pretty Good Privacy (PGP)," IETF RFC 2015, 1996.

[9] D. Senie. "NAT Friendly Application Design Guidelines," IETF Internet draft, March 2001, work in progress.

[10] J. Rosenberg and H. Schulzrinne. "SIP Traversal through Residential and Enterprise NATs and Firewalls," IETF Internet draft, March 2001, work in progress.

[11] D. Yon. "Connection-Oriented Media Transport in SDP," IETF Internet draft, February 2001, work in progress.

[12] A. Johnston, et al. "SIP Call Flow Examples," IETF Internet draft, 2001, work in progress.

[13] For the latest on the MIDCOM IETF Working Group, visit http://www.ietf.org/charters/midcom.html.

[14] P. Srisuresh, J. Kuthan, and J. Rosenberg. "Middlebox Communication Architecture and Framework," IETF Internet draft, 2001, work in progress.

[15] C. Martin and A. Johnston, "SIP Through NAT Enabled Firewall Call Flows," IETF Internet draft, 2001, work in progress.

[16] W. Marshall, et al. "SIP Extensions for Caller Identity and Privacy," IETF Internet draft, 2001, work in progress.

[17] J. Rosenberg. "Architecting SIP Networks for ITSPs," Presentation at the SIP 2001 Europe, Paris conference, March 2001.

CHAPTER 9

# SIP-Based Telephony

In this chapter, the basic telephony services and features will be discussed as implemented in a SIP-enabled network. First, basic telephony will be covered, followed by more advanced features. We will describe the basic and more advanced telephony features for which there are Internet drafts published to support interservice provider and intervendor product interoperability.

## Basic Telephony Services

Basic telephony involves the establishment of sessions between endpoints. The basics of telephony in an all-IP environment are covered in Chapter 5, *SIP Overview*. This chapter will focus on SIP and PSTN interworking for basic telephony services.

### SIP and PSTN Interworking

SIP and PSTN interworking occurs whenever a call originates in one network and terminates in the other network. To accomplish this, the signaling and media transport protocols must be mapped between the two domains. Calls in which an action in one domain causes an action in the other domain, but not the establishment of a session between them, will be discussed in Chapter 13, *Mixed PSTN and Internet Telephony Services.*

Gateways are the network elements bridging the two networks, as shown in Figure 9.1. The gateway is, as a result, part of both the PSTN and SIP network. There are two basic approaches to building these gateways—complete protocol interworking and protocol encapsulation. The latter approach is known as SIP Telephony (SIP-T) [1], which is not a separate protocol, but rather the SIP protocol plus a number of extensions. The gateway appears to the SIP network to be a user agent for many different users, and to the PSTN as a terminating telephone switch, either Class 5 or Class 3 depending on the design.

## Gateway Location and Routing

Since the gateway has multiple users, it does not REGISTER like a normal user agent. A normal registration binds a user's URL with a number of URLs. A gateway instead serves a host of users, either a corporate entity served from a PBX or Centrex group, a local ISP domain, or users associated with a particular geo-

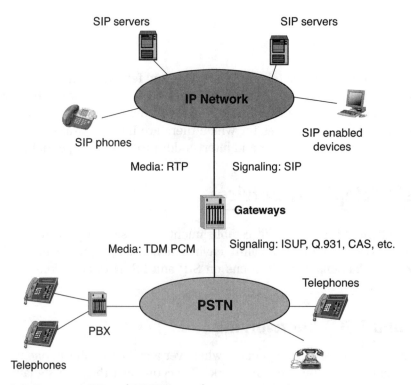

**Figure 9.1** Gateways, SIP, and PSTN Networks.

graphic region, usually identified by a PSTN number range: Country code, Numbering Plan Area (NPA) or area code or NPA-NXX (area code and local exchange). Instead of modifying SIP registration, the problem of gateway location and routing has been tackled in the IETF IP Telephony Working Group (IPTEL WG) with the development of the Telephony Routing over IP (TRIP) [2] protocol. This gateway to the location server protocol, based on Border Gateway Protocol (BGP)—used to advertise IP routes between networks—allows a gateway to advertise what PSTN number range it supports. This information is then available to proxies in routing SIP URLs containing telephone numbers and telephony URLs.

TRIP is designed for interdomain gateway location—it is not specifically designed to be used within a domain. However, the need for this same service within a domain has been identified by the IPTEL WG, which has begun work on a modified protocol called "TRIP Lite" which operates between a gateway and a proxy within a domain.

---

**SIP URLS AND TELEPHONE NUMBERS**

As discussed in Chapter 5 *SIP Overview*, SIP URLs can contain telephone numbers such as sip:+65234213@carrier.com;user=phone. This URL might seem to have enough information present to route the SIP request without needing TRIP or any other protocol, since the carrier identified in the hostname can locate a gateway. However, the user placing a SIP call through a gateway to the telephone number identified in this URL does not have to use the gateways owned by the IP telephony carrier identified in the hostname portion. Since the phone number is a global E.164 number, any number of gateways could be used. Since the call through the gateway will likely involve a charge, the user will probably want the call routed through a gateway operated by the IP telephony carrier of choice. As a result, the request will probably be routed to a different IP address than that specified in the SIP URL. That carrier will then need to locate a termination gateway using TRIP or other schemes.

---

## SIP/PSTN Protocol Interworking

SIP and PSTN protocol interworking has two levels—the media and the signaling. The media interworking is quite straightforward. The PSTN generally uses a 64-kb/s pulse-coded modulation (PCM) encoded time division multiplexing (TDM) channel known as a trunk to carry the voice media. If Integrated Services Digital Network (ISDN) is used, the B channel contains the 64-kb/s PCM media stream. SIP-enabled devices generally have audio capabilities in the form of Real-time Transport Protocol (RTP) packets. The media interworking in a gateway involves terminating a PCM trunk on the PSTN side and bridging the media with an IP port that sends and receives RTP packets. Codec conversion between PCM and another codec is possible in the gateway, or the gateway may simply reuse the 64-kb/s PCM as RTP/audio-video profile (AVP) 0, a common codec supported by nearly every SIP device capable of sending and receiving audio. The gateway refuses SIP sessions that do not contain an audio channel, and will reject all other media types that cannot be mapped into PSTN telephony voice channels.

The signaling interworking is much more complex. While a SIP network is "flat" in terms of not having a different ITU-style user-to-network interface (UNI) and network-to-network interface (NNI), the PSTN uses many different signaling protocols to complete a call. For example, a PSTN call may enter the PSTN as a PBX trunk, in which a Circuit-Associated Signaling (CAS) protocol is used to out-pulse dialed digits as multifrequency (MF) tones. The telephone switch then signals to other telephone switches using ISDN User Part (ISUP) signaling which is carried out-of-band in a dedicated packet switched network known as Signaling System 7 (SS7). Alternatively, ISDN (Q.931) D-channel signaling may be used.

There are also service level gateways for more complete integration of PSTN, mobile phone networks, and SIP services, as are described in Chapter 13, *Mixed PSTN and Internet Telephony Services.*

## Types of Gateways

The PSTN signaling protocol that a SIP/PSTN gateway will use will depend on the way it interfaces with the PSTN. We will consider two types of gateways: (1) network gateways and (2) enterprise gateways. Descriptions of each follow:

1. A *network gateway* is a high port count gateway that is typically owned by a PSTN carrier and interfaces with other PSTN switches using ISUP and ISDN as its network-to-network interface. A network gateway is typically located at a PSTN central office, where other large telephone switches are located.

2. An *enterprise gateway*, on the other hand, is typically a small port count gateway that may be owned by a PSTN customer, and interfaces with the PSTN via user-to-network protocols such as Circuit Associated Signaling (CAS) and ISDN. This device typically will be located on a customer's premises or building.

## SIP and Early Media

A number of Internet drafts have been written to document the basic mapping between SIP and PSTN protocols. However, the base SIP specification was found to be missing one key component of successful SIP/PSTN interworking—support of early media. In the PSTN, call progress indicators are often provided in-band in the media path, such as ring tone, busy signal, re-order tone, etc. These indicators are carried in a one-way speech path that is established as soon as the called party is alerted, but prior to the call being answered. The caller hears the ring tone or busy signal and knows how the call is progressing.

In SIP, the media path is not established until the called party answers (200 OK), and all call progress indicators are assumed to be carried in the SIP responses, not in any media path (180 Ringing, 181 Call is Being Forwarded, 486 Busy Here, 503 Service Unavailable, etc.). This is not a problem in a call from the PSTN to SIP—the gateway simply takes the SIP response code and generates any tones or signals in the PSTN media path. However, for SIP-to-PSTN calling, the SIP phone's local ring tone generated by the receipt of a 180 Ringing response from the gateway masks the in-band progress indicators being received by the gateway. The result is that the call may fail and the SIP caller will never hear any indication, just the locally generated ring tone.

The solution was to add a response code to SIP, called 183 Session Progress [3], which is used to indicate that the call is progressing, but that the user agent server (PSTN gateway) is not able to determine from signaling what is occurring, but that information may be available in the media path. The gateway then sends the call progress tones or signals it is receiving in the one-way speech path in the TDM channel as RTP packets to the SIP phone. The SIP phone receiving a 183 response knows then to play those RTP packets instead of generating local alerting, as shown in Figure 9.2.

This approach works, but has an unfortunate side effect in the case of a SIP call that may have been forked to two different locations in the PSTN. The result of this is that two 183 responses will be received, and the SIP user agent client will have to decide which media stream to play or whether to mix the two together.

Note that the gateway only sends a 183 Session Progress response if it is unable to determine whether ringing is occurring. For example, if the PSTN connection is exclusively ISDN, then the alerting message can be mapped to a 180 Ringing. However, in many cases, especially where some type of non-SS7 signaling path is present in the PSTN, the gateway will not be able to make this determination and will send a 183 Session Progress.

It is also important to note that when the gateway cannot make this distinction, it is not considered early media [3], since the connection on the IP side is unidirectional. The gateway received the INVITE from the user agent so it knows the IP address and port number where the user agent will be listening. The SIP standard requires a calling user agent to immediately begin listening for media on the port as soon as the INVITE is sent. The gateway is then able to send the in-band call progress RTP packets to that address. The

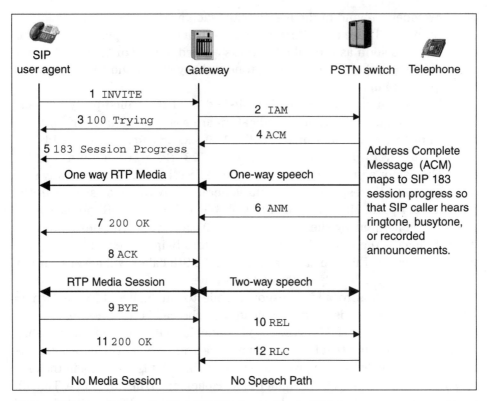

**Figure 9.2** SIP-to-PSTN call with in-band call progress indicators.

actual two-way RTP media session is not established until the called party answers and a 200 OK and ACK have been exchanged between the gateway and user agent.

A SIP-to-PSTN call flow is shown in Figure 9.3. In this case, the called SIP user agent sends a 180 Ringing response to the gateway, which then seizes a trunk in the PSTN and sends an address complete message (ACM). If the PSTN requires in-band alerting such as ring tone, the gateway would generate it. The 183 Session Progress is not used. In this scenario, if the SIP user agent returned an error response, such as 410 The Number is No Longer in Service, the gateway would be responsible for playing a suitable announcement for the PSTN caller. In the long term, this will involve a text-to-speech conversion in which the gateway would speak the error reason phrase. In the short term, the gateway will need to play a prerecorded announcement, or forward an INVITE to an announcement server, which can play the announcement.

Many examples of SIP and PSTN interworking are given in the IETF SIP Call Flows Informational RFC [4]. Detailed information about mapping between SIP and ISUP can be found in Camarillo and Roach [5].

**SIP AND EARLY MEDIA**

In a normal SIP session, the media session is not established prior to the call completing with a 200 OK response. The PSTN supports both one-way and two-way early media (that is, voice connections prior to an answer message (ANM) or connect message) in certain circumstances. For example, some nationwide toll-free routing services prompt the caller and collect dual-tone multifrequency (DTMF) digits prior to routing the call to the final destination.

There are numerous problems in supporting this type of early media in SIP. Early proposals were to include session description protocol (SDP) in the 183 Session Progress response, which would allow a two-way media session to be established. This approach has many problems, mainly with forking. For example:

■ A caller could receive early media from multiple locations at the same time if forking is encountered. Also, there is no way to correlate the media streams with the signaling information.

■ The 183 needs to be delivered reliably, so the PRACK method is needed.

■ There is no way to put an early media stream on hold—a re-INVITE cannot be sent until the initial INVITE is completed.

For these and other reasons, other early media approaches are being developed to overcome these problems. However, this approach will be an extension to SIP and will require the use of a Supported header.

However, basic PSTN interworking does not require the support of early media extensions, since a one-way media stream established prior to the call being answered is supported in the base SIP specification RFC 2543.

## SIP Telephony and ISUP Tunneling

SIP interworking with the PSTN at the signaling level involves a mapping of message types and parameters from one network to another. For example, consider the PSTN-to-SIP call in Figure 9.3. The ISUP IAM message 1 in Figure 9.3 is shown in Table 9.1, along with a description of each field.

The IAM can be mapped to the SIP INVITE message 2 of Figure 9.3 as shown here:

```
INVITE sip:+1-972-555-2222@proxy.carrier.com;user=phone SIP/2.0
Via: SIP/2.0/UDP gw1.carrier.com:5060
From: sip:+1-314-555-1111@gw1.carrier.wcom.com;user=phone
To: sip:+1-972-555-2222@proxy.carrier.com;user=phone
Call-ID: 12345602@gw1.carrier.com
CSeq: 1 INVITE
Contact: sip:+1-314-555-1111@gw1.carrier.com;user=phone
Content-Type: application/sdp
Content-Length: 156
```

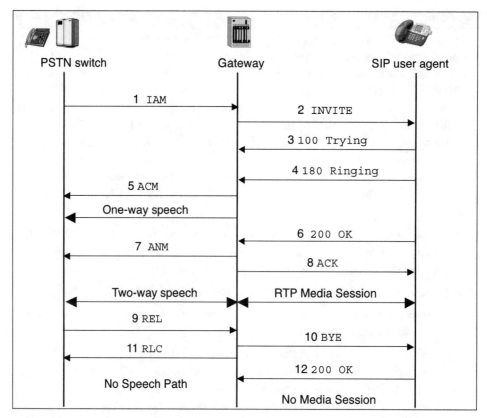

**Figure 9.3**  PSTN-to-SIP call.

```
v=0
o=GATEWAY1 2890844527 2890844527 IN IP4 gatewayone.carrier.com
s=Session SDP
c=IN IP4 gatewayone.carrier.com
t=0 0
m=audio 3456 RTP/AVP 0
a=rtpmap:0 PCMU/8000
```

Some field mapping is obvious, such as Calling Party Number to `From`, but others are not so obvious. In particular, there are generally many more parameters in a PSTN signaling message than can be mapped to a SIP message. (For example, how is the Forward Call Indicator mapped to SIP?) The result is some information loss. However, if the call routes over the SIP network to the destination, there is no net effect on the call completion, since all information *usable* in the SIP network has been mapped. The additional parameters that are not mapped from ISUP to SIP are designed for PSTN routing, not SIP routing, and their loss has no effect. Similarly, mapping from SIP to ISUP (shown in Figure 9.2) does not cause a loss in functionality. In

**Table 9.1** ISUP IAM Message and Field Description

| | |
|---|---|
| `IAM` | Initial Address Message |
| `CgPN=314-555-1111,`<br>`NPI=E.164, NOA=National` | Calling Party Number, Numbering Plan Indicator, Nature of Address |
| `CdPN=972-555-2222,`<br>`NPI=E.164, NOA=National` | Called Party Number, Numbering Plan Indicator, Nature of Address |
| `USI=Speech` | User Service Information |
| `FCI=Normal` | Forward Call Indicator |
| `CPC=Normal` | Calling Party's Category |
| `CCI=Not Required` | Call Charge Indicator |

this case, some ISUP parameters that have no counterpart in SIP will need to be created for the mapped IAM. These values are set to default values, typically on a trunk group basis.

However, should a call be routed from the PSTN to SIP then back to the PSTN, some of the lost parameters from the first PSTN leg could be useful in routing in the second PSTN leg. To solve this problem for networks designed to do this, the encapsulation of PSTN signaling messages, in addition to interworking, was developed. This application of SIP, known as SIP Telephony (SIP-T) [1], carries the PSTN signaling information in the SIP signaling message as a MIME message body [6]. The terminating gateway then constructs the second leg PSTN signaling based on the SIP signaling parameters and the attached message body of the original PSTN signaling. The resulting network offers the possibility of making the SIP leg of the call transparent to the PSTN. Put another way, SIP-T enables the ISUP transparency across a SIP network. This call flow is shown in Figure 9.4.

SIP-T also uses the `INFO` method to carry midcall signaling information, as shown in Figure 5.7.

The advantages of implementing SIP-T are obvious—it allows a carrier to build a PSTN network using a SIP IP telephony core, and provide transparency and full features. The disadvantages are not so obvious, but can be seen on closer examination. For instance, the complexity of gateways implementing SIP-T is much greater than a normal gateway, since a SIP-T gateway must still do all the PSTN-to-SIP mapping of a regular gateway, plus the additional encoding, decoding, and parsing of the ISUP attachments. For example, the `INVITE` message 2 of Figure 9.4 would be:

```
INVITE sip:+1-972-555-2222@proxy.carrier.com;user=phone SIP/2.0
Via: SIP/2.0/UDP carrier.wcom.com:5060
From: sip:+1-314-555-1111@carrier.wcom.com;user=phone
To: sip:+1-972-555-2222@ss1.wcom.com;user=phone
Call-ID: 12345602@ngw1.carrier.com
```

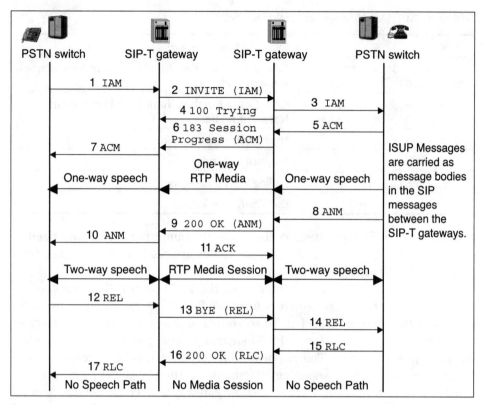

**Figure 9.4** SIP-T call flow with ISUP tunneling.

```
CSeq: 1 INVITE
Contact: sip:+1-314-555-1111@ngw1.carrier.com;user=phone
MIME-Version: 1.0
Content-Type: multipart/mixed; boundary="--***"
Content-Length: 318

--***
Content-Type: application/sdp

v=0
o=GATEWAY1 2890844527 2890844527 IN IP4 gatewayone.carrier.com
s=Session SDP
c=IN IP4 gatewayone.carrier.com
t=0 0
m=audio 3456 RTP/AVP 0
a=rtpmap:0 PCMU/8000

--***
Content-Type: mime/isup

7452a43564a4d566736fa343503837f168a383b84f706474404568783746463ff
```

Compared to the example INVITE of message 2 of Figure 9.3 shown previously, the message body is now a multipart MIME attachment. The first part contains the SDP of the gateway, while the second part contains the binary encoded IAM of message 1 in Figure 9.4. In creating the Initial Address Message (IAM) of message 3 in Figure 9.4, the terminating SIP-T gateway uses information from both the SIP headers of the INVITE and the ISUP attachment. In a SIP-T network, the complexity and intricacies of the PSTN are not absorbed in the gateways, but distributed throughout the network. All gateways must be able to parse the ISUP attachments, or true ISUP transparency will not occur. For international networks, there are many different incompatible "flavors" of ISUP. International gateway PSTN switches are extremely complicated and expensive due to the requirements that they be able to use and convert all these different incompatible protocols. In an international SIP-T network, what "flavor" of ISUP will be used? If multiple versions are allowed in the SIP network, every gateway will need to be able to deal with all versions of ISUP. If only a single version is allowed, there will be information loss as the ISUP is converted, leading to a failure in true transparency. Finally, in a mixed SIP and SIP-T network (one involving both SIP-T gateways, conventional gateways, and SIP phones and end devices), the ISUP will need to be encrypted due to the sensitivity of some information present there (such as the Calling Party Number of a private call), leading to additional complexity in gateways. Alternatively, a network of screening proxies will be needed to selectively remove ISUP attachments. (These proxies will have to decode the multipart MIME attachment composed of the SDP and the ISUP, extract only the SDP, recalculate the octet count, then forward the message.) This adds delay and complexity to the SIP network.

The simplest argument against SIP-T is the fact that SIP phones cannot easily talk to SIP gateways and there are now really two types of SIP endpoints that cannot talk to each other. As a result, SIP gateways can talk only directly to other SIP gateways, and SIP phones can talk only to other SIP phones.

Some early SIP networks will implement SIP-T, especially in so-called "softswitch" networks. However, for truly scalable and cost-effective telephony, the complexity and protocols of the PSTN must not be carried into the IP domain—a true SIP/PSTN interworking gateway is required and ISUP tunneling or encapsulation is not required.

A summary of SIP-to-PSTN protocol mapping is shown in Table 9.2. Note that this table is greatly simplified, and actual mapping is more complex, depending on the version of ISUP used (ETSI, ANSI, etc.).

# Enhanced Telephony Services

One remarkable promise of SIP-enhanced telephony services is that they can be implemented across the open Internet environment, working effectively

**Table 9.2** SIP-to-ISUP and ISDN Message Mapping

| SIP MESSAGE OR RESPONSE | ISUP MESSAGE | ISDN MESSAGE |
|---|---|---|
| INVITE | IAM or SAM | Setup |
| INFO | USR | User |
| BYE | REL | Release |
| CANCEL | REL | Release |
| ACK | — | — |
| REGISTER | — | — |
| 18x | ACM or CPG | Alerting |
| 200 (to INVITE) | ANM or CON | Connect |
| 4xx, 5xx, 6xx | REL | Release |
| 200 (to BYE) | RLC | Release Complete |

across service provider boundaries and between equipments and software from many vendors. It remains to be seen to what extent this promise of extending PBX-like rich call features across the Internet will be fulfilled.

Enhanced services in telephony come in three possible forms: (1) PBX or Centrex features, (2) Custom Local Area Signaling Services (CLASS) features, and (3) Advanced Intelligent Network (AIN) services.

Features have very specific names and definitions in the PSTN and PBX world. However, to discuss their analog in SIP, we will use generic names, which may or may not exactly map to the PSTN or PBX features. Although the IETF does not standardize features or services, many of these services implemented using SIP are described in Johnston [7].

Standardizing the key PBX functions across the Internet may herald a significant disruption in the PBX market where all products are vendor proprietary and interoperability, as with the ITU QSIG standard, is difficult to achieve. Also, PBX phones from different vendors are not interchangeable. IP PBXs based on SIP have the potential of basic standards-based interoperability and also the potential of interchangeable SIP phones for baseline PBX features. We will take a closer look at baseline PBX features.

PBX or CLASS features generally include the following:

**Call transfer.** There are three types of call transfer services: (1) blind, (2) unattended, and (3) attended that can be implemented using the REFER method. In a blind transfer, the transferor sends a REFER then immediately sends a BYE and terminates the existing session without waiting for the outcome of the transfer. In an unattended transfer, the transferor may keep the transferee on hold pending the outcome of the REFER request. Once the transferor receives notification that the transfer has succeeded, a BYE is sent to tear down the existing session. Finally, the attended transfer involves a temporary conference call between the three parties in which the transferor knows the exact progress of the transfer. Once the transfer is complete, the transferor can then drop out of the call. The types of call transfer are described in Table 9.3.

**Call waiting.** This is a service implemented on single-line telephones. Since there is no such thing as a "line" in a SIP network, this feature does not have an exact analog. However, a SIP phone that offers multiple "line" behavior would return a 180 Ringing response and initiate alerting even when there is an active session established. The called party can then either place the session on hold and answer the second call or ignore the second caller.

**Call hold.** This feature has many forms in the PSTN, from a button on a telephone set that simply cuts the speaker and microphone, to advanced features in PBX or ISDN systems. In a SIP network, a call is placed on hold by sending a re-INVITE with a connection IP address of 0.0.0.0 in the SDP. This causes the recipient to stop sending media packets. The 200 OK response to the hold re-INVITE usually also has a connection IP address of 0.0.0.0, which then stops all media packets for the session. The call is taken off hold when either party sends a re-INVITE with a nonzero connection IP address.

**Call park and pickup.** In this feature, a call is placed on hold at one location, and then retrieved (picked up) at another location. There are a number of proposals to implement these features in SIP. Some of them use a REGISTER request and a re-INVITE, while others use a REFER, and then a redirect.

**Call forwarding.** There are three options with this feature: (1) forward on busy, (2) don't answer, and (3) unconditional. Forwarding can be done in SIP either in a proxy or in a user agent, as shown in Chapter 6, *SIP Service Creation*. A proxy can translate one URL for another,

**Table 9.3** Types of Call Transfer

| TRANSFER OR ACTION | TRANSFER | CONSULT NEW PARTY | TALK TO BOTH PARTIES |
|---|---|---|---|
| Unattended | Yes | No | No |
| Consultation Hold | Yes | Yes | No |
| Attended | Yes | Yes | Yes |

resulting in a forward that is transparent to the calling user agent. Alternatively, a user agent or a proxy can issue a redirection response (302 Moved). A proxy receiving a 486 Busy Here response can invoke a call-forward-on-busy feature by generating an ACK and then forwarding the INVITE to another URL. A proxy can also start a ring timer upon receipt of a 180 Ringing response, then send a CANCEL and proxy the INVITE to another URL to implement a call-forward, don't-answer service.

**Calling line identification.** The ability to display calling line identification is a useful feature in the PSTN to aid the caller during alerting in deciding whether to answer a call or to implement automated screening services. For example, a feature could be implemented to block incoming SIP calls in which the calling party has not identified themselves. The basic functionality is built into SIP to accomplish this, using the From header. However, since the From header is populated by the calling user agent, and not by a trusted source such as a carrier, this calling line identification is not verified or guaranteed to be accurate. Instead, an extension header to SIP has been proposed called Remote-Party-ID, which would be inserted and verified by a trusted source, such as an IP telephony carrier. The value of this header is more analogous to calling line identification in the PSTN. However, this header is only valid as long as there is a trust relationship over the entire signaling path.

**Incoming and outgoing call screening.** Incoming and outgoing call screening can be implemented in either a proxy or user agent. A Request-URI or From header is compared to a list of allowed or blocked URIs, and an appropriate response generated, such as 403 Forbidden, in the event of a call being blocked. The outgoing call screening feature can only be implemented in a proxy if the user agent is configured to always use that proxy as an outgoing proxy. The incoming call screening feature can only be implemented in a proxy if the user agent is configured to accept only requests from an incoming proxy, redirecting all other requests with a 305 Use Proxy response.

**Automatic callback and recall.** Automatic recall allows a PSTN user to return a missed call based on calling line identification. This is easily implemented in a user agent by caching the From header from the previous failed INVITE request. Automatic callback allows a PSTN user whose call fails due to a busy signal to have the call automatically placed, as soon as the called party becomes free. This can be implemented in a SIP network using a simple presence service, in which a SUBSCRIBE is sent to request notification when the called user agent is no longer busy. The NOTIFY response would then automatically generate a new INVITE to complete the call. This was shown as an example in Figure 5.11 in Chapter 5, *SIP Overview*.

**Speed dial.** Speed dial allows a user to place a call by dialing a shorter digit string, often stored in the network or in the telephone set. A SIP user agent can use any speed dial method. Alternatively, a mapping from a "nickname" to a full URI is possible to allow easier "dialing" in a similar way that nicknames are useful in e-mail.

**Conference calling.** Conference calling is described in Chapter 12, *SIP Conferencing*.

**Voice mail.** This important service is described in Chapter 10, *Voice Mail and Unified Messaging*.

Besides emulating PBX features, SIP also can emulate AIN services found in the PSTN. Both capability sets CS-1 and CS-2 defined by the ITU are discussed and illustrated for SIP in Lennox, et al. [8]. AIN or advanced features in the PSTN often take one of the following forms:

**Interactive voice response (IVR) system.** These "voice menu" or "auto prompt" systems allow an automated attendant to answer a call, play prompts, collect information using either spoken words or DTMF digits, and then route the call to its final destination. This typically is accomplished using a third-party control mechanism discussed later in this chapter.

**Specialized routing services.** Call routing is performed based on time of day, origin number, traffic load, and other factors. This type of routing decision is routinely made in proxy servers in a SIP network.

**Database query and information retrieval services.** These services are extremely primitive in the PSTN due to the separation of the PSTN from the databases in which the information is stored. For a SIP-enabled network, retrieval and return of information from the biggest database of all, the Internet, is trivial using HTTP, FTP, etc. Simple query services can be built using a SIP redirect server.

# Call Control Services and Third-Party Call Control

Call control services and third-party control are important topics in telephony, as they enable many advanced services and features. For example, automated dialers and interactive voice response (IVR) systems can be built using SIP third-party control.

## Problem Statement

Circuit-switched telephony services in the PSTN historically have been augmented by advanced services in private voice networks by innovative PBX vendors. Where even PBX technology failed to provide adequate solutions, such as in PC-phone interaction and especially for call center applications, the computer telephony industry (CTI) has come to the rescue. Advanced services, however, were created at significant cost and had the drawbacks of: (1) local reach only due to lack of global standards, (2) tremendous complexity that translated into very high cost of ownership, and (3) long time to market. Finally, new telephony applications and other communications have emerged with the advent of the Internet.

A list of call scenarios in use at present would include:

- Managing telephony applications from the desktop PC
- Click-to-connect
- Internet call waiting
- Instant communications

More complex call control models, however, are used at present in conventional telephony systems. Call control, especially in private voice networks, can be extremely complicated. Some examples are given here, with increasing degrees of complexity:

- Pick up a call that was ringing someone else's phone
- Monitor a call in progress such as for call center operations
- Join a conference call (whether scheduled or spontaneous)
- Transfer a call to another party
- Receptionist and secretary model: A caller on the PSTN calls an employee accessible via a private voice network. The call will first reach the receptionist who will inquire about the nature of the call and forward it to the desired party. The called party may have a secretary who may screen the call before connecting it to the boss.
- Call center applications

In a call center scenario, a customer call for support to an 800 number may be routed to an enterprise call center by a public carrier, depending on the call's origin and time of day. The call reaches the call center and, depending on the interaction of the caller with an IVR, the call may be routed according to load and skill set to an appropriate agent group. The agent taking the call may refer the caller to a subject expert in another location and may stay online to make sure the call has been routed to the customer's satisfaction. This complex scenario is accomplished at present with quite expensive call software on various carrier and private network switches, using a rather high count of circuit switch ports both on the carrier side and within the private voice network that owns the call center.

The complexity in the preceding scenarios addresses real business requirements for customer, vendor, and partner relations and were addressed by circuit-switched telephony in combination with CTI. Though Internet engineers promote simplicity as an engineering design goal, it is felt SIP-based solutions have to deal with such complexity as well.

> **NOTE** Examination of the preceding scenarios for call control shows that protocols and standards from conventional telephony models—IN/AIN, PBXs, and softswitch devices—control protocols cannot meet the requirements for Internet standard advanced voice services.

SIP can be applied for extremely complex call scenarios for all of the call scenarios presented here. The question is: Is there a consistent mechanism to deal with such scenarios, with no unnecessary complexity beyond doing the job right and based on public standards for a large degree of interoperability?

The problem was first addressed in the SIP community in the paper on Third-Party Call Control in SIP [9] and then formulated within a framework for SIP Call Control Extensions [10]. The desire was to achieve functionality with extensions and without burdening the base SIP protocol implementations that do not require functions that are more complex. The transfer services were treated in more detail in Sparks [11], after which some interesting new applications emerged, most notably controlling a SIP phone from a desktop PC [12],[13] using SIP third-party call control. A useful method for SIP, called REFER, turns out to be appropriate to handle most complex call control scenarios. Readers having some insight into the complexity of the IN/AIN, PBXs, H.323, and MEGACO/H.248 protocols may find the simplicity of the REFER method outlined here especially intriguing.

## The REFER Method

The REFER method allows a third party, such as a controller, to request the caller set up a call with a resource. The resource is identified in a new SIP header called Refer-To. Note that the resource is a URL, not necessarily a SIP URL. For example, the Refer-To header could contain an HTTP URL which would result in the Web page being retrieved instead of a new SIP call being initiated. Also, a SIP URL in a Refer-To header may contain the method type, which defaults to INVITE if not specified. Thus, a REFER request could be used to request a BYE be sent instead of an INVITE. A REFER request must contain a `Referred-By` header which identifies the referring party. In the new request generated as a result of the `REFER` request, this `Referred-By` header can be used to inform the called party by whom it was referred to make this call. Examples of the the Refer-To header are:

1. To request a party to call John Doe, a `REFER` request is sent containing:
   `Refer-To: sip:john.doe@isp.com`

2. The same request containing the header
   `Refer-To: sip:john.doe@isp.com?`

   `Accept-Contact=sip:jdoe@100.101.102.103;only=true`

   ensures that the right John Doe device (instance) is reached by the request. For example, the referred request could encounter a forking proxy, or some other service logic in which there are multiple possible `Contact` URLs for John Doe. The `Accept-Contact` header along with the `only=true` parameter ensures that the right one is reached.

Examples of the `Referred-By` header are:

1. `Referred-By: sip:manager@isp.com;ref=http://headhunters` `.com` provides the reference source for "headhunters," which is a Web page.

2. `Referred-By: sip:john.doe@isp.com; ref=<htpp://` `headhunters.com>;scheme=pgp;pgp-version="5.0";` `signature= "34a6e328d7cc710f8382"`

also provides a Pretty Good Privacy (PGP) signature computed across the URL of referee and the reference URL. It is recommended that `Referred-By` headers be signed to prevent unauthorized parties from hijacking calls.

Informational reply status codes have been proposed [13] to provide information about the progress of the call. Other approaches are also being considered, including the use of `SUBSCRIBE` and `NOTIFY` requests to request and receive notification about the final outcome of a `REFER` request.

## SIP Third-Party Call Control

As mentioned, by contrast to the ITU and CTI standards, the SIP third-party control presumes intelligent IP end devices instead of dumb terminals, keeping pace with the advent of highly distributed computing. We will show here how intelligent IP endpoints can be controlled for communication services using SIP only. The central idea is loose coupling between intelligent IP endpoints and using SIP call setup only to invoke the necessary functions in the devices, such as phones and desktop and Palm computers. The details of the device operation are then left to the device itself.

Third-party call control is a basic telephony function and is used for many services such as call setup by a controller and call transfers. SIP third-party call control also can be used to control many other services and integrate communications with various other applications and transactions, as shown in the application services architecture. No other standard or proprietary protocols are necessary besides SIP.

**NOTE** Readers familiar with computer telephony integration (CTI) can appreciate the complexity of the technology involved in controlling phones from computers and desktop PCs. CTI relies on complex schemes that are based on special application programming interfaces (APIs) that, in turn, depend on:

  (1) proprietary system implementations and

  (2) proprietary operating systems.

Any "open" API has, therefore, two claimants on intellectual property rights and change by the owners at their convenience. We will show here that computers can control phones in a very simple and completely open, standard manner using SIP. It is the opinion of the authors that CTI is made obsolete by SIP.

### Basic Third-Party Call Control

The concept for basic third-party call control is shown in Figure 9.5, where a controller will set up a call between two parties, A and B, without participating in the conversation in any way.

The operation is as follows:

1. The controller sets up a call with the first party (party A) by sending an INVITE message (message 1 in Figure 9.5). This INVITE does not have an SDP message body. Party A responds with a 200 OK containing the media information of party A. The controller then sends an ACK containing an SDP message body part with a connection address set at IP 0.0.0.0. This is, by convention, a media stream "on hold." No media exchange is possible in this step. The controller stores the SDP data from party A for the next step.

2. The controller will now set up a call with the second party (party B) by sending a second INVITE (message 4 in Figure 9.5) also without any SDP present. This time the controller stores the SDP data received from party B in the 200 OK message (message 5). The controller holds off sending the ACK to party B until this media information is communicated to party A in the next step.

3. Next, the controller re-INVITEs party A from the media "on hold" state using the SDP connection and media data supplied by party B in the previous 200 OK message (message 5 in Figure 9.5). Party A responds with new media information in the 200 OK (message 7). This SDP infor-

mation is then passed back to party B in an ACK (message 8). An ACK without SDP to A completes the session setup. Parties A and B can now exchange real-time protocol RTP media, since they both have the required SDP connection and media data from each other.

4. From a signaling perspective, parties A and B are still communicating with the controller and not with each other. To terminate the call, any party can send a BYE message to terminate the connection to the controller, as shown in (message 11 in Figure 9.5). The controller will follow up by sending a BYE to the other party (message 12). Both BYE messages are followed by 200 OK messages (messages 13 and 14) and the call is terminated.

## Security for Third-Party Call Control

Third-party call control is simple to implement in well-secured IP networks where no security risks are assumed within the trusted environment. In a larger context, however, additional steps have to be taken to authenticate the controller to the controlled parties and to make the controlled SIP endpoints exchange RTP media with each other. In case of encrypted media, the parties need to have a

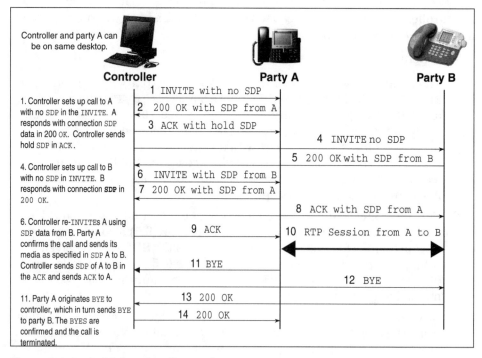

**Figure 9.5** Basic third-party call control.

cryptographic key exchange, which has to be facilitated by SIP call setup. Firewalls and network address translators also will add complexity to third-party call control when the parties reside in different secured networks.

### Peer-to-Peer Third-Party Call Control

SIP can be used for complex call control applications in the peer-to-peer control model. We will discuss an example where a dialer application on a desktop computer of a secretary can control his or her own phone and also can be used to set up calls between two other phones, such as between the boss and a customer, as shown in Figure 9.6. In this application, SIP for presence is used to display on the computer the state of the secretary's own phone. For

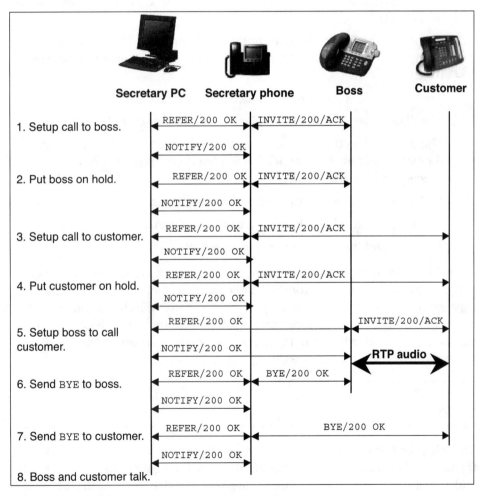

**Figure 9.6** Example of peer-to-peer third-party call control.

simplicity, it is assumed that the presence publisher for the phone is located in the phone itself. This is quite doable with intelligent SIP phones and does not require more complex message exchanges with a dedicated presence server.

SIP servers that normally route all calls are not shown in Figure 9.6 so as to focus the example on only peer-to-peer third-party call control. Also, complete message transaction sequences, such as REFER/200 OK and INVITE/200/ACK are grouped and represented by single, two-headed arrows. The dialer will now use third-party call control to go through a number of steps to set up a call between the boss and a customer:

1. The dialer refers the phone to set up a call to the boss using a REFER request. The result of the REFER is sent in the NOTIFY response. This occurs after each REFER and enables the dialer to know the exact state of the call.

2. The dialer refers the phone to put the boss on hold. This is accomplished by sending a REFER to the phone with the connection address 0.0.0.0.

3. The dialer refers the phone to place a call to the customer.

4. The dialer refers the phone to place the customer on hold.

5. The dialer refers the boss's phone to call the customer. The boss and the customer now have an RTP voice "call" established. The dialer now proceeds to get out of the loop.

6. Dialer refers the phone to send a BYE to the boss.

7. Dialer refers the phone to send a BYE to the customer.

8. The boss and the customer continue to talk.

Real-life scenarios would look more complex, since we have omitted several messages in this example for the sake of clarity. There would be extra message exchanges for presence to display more extensive information about the status of the phone, and messages with SIP servers to route the calls. Also, as discussed in Chapter 8, *Security, NATs, and Firewalls*, the existence of firewalls and NATs will complicate third-party call control.

## Summary

This chapter has examined SIP telephony, interworking with the PSTN, and feature implementations. Even though SIP uses a radically different call model and structure, basic and enhanced telephony services can easily be implemented in a SIP-enabled network.

# References

[1] E. Zimmerer, et al. "SIP Best Current Practice for Telephony Interworking," IETF Internet draft, 1999, work in progress.

[2] RFC 2871: "A framework for Telephony Routing Over IP," J. Rosenberg, et al., IETF, June 2000.

[3] S. Donovan, et al. "SIP 183 Session Progress Message," IETF Internet draft, 1999, work in progress.

[4] A. Johnston, et al. "SIP Call Flow Examples," IETF Internet draft, June 2001, Work in Progress.

[5] G. Camarillo and A. Roach, "SIP to ISUP Mapping," IETF Internet draft, 2001, work in progress

[6] E. Zimmerer, et al. "MIME Media Types for ISUP and QSIG," IETF Internet draft, 2000, work in progress.

[7] A. Johnston, et al. "SIP Service Examples," IETF Internet draft, June 2001, work in progress.

[8] J. Lennox, H. Schulzrinne, and T. La Porta. "Implementing Intelligent Network Services with the Session Initiation Protocol," Columbia University Computer Science Technical Report CUCS-002-99, January 1999.

[9] J. Rosenberg, J. Peterson, and H. Schulzrinne. "Third Party Call Control in SIP," IETF Internet draft, November 2000, work in progress.

[10] B. Campbell. "Framework for SIP Call Control Extensions," IETF Internet draft, July 2000, work in progress.

[11] R. Sparks. "SIP Call Control Services," IETF Internet draft, November 2000, work in progress.

[12] R. Mahy "Using SIP for Peer-to-Peer Third Party Call Control," IETF Internet draft, November 2000, work in progress.

[13] R. Mahy."A SIP Extension: Informational Responses to the REFER Method," IETF Internet draft, November 2000, work in progress.

# Voice Mail and Unified Messaging

The proliferation of messaging services, such as voice mail on PBXs, for PSTN phones, mobile phones, e-mail, fax, instant messaging, and paging creates challenges for:

**End users**. To manage and keep track of their messages on multiple
   devices and systems.

**Service providers and network administrators.** To manage multiple
   message systems.

This challenge has prompted vendors and service providers to offer various solutions for unified messaging, but a closer look will reveal these systems to be proprietary. Service integration is accomplished by "brute force" with its resulting high complexity.

We will show in this chapter how SIP-based voice mail, presence, and instant messaging can also support unified messaging on the same infrastructure at much reduced complexity, while at the same time providing enhanced functionality.

## Problem Statement

Messages are on disparate networks with network-specific systems and devices. There are incompatible PBX voice mail systems, PSTN voice mail, mobile voice mail, fax, and pagers. There are different email clients and Web clients, including multiple media (text, voice, fax, whiteboard, Web pages, ...) and individual user preferences.

A very short summary of key system properties would look like the following:

- Full user control of messaging features and personalization
- Full user control of recording and playback
- Options for receiving notifications: email, IM, pager, Web browser
- Scalability for very large systems and multiple accounts
- Media agnostic (text, voice, fax, video, whiteboard, etc.)
- Device agnostic (email, Web, phones, fax, pager)
- Use existing infrastructure:
  - Data types and records
  - Network protocols between network elements
  - Network elements
    - IP telephony gateways
    - SIP servers: Registrar, redirect, proxy, forking
    - Component servers: Media servers, voice portal, or IVR
    - Directory
  - Security infrastructure

The main new network element in the design of a unified message system is the universal message store, under control of a unified message server. The unified message server and store can be implemented in various ways to meet these requirements, but it also needs to present a uniform approach for the three message store access phases:

1. User and system access for managing the "mailbox"
2. Message deposit
3. Message retrieval

## Example of Unified Message Operation and Architecture

An example is appropriate at this point to illustrate the SIP, SMTP, HTTP, and RTSP-based open architecture for unified messaging. The example is shown in Figure 10.1.

The example in Figure 10.1 shows the following steps for a voice mail application [1]. The high-level message flow is as follows:

1. A caller on the PSTN or mobile network places a call to a SIP phone.

2. The VoIP gateway sends the INVITE message to its outgoing SIP server.

3. The SIP server forks the call to the called party and to the unified message (UM) server.

4. The called party does not answer the call.

5. The UM server takes the call after a 10-second timeout and the caller leaves a message that is stored in the UM store.

6. The UM server sends an e-mail notification to the called party.

7. The UM server sends a NOTIFY message to the SIP phone for message waiting.

The notification for message waiting will be delivered:

- Via email to the mail client,
- To the IM client (not shown in Figure 10.1) as a NOTIFY message,
- To the SIP phone as a NOTIFY message,
- Can be displayed on the browser by accessing the UM store via HTTP,
- Can be announced via PSTN phone when the called party calls the mailbox.

The voice message can be retrieved by PSTN, PBX, or SIP phones and also by Web browsers that have an RTSP-enabled media player, native or plug-in.

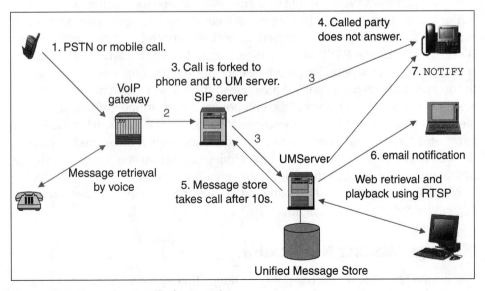

**Figure 10.1** Example of unified messaging.

We have not shown for simplicity other network elements that may be involved in this voice mail application, such as various VoIP gateways; SIP servers performing registration, rendezvous, and routing; and component servers such as VoiceXML voice portals and IVRs.

These network elements are part of the SIP infrastructure and can be reused without modification.

## RTSP-Enabled Voice Message Retrieval

The Real-Time Streaming Protocol (RTSP), defined by RFC 2326 [2], allows the remote recording and replay of various media across the Net and provides similar functionality to the familiar VCR for video. The most popular Internet media players, such as the RealPlayer, WindowsMedia, or QuickTime, support RTSP.

Users will quickly appreciate the advantage of listening to their voice mail using an RTSP-enabled media player instead of using a phone: Lengthy voice mail messages can be replayed selectively, so as to listen to certain parts with relevant information, instead of having to replay the whole message. Replay control is exercised by moving the cursor to the desired message part marked by timestamps.

PC retrieval of voice mail can be a valuable component of a package of desktop and laptop PC applications for IP communications, possibly bundled with call management using third-party call control of SIP phones, as described in Chapter 9, *SIP Telephony*.

Figure 10.2 shows an example of a complete unified messaging system.

The UM system in Figure 10.2 supports Web, email, IM, and phone clients and uses only the core protocols for the transport and control of these applications: HTTP, SMTP, SIP, and RTSP. Media (voice, fax, and video) is carried in RTP packets. Application programming interfaces are *not* required for interoperability in the open, standards-based unified message system. This unified message system is built entirely along the lines of the component server architecture described in more detail in Chapter 17, *The Component Server Architecture*, where the only parameter the individual servers have to know about each other are the respective URLs. Each server can be developed independently, without any knowledge of the internal working of the other corresponding servers.

We will exemplify in the following paragraphs some relevant message exchanges for unified messaging.

## Message-Waiting Notification

Traditional analog and PBX phones have lamps that signal when there are voice messages to be retrieved. Users content to have a similar experience with SIP-

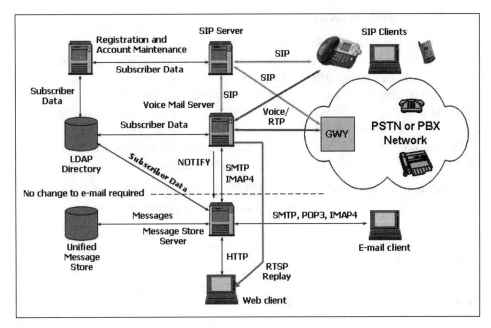

**Figure 10.2** Unified message system.

based systems will require only a minimum of information when alerted by a message-waiting signal.

The user agent, typically a SIP phone, a PC client, or other type of device will use the SIP SUBSCRIBE method to receive NOTIFY messages for changes of state in the mailbox. The user agent also can explicitly fetch the status of the mailbox.

The user agent can subscribe to multiple mailboxes distinguished by the URLs in the To headers.

Multiple user agents can subscribe to the same account. This allows the use of several devices to retrieve waiting messages.

We will exemplify in the following several message flows that highlight the tight integration of SIP-based unified messaging with instant messaging and voice mail. This integration allows many unified message components to be made available on a common SIP infrastructure.

## Simple Message Notification Format

The simple message waiting format [3] can convey only summary information about the status of the mailbox:

- Media type: email, voice mail, fax, and video mail
- Message status: new/old mail

■ Urgent/normal messages

For example, the message-waiting summary *Voice mail: 1/3 (0/1)* conveys the information that there is one new message and three old messages, of which zero new messages are urgent and one old message was urgent. If no such details are required, the message-waiting summary could simply be *Messages-Waiting: yes*. Figure 10.3 shows the message exchange required to subscribe the user agent to the mailbox and the notification messages.

Writing out in full the first three messages from Figure 10.3 will explain the use of SIP SUBSCRIBE, 200 OK, and NOTIFY [4] messages.

**1. Subscriber (Henry's PC) to Notifier (Henry's voice mail server) Subscribe to Henry's message summary status for 1 day.**

```
SUBSCRIBE sip:henry@mail3.wcom.com SIP/2.0
Via: SIP/2.0/UDP henrys-phone.wcom.com:5060
To: <sip:henry@mail3.wcom.com>
```

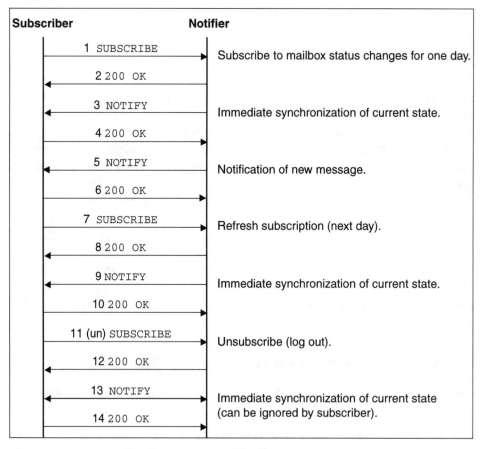

**Figure 10.3** Message flow for message notification.

```
From: <sip:henry@wcom.com>;tag=312
Date: Thu, 12 Apr 2001 15:00:00 GMT
Call-ID: 314@henrys-phone.wcom.com
CSeq: 4 SUBSCRIBE
Contact: <sip:henry@henrys-phone.wcom.com>
Event: simple-message-summary
Expires: 86400
Accept: application/simple-message-summary
Content-Length: 0
```

### 2. Notifier to Subscriber

```
SIP/2.0 200 OK
Via: SIP/2.0/UDP henrys-phone.wcom.com:5060
To: <sip:henry@mail3.wcom.com>
From: <sip:henry@wcom.com>;tag=312
Date: Thu, 12 Apr 2001 15:00:00 GMT
Call-ID: 314@henrys-phone.wcom.com
CSeq: 4 SUBSCRIBE
Event: simple-message-summary
Expires: 86400
Content-Length: 0
```

### 3. Notifier to Subscriber: Immediate synchronization of current state. Two new and eight old messages of which two old messages are urgent.

```
NOTIFY sip:henry@henrys-phone.wcom.com SIP/2.0
Via: SIP/2.0/UDP henrys-phone.wcom.com:5060
To: <sip:henry@mail3.wcom.com>
From: <sip:henry@wcom.com>;tag=313
Date: Mon, 10 Jul 2000 03:55:07 GMT
Call-ID: 314@henrys-phone.wcom.com
CSeq: 20 NOTIFY
Contact: <sip:henry@vmail.wcom.com>
Event: simple-message-summary
Content-Type: application/simple-message-summary
Content-Length: 145
```

**Messages-Waiting: yes**
```
Voicemail: 2/8 (0/2)
```

## Rich Message Notification Format

The notification, however, can be expressed with much richer content by using XML message summary formats, as shown here [5]:

```
<DOCTYPE message_summary SYSTEM xml_mwi.dtd>

<MESSAGE_SUMMARY>
    <MAILBOX_IN>
      <NAME>Inbox</NAME>
```

```
<VOICEMAIL>
            <UNTOUCHED urgent="1">2</UNTOUCHED>
            <SKIPPED>1</SKIPPED>
            <READ>3</READ>
            <DELETED>2</DELETED>
   </VOICEMAIL
   <FAX>
            <READ>1</READ>
   </FAX>
   <VIDEO/>
  </MAILBOX_IN>
  <MAILBOX_IN>
   <NAME>Inbox.Priority</NAME>
   <VOICEMAIL/>
   <EMAIL>
            <UNTOUCHED urgent="1">101</UNTOUCHED>
            <SKIPPED/>
            <FLAGGED urgent="2">4</FLAGGED>
            <READ>3</READ>
            <ANSWERED>2</ANSWERED>
            <DELETED/>
   </EMAIL>
  </MAILBOX_IN>
 </MESSAGE_SUMMARY>
```

A text-to-speech converter can read this document providing the following voice message summary:

"You have reached the mailbox of <Name>"

"Inbox:"

"You have the following voice messages:"

"You have two skipped messages"

"You have three read messages"

"You have two deleted messages"

"This was the summary of your voice mail"

"You have the following fax mail:"

"You have one read fax"

"This was the summary of your fax mailbox"

"You have no video mail"

"Priority inbox of <NAME>"

"You have the following email:"

"You have 101 untouched email messages, one urgent message"

"You have no skipped email messages"

"You have four messages flagged urgent two"

"You have two answered messages"

"You have no deleted messages"

"This is the end of your email inbox"

"This was the complete message summary"

It is interesting to note that the same XML script can be used by a graphic application to paint the graphic user interface, showing the folders for email, voice, fax, and video mail with subfolders for normal and priority mail and the respective icons for normal, urgent, skipped, and deleted messages.

A standard document type definition (DTD) for XML message waiting notification has been proposed in Mahy and Slain [5].

# Summary

SIP-based voice mail can be integrated to run on a common infrastructure with SIP-based presence, instant messaging, voice, and other IP communication services. The resulting unified messaging system has a rich portfolio of services and works seamlessly across the domain's e-mail, the Web and also includes voice mail.

# References

[1] H. Schulzrinne and K. Singh. "Unified Messaging Using SIP and RTSP," IP Telecom Services Workshop, Atlanta, Georgia, September 11, 2000.

[2] H. Schulzrinne, A. Rao, and R. Lanphier. "Real-Time Streaming Protocol (RTSP)," IETF RFC 2326, 1998.

[3] R. Mahy and I. Slain. "SIP Event Package for Message Waiting Indication," IETF Internet draft, February 2001, work in progress.

[4] A. Roach. "Event Notification in SIP," IETF Internet draft, November 2000, standards track.

[5] R. Mahy and I. Slain. "SIP Extensions for Message Waiting Indication," expired Internet draft, IETF, July 2000.

**CHAPTER**

# Presence and Instant Communications

This chapter covers the new concepts of presence and instant communications, and shows how they can be implemented using SIP. Polite calling, automatic call-back, avoiding unsuccessful calls, and legitimate tracking of specialized workforce members are some of the new communication services enabled by presence and using SIP.

## The Emergence of Instant Messaging

It is not practical to write the very short history of the emergence of instant messaging (IM) on the Internet, since any data would be obsolete by the time of the printing of this book. IM is, at present, the technology, competitive, and regulatory battleground for the largest and smallest software companies and service providers alike.

We will provide in this chapter the technology concepts on which instant messaging and its successor, instant communications (IC), are based, and describe how IC can be implemented with SIP.

The first widespread use of IM was AOL's Instant Messenger, which proved to be so popular that many non-AOL customers signed up for a free IM account. The companion "Buddy List," which allows a user to be notified when a specified set of users is active, also represents a primitive presence client. However, the first IM products used proprietary protocols and centralized server architecture. Efforts by various IM developers to internetwork have not been successful. As a result, there has been a strong push in the industry to develop an open standard, interoperable, and scalable protocol for IM. This has lead to the formation of the IETF Instant Messaging and Presence Protocol Working Group (IMPP WG). To date, this group has produced two key documents on requirements [1] and a model [2] for presence and instant messaging. It soon became apparent, however, that:

1. The newly discovered presence service may be used for all other communication services, beyond short text messaging.

2. IM by itself can be implemented using various protocols. Three contending protocols emerged in the IMPP WG:

   a. SIP for general communications applications, or SIMPLE (SIP for Instant Messaging and Presence), as the extensions to SIP are known.

   b. IMXP [3] to keep IM the simplest it can be and to build on email,

   c. PRIM [4] also to keep IM lightweight, but using TCP transport.

The commonalities and differences were clearly articulated [5] and it was felt the different approaches may meet different needs and should have only a common model and data exchange format for interoperability between the various protocols. Another key document, the Common Profile for Instant Messaging (CPIM) [6], was the result of this agreement in the IMPP WG.

In conclusion, the internal protocols and data formats of various IM systems are a local design decision, but interoperability between IM systems should be possible via CPIM.

## The IETF Model for Presence and Instant Messaging

Presence and instant messaging are made possible by the packet nature of the Internet and may merit dedicated tutorials on their own. We will attempt here only to give some basic notions that help in understanding the new service and its potential. The model for a presence service is shown in Figure 11.1a[2].

The model for instance instant messaging is similar and is shown in Figure 11.1b. Both services have other similarities such as the notions of *principals* that can be either people or software that appear to the service as a single enti-

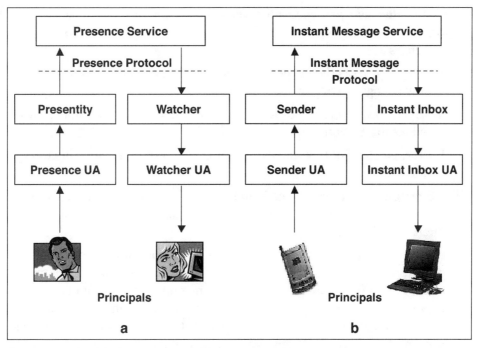

**Figure 11.1** Models for presence and instant messaging.

ty. Principals interact with the system via *user agents*. A user agent is the coupling between the principal and some core entity in the system.

The document defines a standard data format for presence, which is composed of so-called presence tuples. Each presence tuple consists of the following fields:

**Status.** Online, offline, busy, away, do not disturb

**Communication address**. Includes the:

> **Contact means.** Such as messaging (short, email), pager, PSTN, etc.
>
> **Contact address.** The service-specific URL

**Other Markup.** Not yet specified.

The document defines a *presentity* as the software that provides presence information to the presence service. While the presence service handles distribution of the information, it is the presentity that generates a message called a *notification* about the presence information of the principal. Contained in the notification is the *status* of the principal, defined in the document as *open* or *closed*, or other mutually exclusive values. The nature of these status values depends on the nature of the service. Requests to the presentity are sent by a *watcher*. These terms are defined as follows:

**Watcher.** Requests presence information about one or more presentities or about other watchers from the presence service. Special types of watchers are:

**Subscriber.** Asks the presence service to be immediately notified of any changes to one or more presentities.

**Fetcher.** Makes a request for presence information, but has not requested a subscription to the presence service.

**Poller.** Is a fetcher that makes regular requests to update presence information.

**Notification.** Is a message sent from the presence service to a subscriber when there is a change of presence information by some presentity of interest to the watcher.

**Status.** Is a distinguished part of the presence information about presentity. Status can have at least two mutually exclusive values: *open* or *closed*. Open or closed has meaning for instant messaging and there may be equivalent notions for other means of communications such as free or busy in circuit switched telephony. Other means of communications also can have different status values, in addition to open or closed.

**Presence service.** Accepts, stores, and distributes presence information.

**Instant message service.** Accepts and delivers instant messages.

Both the presence and the instant message services may have complex internal structures with specific servers and/or proxies with quite complex security implementations. In keeping with the end-to-end control principle of the Internet, these services also can be implemented in the endpoints, without dependence on intermediate elements in the network, as is the case with SIP.

## Security for Presence and IM

Security considerations for presence and instant messaging deal with:

**Spam.** Unwanted instant messages. Delivery rules are intended to deal with Spam.

**Spoofing.** The imitation of a principal by another principal. Authentication rules are intended to deal with spoofing.

**Stalking.** Using presence information about the whereabouts of a principal for illegal or malicious purposes. Access rules, visibility rules, and rules for the distribution of watcher information are intended to deal with stalking.

# The Common Profile for Instant Messaging

As mentioned, IM systems can use different protocols and different data formats, but should meet the definition of the Common Profile for Internet Messaging (CPIM) for interoperability. CPIM interoperability is expressed in terms of an abstract presence service and an abstract instant message service.

The documents define a new URL scheme—"im"—which represents the resource of the specified user's instant message inbox. The addresses use the familiar e-mail form of user@host or user@domain. The URL of an IM recipient could be, for example: im:student@college.edu.

Note that this URL does not define the transport protocol. As a result, the IP address lookup for the URL depends on the particular transport protocol used by the local IM system. If SIP is used for transport, the DNS resource record (RR) is found by executing a service lookup (SRV) for the address of the SIP proxy for the *college.edu* domain to determine the next hop for the message. See Chapter 14 on DNS lookup for SIP.

The abstract models for presence and instant message services in CPIM are of a very simple nature and are represented in Figure 11.2.

Figure 11.2a shows the message exchange to subscribe and Figure 11.2b shows the basic message exchange for a subscribed user. There also is a corresponding *Unsubscribe* message, not shown in Figure 11.2.

We will reproduce here the message flows as specified in CPIM, since they illustrate the minimalist requirements for interoperability. HTML is used in the example, though it is not a requirement to be used between systems or inside any particular system. Gateways may be necessary if the interworking systems use different data representations, though the systems may internetwork directly, depending on their implementation.

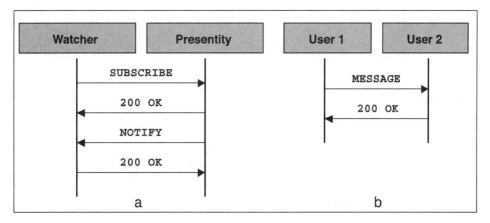

**Figure 11.2** CPIM models for presence and instant message services.

## Presence Service

A watcher friend1 subscribes to the presence service associated with presentity of friend2. The requested time in the example is 24 hours (86,400 seconds), but only 1 hour is returned in the response.

### Subscribe

The subscribe is:

```
<subscribe watcher='pres:friend1@isp1.com'
              target='pres:friend2@isp2.com'
               duration='64000'  transID='1' />
```

### Response

The response is:

```
<response status='success' transID='1' duration='3600' />
```

The successful subscription will enable the notify operation to communicate the presentity information to the watcher.

### Notify

The notify is:

```
<notify watcher='pres:friend1@isp1.com'
              target='pres:friend2@isp2.com'
              transID='1' />

    <presence entityInfo='http://www.isp2.com/friend2' />

        <tuple destination='im:friend2@isp2.com'
                            status='open' />
</notify>
```

A watcher can unsubscribe from the presence service (not shown in Figure 11.2):

### Unsubscribe

The unsubscribe is:

```
<unsubscribe watcher='pres:friend1@isp1.com'
                target='pres:friend2@isp2.com'
                transID='1' />
```

and, if successful, will be informed:

```
<reponse status='success' transID='1' />
```

## Instant Message Service

The watcher can now send a message, knowing the open presence status of the inbox.

### *Message*

The message is:

```
<message source='im:john.doe@isp1.com'
         destination='im:mary.king@isp2.com'
         transID='1' />

Content-Type: text/plain; charset="us-ascii"

Hello! How are you?
```

### *Response*

The response is:

```
<response status='success' transID='1' />
```

In case of success, the response will be:

```
<response status='success' transID='1' />
```

Though of minimalist nature, CPIM interworking between instant message systems will still meet the requirements described in RFC 2778[2] for interoperability.

# Why SIP for Presence and Instant Messaging?

At the time of this writing, there is an abundance of instant messaging products and services on the market, mostly implemented on centralized servers. None of these IM services interoperate, and none uses a standard, open protocol. The development of the requirements for a standard, open, interoperable protocol in the IETF has resulted in multiple standards proposals in the IMPP WG [7], out of which only one was based on SIP. Why use SIP for presence and instant messaging? There are a number of reasons to choose SIP for commercial grade presence and instant communications:

- Presence is useful for any type of communications, not only short text messaging.

- SIP already solves the tasks required for presence and instant communications:

- User agent registration
- User agent authentication

- Rendezvous between parties via call routing. SIP call setup and presence are dual aspects of the rendezvous feature. In call setup, the message is routed from the caller to the called party at the request of the caller, while in presence the notification of status change is routed to the watcher, whenever it happens.
- Use of existing infrastructure. Clients and servers, software and databases, and, last but not least, the security mechanisms deployed for SIP.
- SIP has a decentralized, highly scalable architecture.

A large number of IETF drafts, each dealing with a particular topic, have provided the complete information required to build presence and IM using SIP [8-15]. Since it is not possible to describe here in complete detail the content of this work, we will illustrate only the basic concepts.

As we will show, SIP requires three methods, called SUBSCRIBE, NOTIFY, and MESSAGE to support presence and instant communications of any form such as text, voice, data, video, or for interactive games.

# New Services Based on SIP for Presence

The most popular application from the family of services based on presence is instant messaging for short text messages. Other media, such as voice, video, and games, have also emerged. Besides the various media types, however, significant new communication models are now possible.

## Polite Calling

We will exemplify here a communication scenario based on the new notion of "polite calling." Using the Internet, the caller can, for the first time, "be polite" and find out if the called party is available and willing to communicate. The called party may have used a service with SIP user preferences and:

- Has indicated he or she is away on business and thus available only by mobile phone or some other mobile device.
- May be in a meeting or in a theater and indicate the preference for text-based communications only and also only for certain callers.

By using the presence service, the caller may find out information about the called party:

- Is the called party reachable by the network? The mobile phone service may not work, for example, in an airplane or in certain geographic locations, but other devices, such as satellite-based pagers or palm computers, may be reachable. By stepping off an airplane, the caller may be notified that the called party is again reachable by mobile phone.

■ The complete presence information also may indicate if the called party is already in a conversation, and if so, the caller may find out the answer to the question: May I join the call or conference? Who is already online?

A secretary or close friend or relative may be permitted to join conversations for calls categorized as for business, private, or relating to interest groups. A chat room for an interest group may display the presence of other community members online. A business conference will support the authenticated display of all participants and thus provide the necessary confidence to discuss sensitive topics.

## Avoiding Unsuccessful Calls

A very mundane, but highly effective application may turn out to be the avoidance of unsuccessful calls, especially those experienced during business hours in the workplace. Often, the called parties are away from their desks, in meetings, or otherwise unreachable. Simple applications using presence can avoid such frustrations.

## Automatic Call-Back on Presence

A caller can be alerted that the called party is not reachable on the cell phone (may have boarded an airplane), but the application can automatically initiate a new call as soon as a notification is received that the cell phone is reachable again.

## Legitimate Tracking of the Workforce

Certain types of business depend on critical information on the whereabouts of their workforce, such as for messenger and delivery services. Presence can be used to track couriers, for example.

## Replacing Traditional Telephony Services and Devices

Instant communications based on presence is still a fertile field for many not-yet-invented communications services and devices.

### Services

Scheduled voice conferencing is a significant driver for business-oriented services provided by telephony carriers. Instant voice chat, however, may complement and partially replace scheduled voice conferences. We believe that a continuous spectrum of conferences may have its place in the service portfolio of ISPs, from scheduled and managed voice calls to instant conferencing started on impulse and with polite calling enabled by presence.

Another example for possible innovation is the replacement of the automatic call distributor (ACD) that is a core component of existing telephony call centers. Users calling an 800 number for support may experience frustratingly long waiting times before reaching an operator. The ACD could be potentially replaced with a presence service for the desired operator, so that a notification is received when the operator becomes available. Also, the presence state could show the length of the queue of customers waiting in line. Presence, and other SIP services, can thus be used for a complete rearchitecting of call centers.

### Devices

Since the graphic user interface (GUI) for presence and instant communications has a small footprint, the same GUI can be used on more than one device type: PC, laptop, SIP phone, palm computer, bidirectional pager, and also for IP appliances. Future phones may have much more in common with the IM GUI than with the existing numeric keypad.

We call this new suite of services *Instant IP Communications*.

## Architecture for Instant IP Communications

The architecture for SIP for presence is shown in Figure 11.3. It is fully distributed, and highly scalable as mentioned, since the upper layer SIP proxy servers can be stateless. The same architecture is used for all other types of instant communications based on SIP for presence.

The architecture in Figure 11.3 is extremely flexible. At one end of the spectrum, SIP end devices can communicate directly with each other and serve as registrar, as well as presence user agent (PUA) in the roles of watcher and presentity. Direct end-to-end user rendezvous is not scalable, however, and may have more limited features than can be provided by servers.

At the other end of the spectrum, full use of SIP proxy servers in the network can be made and the hierarchy of SIP proxies in the network provides the rendezvous, transport, and security functions. Thus, for security, the local SIP proxy servers in private IP networks enable firewall transversal for RTP packets for various media types, such as voice and video.

The SIP proxy server infrastructure can be used for presence and instant messaging without any additional modifications, though some features are not used, as will be shown later in this chapter.

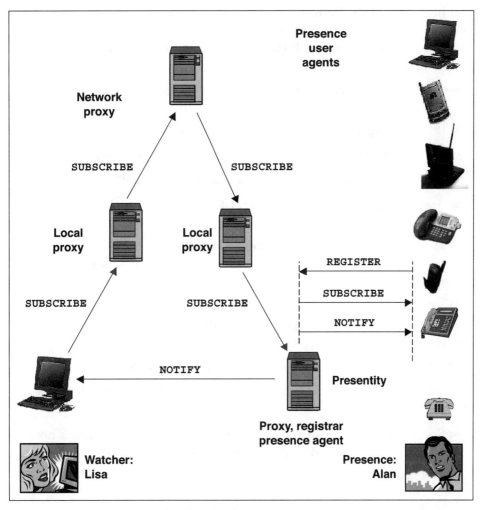

**Figure 11.3** Scalable architecture for SIP for presence.

The presence agent server for the principal, Alan, on the right side in Figure 11.3 may convey presence for many devices, as shown. Connectivity to the network by any device is logged in the SIP proxy registrar and presence agent server on a dynamic basis. Lisa, who is a watcher on the left, can find the presence information for Alan by having the SUBSCRIBE message forwarded by the SIP proxies in the network to the SIP proxy registrar for all the devices that Alan may have. The presence agent server can accept SUBSCRIBE requests on its own or forward the request to any of the active devices, so that Alan can make the decision to accept or reject Lisa as a new watcher. SIP user preferences can determine to which of several possible devices the SUBSCRIBE message should be routed. NOTIFY messages can then be sent directly from the presentity user agent on one of the devices owned by Alan to the watcher, Lisa.

The architecture shown in Figure 11.3 inherits the following features from the SIP infrastructure:

- Scale for instant communications on a distributed, scalable, and global basis.
- Soft state ensures fast processing in the network.
- Rendezvous function to find entities across the entire Internet.

SIP REGISTER to publish presence can support the following features:

- Any communication type based on URL addressing, such as HTTP and SMTP.
- Multiple devices can update independently the state for the various communication addresses for the same presentity, in a fully distributed manner.
- One party can update presence for another in third-party updates.
- Caller preferences are supported for different addresses and for other distinctions.
- Arbitrary text can be used to express caller preferences.

Access control to presence information by end users can be accomplished in various ways:

- Secure Web-based entries by users. Web-based entry, however, is not suitable for automated entries from service support systems.
- Call processing language (CPL) scripts can be uploaded in the SIP REG-ISTER request.
- An ISP can use the Common Open Policy Service (COPS) protocol in third-party service provider scenarios such as for virtual private network services.

SIP security applies to the following aspects of presence and instant communications:

- Privacy. Subscribers may not want to reveal they have:
  - Subscribed to certain users
  - Accepted subscriptions from certain users

Security: Notification messages may contain sensitive information and there may be problems with NATs and firewalls:

- Message integrity and authentication

- Replay prevention
- Denial of service (DOS) attacks
- Firewall transversal

SIP supports a combination of end-to-end security and hop-by-hop security that is reused for instant communications.

What SIP features are required and what SIP features are not used?

Required SIP features for IM are:

- Parsing and processing for To, From, Call-ID, CSeq, Via, Route, Record-Route, and Proxy-Require headers
- SIP REGISTER
- Proxy server functions: connection management, Via processing, loop detection, and message forwarding

A number of SIP features are not required to be supported by user agents for instant messaging:

- Processing of INVITE, re-INVITE, ACK, CANCEL, and BYE requests
- Session description protocol (SDP) processing

Note that this represents a significant reduction in the complexity of the protocol since most of the complexity in SIP relates to these two topics.

## Basic Call Flows for SIP IM

Basic messages used by SIP for presence are shown in Figure 11.4a. The following are examples of call flows showing the messages for SUBSCRIBE and NOTIFY.

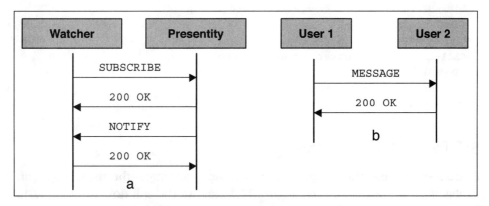

**Figure 11.4** Presence and instant messaging using SIP.

## *SUBSCRIBE*

Watcher to presentity:

```
SUBSCRIBE sip:presentity@pres.example.com SIP/2.0
Via: SIP/2.0/UDP watcherhost.example.com:5060
From: User
To: Resource
Call-ID: 3248543@watcherhost.example.com
CSeq: 1 SUBSCRIBE
Expires: 600
Accept: application/xpidf+xml, text/lpidf
Contact: sip:user@watcherhost.example.com
```

## *200 OK*

Presentity to watcher:

```
SIP/2.0 200 OK
Via: SIP/2.0/UDP watcherhost.example.com:5060
From: User
To: Resource
Call-ID: 3248543@watcherhost.example.com
CSeq: 1 SUBSCRIBE
Expires: 600
Content-Type: application/xpidf+xml
Content-Length: 351
```

## *NOTIFY*

Presentity to watcher:

```
NOTIFY sip:user@watcherhost.example.com SIP/2.0
Via: SIP/2.0/UDP pres.example.com:5060
From: Resource
To: User
Call-ID: 3248543@watcherhost.example.com
CSeq: 1 NOTIFY
Content-Type: application/xpidf+xml
Content-Length: 352
```

# SIP for Instant Messaging

In case of success for the preceding message exchange, the users now can exchange short text messages. Figure 11.4b shows the call flow for MESSAGE. The messages are as follows:

### MESSAGE

User1 to user2:

```
MESSAGE sip:user1@user1pc.domain.com SIP/2.0
Via: SIP/2.0/UDP user2pc.domain.com
To: sip:user1@domain.com
From: sip:user2@domain.com;tag=ab8asdasd9
Contact: sip:user2@user2pc.domain.com
Call-ID: asd88asd77a@1.2.3.4
CSeq: 1 MESSAGE
Content-Type: text/plain
Content-Length: 29

My name is User One
```

### SIP/2.0 200 OK

User2 to user1:

```
SIP/2.0 200 OK
Via: SIP/2.0/UDP user2pc.domain.com
To: sip:user1@domain.com
From: sip:user2@domain.com;tag=ab8asdasd9
Call-ID: asd88asd77a@1.2.3.4
CSeq: 1 MESSAGE
Content-Length: 0
```

## Lightweight Data Formats

Depending on the type of service, a lightweight data format can be used for presence [15]. The following is an example of a lightweight presence information data format (LPIDF):

```
To: sip:presentity@example.com
Contact: sip:presentity@example.com;
         methods="INVITE,BYE,OPTIONS";
         mobility=fixed;features="voicemail"
Contact: mailto:presentity@example.com
Contact: http://www.example.com
```

This message from a presence user agent to a presence server indicates that the user has published availability for full SIP-based communications that use INVITE, BYE, and OPTIONS. The indicated contacts are voice mail, email, and a Web site as the contact of last resort.

## Communications Based on Presence

As mentioned, all interactive communications, not only short text messages, can be supported by SIP for presence. At the writing of this book, a number of products have emerged that support the following types of communications:

- Text
- Voice
- Video
- Web page sharing
- Desktop application sharing
- Interactive games

Figure 11.5 shows "Windows Messenger," which is an example of a soft client that provides presence-based: (1) IP communications and (2) data collaboration for:

- Text-based instant messaging (IM)

**Figure 11.5** PC SIP user agent combining presence, Instant text messaging, voice, video with whiteboard, and application sharing.

- Voice
- Video
- Shared whiteboard
- Application sharing

using SIP (courtesy Microsoft Corporation).

We believe similar applications will also be deployed for emerging wireless devices.

In other industry segments, new services for conferencing and call centers, as discussed in the beginning chapters of this book, may completely redefine telephony and other types of communication services.

## References

[1] M. Day, S. Aggarwal, G. Mohr, and J. Vincent. RFC 2779: "Instant Messaging and Presence Protocol Requirements," IETF, February 2000.

[2] M. Day, J. Rosenberg, and H. Sugano. RFC 2778: "A Model for Presence and Instant Messaging," IETF, February 2000.

[3] M.T. Rose, G. Klyne, and D.H. Crocker. The IMXP Presence Service, IETF Internet draft, March 2001, work in progress.

[4] F. Mazzoldi, A. Diacakis, S. Fujimoto, G. Hudson, J.D. Ramsdell, and H. Sugano. Presence and Instant Messaging Protocol (PRIM), IETF Internet draft, September 2000, work in progress.

[4] D. Crocker, D. Athanasios, C. Huitema, G. Klyne, F. Mazzoldi, M. Rose, J. Rosenberg, R. Sparks, and H. Sugano. A Framework for Moving IMPP Forward, IETF Internet draft, August 2000, work in progress.

[5] D. Crocker, D. Athanasios, C. Huitema, G. Klyne, F. Mazzoldi, M. Rose, J. Rosenberg, R. Sparks, and H. Sugano. "A Common Profile for Instant Messaging (CPIM)," IETF Internet draft, November 2000, work in progress.

[6] D. Crocker. RFC 822: "Standard for the Format of ARPA Internet Text Messages," August 1982.

[7] The Instant Messaging and Presence Protocol (IMPP) Working Group of the IETF http://ietf.org/html.charters/impp-charter.html.

[8] J. Rosenberg, D. Willis, R. Sparks, B. Campbell, H. Schulzrinne, J. Lennox, B. Aboba, C. Huitema, and D. Gurle. A Protocol for Presence Based in SIP, IETF Internet draft, June 2000, work in progress.

[9] J. Rosenberg, D. Willis, R. Sparks, B. Campbell, H. Schulzrinne, J. Lennox, B. Aboba, C. Huitema, and D. Gurle. A Protocol for Instant Messaging Based on SIP, IETF Internet draft, June 2000, work in progress.

[10] J. Rosenberg, D. Willis, R. Sparks, B. Campbell, H. Schulzrinne, J. Lennox, B. Aboba, C. Huitema, and D. Gurle. "SIP Extensions for Presence," IETF Internet draft, June 2000, work in progress.

[11] J. Rosenberg, D. Willis, R. Sparks, B. Campbell, H. Schulzrinne,
J. Lennox, B. Aboba, C. Huitema,  D. Gurle, and D. Oran. "SIP
Extensions for Instant Messaging," IETF Internet draft, June 2000, work
in progress.

[12] J. Rosenberg, D. Willis, R. Sparks, B. Campbell, H. Schulzrinne,
J. Lennox, B. Aboba, C. Huitema, and D. Gurle. "An XML Format for
Presence Buddy Lists," IETF Internet draft, June 2000, work in progress.

[13] J. Rosenberg, D. Willis, R. Sparks, B. Campbell, H. Schulzrinne,
J. Lennox, B. Aboba, C. Huitema, D. Gurle, and D. Oran. "SIP Extensions
for Presence Authorization," IETF Internet draft, June 2000, work in
progress.

[14] A. Roach. "Event Notification in SIP," IETF Internet draft, November
2000, work in progress.

[15] J. Rosenberg, D. Willis, R. Sparks, B. Campbell, H. Schulzrinne,
J. Lennox, B. Aboba, C. Huitema, D. Gurle, and D. Oran. "A Lightweight
Presence Information Format (LPIDF)," IETF Internet draft, June 2000,
work in progress.

# CHAPTER 12

# SIP Conferencing

We will present in this chapter conferencing services based on SIP. Readers interested in this topic may also want to refer to Chapter 4, *Internet Multimedia and Conferencing*, on which SIP conferencing is based.

Though the interest in SIP is at present due mostly to telephony and other IP communication services, it is useful to remember that SIP has been developed initially in the IETF MMUSIC Working Group for large-scale multimedia conferencing over the Internet within the Internet Multimedia Conferencing Architecture [1].

## Introduction

Present commercial conferencing products and services are mainly of two types:

- PSTN-based telephone conferences which are the most widely used.
- Various video conferencing products, based on the ITU H.3xx series of recommendations that support voice, video, and also document sharing, using the T.120 standard. Contrary to voice conferencing, most video

and data conferencing products are not fully interoperable, though they may be advertised as being in compliance with the previous standards. This is due to the large number of options permitted in ITU conferencing standards and the fact that various products may support different sets of options, besides some proprietary enhancements.

The main issues the authors have with the H.3xx type of conferencing products is the way they are architected, based on ITU network models, and their technology which makes them a poor fit for the Internet and the World Wide Web. Thus, integration with other communication and Web services is difficult, and there are a number of divergent approaches, such as for security and scalability.

Considerable effort is expended in both the ITU and IETF on interoperability between SIP and H.323 signaling, but this work is mainly for telephony. A summary on H.323-SIP interworking aspects is provided in Schulzrinne and Sing [2].

Most commercial telecom conferencing services are based on a central multipoint control unit (MCU) that serves both as the central signaling control point and media mixer. Rosenberg [3] provides a detailed review of SIP conferencing models.

We will present in this chapter the Internet conferencing models and services based on SIP that include the MCU model but also have other flexible approaches for various other conferencing models.

# SIP Conferencing Models

IP conferences may differ in many respects, depending on the signaling to set up the conference and the way media is transported and mixed for the conference participants. Table 12.1 shows the main conference models possible. The models are roughly ordered by the possible scale of the conference. We will use the generic term "conference bridge" in the table, since the conferencing network element is sometimes a SIP server only and sometimes a SIP server combined with an RTP media mixer. Telephony conferencing network elements are sometimes called multipoint controlled units to emphasize the control aspects for certain telephony conference types.

Each conference model shown in Table 12.1 differs from the other models by one or more of the following:

- Scale of the conference
- Call flows for users to join the conference
- How and where the media is sent and mixed
- Location of the service logic: In endpoints or in servers

**Table 12.1** SIP Conference Models

| CONFERENCE MODELS | HOW IT WORKS |
|---|---|
| 1. Endpoint mixing 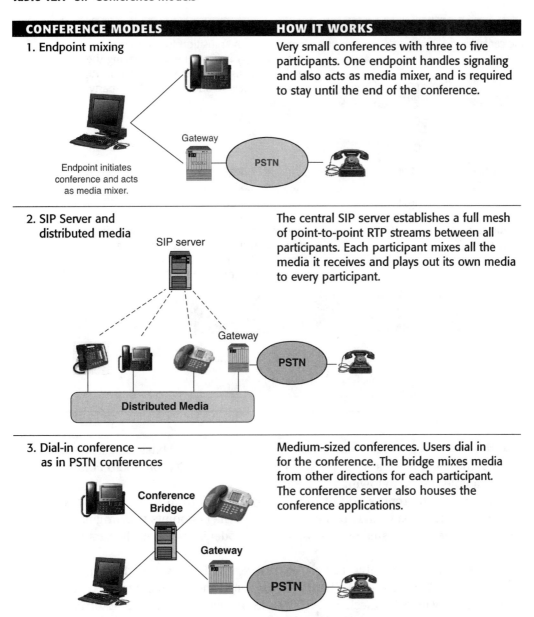<br>Endpoint initiates conference and acts as media mixer. | Very small conferences with three to five participants. One endpoint handles signaling and also acts as media mixer, and is required to stay until the end of the conference. |
| 2. SIP Server and distributed media | The central SIP server establishes a full mesh of point-to-point RTP streams between all participants. Each participant mixes all the media it receives and plays out its own media to every participant. |
| 3. Dial-in conference — as in PSTN conferences | Medium-sized conferences. Users dial in for the conference. The bridge mixes media from other directions for each participant. The conference server also houses the conference applications. |

*continues*

The conference models apply equally well for both audio-only, as in telephony conferences, and for mixed media conferences for audio and video. Depending on the quality of video that users may send and receive due to bandwidth limitations, several IP addresses may be required for layered video codecs. Users

**Table 12.1** (*Continued*)

| CONFERENCE MODELS | HOW IT WORKS |
|---|---|
| 4. Ad hoc centralized conference 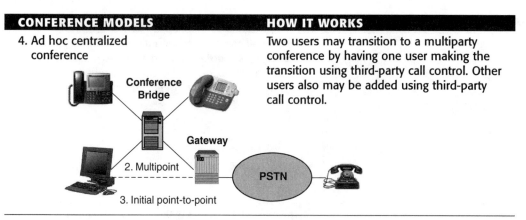 | Two users may transition to a multiparty conference by having one user making the transition using third-party call control. Other users also may be added using third-party call control. |
| 5. Large multicast conference 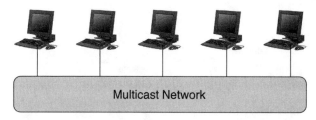 | Very large-scale conferences, up to millions of users. Users join a multicast address announced on the Web, by email or SAP, or are invited to join using SIP. |

with the lowest bandwidth may send and receive only the basic video layer, suitable for small images only. We will focus, for simplicity, on audio conference examples in the following.

Small-scale conferences do not require any support from network servers, since a few RTP streams may be mixed in one of the endpoints that originates the conference. Such a small-scale conference model is shown in the first row of Table 12.1.

In the second row of Table 12.1 a pure SIP service is shown, with no media mixing provided in a server. A SIP server for conferences can support conferences by setting up a full mesh of RTP streams between participants. Each participant mixes all incoming streams for their own use. Since it is unlikely to experience more than one or two speakers at the same time, the required RTP processing in the user endpoints is quite modest.

Telephony-style conferencing is shown in the third row in Table 12.1. The conferencing bridge is a conceptually simple device, consisting of a SIP user agent to handle signaling, an RTP mixer to handle the media streams, and a conference application layer for the authentication, authorization, and accounting (AAA) service, and possible conference control functions, as shown in Figure 12.1. The RTP mixer will send out to each participant the mix of media streams from all other participants.

An important requirement for commercial conference bridges is the capability to convey with confidence the list of all participating users in the conference to ensure participants the conference is private, with no undesirable parties listening in. The list of participants is transmitted by the RTP mixer, using the RTP capability to transmit the name of all registered participants. The CNAME in the Source Description (SDES) is transmitted to inform about participating users. It is the responsibility of the conference bridge to authenticate all participants (the AAA function) and to communicate the list on a dynamic basis using RTP.

The conference model number 5 in Table 12.1 is for large multicast conferences, for the case where IP multicast is available. Multicast conferences can scale up to millions of users and do not really require any SIP signaling. Users can join the multicast conference by addressing their RTP streams to/from the multicast addresses belonging to the particular conference. SIP may be used to inform users of the multicast conference address, though any other means to convey this information, such as Web pages, email, and the Session Announcement Protocol are just as adequate.

## Ad Hoc and Scheduled Conferences

Presence and instant messaging can support the setup of spontaneous conferences, in contrast to the more customary scheduled conferences, as used on the PSTN. It is of interest to note that SIP enables a continuous transition of conferences from ad hoc to scheduled conferences.

Users of an ad hoc conference could agree, for example, they need more time and would like to invite other participants, so they set up a scheduled conference to discuss a topic in more depth. The list of the ad hoc conference

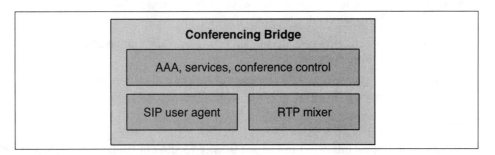

**Figure 12.1** Generic conferencing bridge.

participants can be included by the application to set up the scheduled conference.

## Changing the Nature of a Conference

If users in an ad hoc conference with endpoint mixing (row 1 in Table 12.1) decide to increase the number of participants, they can move the conference to a central conference server so as to benefit from a dedicated RTP mixer, as shown in row 4 of Table 12.1. One of the parties needs to assume responsibility to move existing participants to the centralized conference. The example provided here also is valid for moving from a two-party call to a centralized conference. The following steps involve the move from an ad hoc to a centralized conference:

1. Discover a server that supports ad hoc centralized conferences, such as adhoc.conference.wcom.com.

2. Set up a call with the conference server by sending an INVITE to create the conference.

3. The conference server can create the unique conference ID by assigning it a random number or by combining the name of the user with time/date and its own domain name: johndoe_april1_2001@adhoc .conference.wcom.com.

4. The application of the user in charge of migrating the ad hoc conference to the centralized server can now use the Refer-To method in SIP third-party call control to set up calls between the existing and new participants and the conference server. See Chapter 9 on third-party call control.

John Doe initiates the call setup for Mary Higgins:

```
REFER sip:maryhiggins@wcom.com SIP/2.0
From: <sip:johndoe@wcom.com>
To: <sip:maryhiggins@wcom.com>
Refer-To: <johndoe_april1_2001@adhoc.conference.wcom.com>
Referred-by: <sip:johndoe@wcom.com>
```

As a result, Mary Higgins sets up her call to the conference server:

```
INVITE sip:johndoe_april1_2001@adhoc.conference.wcom.com
   SIP/2.0
From: <sip:maryhiggins@wcom.com>
To: <sip:johndoe_april1_2001@adhoc.conference.wcom.com>
Referred-by: <sip:johndoe@wcom.com>
```

Other users will be migrated in the same way to the centralized conference.

# Summary

This chapter has introduced a number of models of SIP conferencing such as endpoint mixing, SIP server and distributed media, dial-in conferences, and ad hoc centralized and large-scale multicast conferences. We have also shown how SIP can support changes in the nature of conference services.

# References

[1 ] M. Handley, J. Crowcroft, and C. Borman. "The Internet Multimedia Conferencing Architecture," Internet draft, work in progress, IETF, July 2000.

[2] H. Schulzrinne and K. Sing. "Interworking Between SIP/SDP and H.323," work in progress Internet draft, IETF, January 2000.

[3] J. Rosenberg and H. Schulzrinne. "Models for Multi Party Conferencing in SIP," Internet draft, work in progress, IETF, November 2000.

CHAPTER 13

# Mixed PSTN and Internet Telephony Services

SIP interaction with the PSTN has two main forms: (1) interworking, in which a call from one network completes through a gateway to the other network and (2) services, in which devices in one network control initiate operations in the other network. In this chapter, the service interaction between SIP and the PSTN will be discussed in terms of **PSTN** and **INT**erworking (PINT) and the IETF WG's **S**ervers in the **PSTN I**nitiating **R**equests to In**T**ernet **S**ervers (SPIR-ITS). SIP and PSTN interworking has already been discussed in Chapter 9, *SIP Telephony*.

## Introduction

It became clear to many engineers and entrepreneurs soon after the appearance of IP telephony that there is a significant potential in combining it with PSTN for interesting new services. The best known of such early combined services, named here in a generic manner, are Click-to-Connect and Internet (Alert for) Call Waiting.

## Click-to-Connect: An Action on the Web Initiates a Call on the PSTN

To avoid customers abandoning shopping carts on e-commerce sites because of lack of information, a click-to-connect button on the Web page enables the user to initiate a call between his or her phone and an agent in the customer support center. The basic call-to-connect service has been enhanced with:

- Letting the agent see the Web page at which the user is looking,
- Pushing Web pages to the user with relevant information.

## Internet (Alert for) Call Waiting: An Incoming PSTN Call Is Signaled on the Web

Internet users of Internet (alert for) Call Waiting (ICW) with a single phone line and dial access to the Internet can avoid missing incoming phone calls while browsing the Web or exchanging email. An incoming call is signaled from the PSTN to the Web and, as a result, a panel pops up on the browser, alerting the user. Besides displaying the caller ID, when available, the user also may be given some options:

- A selection of voice messages to send to the caller.
- An option to reject the call or forward the call to voice mail or take some other action.

Though such mixed Internet-PSTN services are quite powerful, initially they have had little impact in the industry, since the proprietary nature of early implementations and the resulting lack of interoperability proved not to be practical in the marketplace. Enough prototyping and operational experience was gained, however, and authors from large telecom vendors published their experience, although we have to note the fact that small companies launched most early production systems on the market.

IETF working groups developed standards for interoperability, by specifying extensions to SIP required for interworking with the PSTN.

Prestandard implementations of click-to-connect and Internet call waiting had a heavy dependence on the local specifics of the PSTN. The IETF working groups decided to standardize only the protocols on the Internet side, so as not to depend on various regional or proprietary telecom architectures and signaling variants.

# Introduction to PINT

The PINT protocol allows invoking certain telephone services from an IP network. Examples of possible PINT services are:

- Click to connect
- Click to fax
- Click to receive information over the phone
- Click to send a page
- Click to receive a callback

Figure 13.1 shows the interaction between the Internet and the PSTN for PINT services. The basic idea is that an event on the Internet initiated by a PINT client triggers an action on the PSTN, such as completing a phone call between PSTN devices, such as between phones or fax machines.

The IETF PINT WG has developed SIP with extensions (shown as SIP**ext** in Figure 13.1). The extensions actually do not refer to SIP itself, but to the session description protocol (SDP) body part. This means that a major part of the SIP infrastructure—client registration and call routing by SIP servers—can be used without any changes. The SIP**ext** message set is referred to as the PINT protocol. Other signaling protocols could be used as well, as is the case in proprietary implementations found in various early click-to-connect products.

The PINT standard does not represent a new protocol—it uses SIP Version 2.0 with some extensions and some extensions to SDP. However, PINT does redefine the meaning of some SIP request messages, and introduces three new message types or methods: SUBSCRIBE, NOTIFY, and UNSUBSCRIBE. In standard SIP, an INVITE request is generated by a SIP user agent and is sent to another user agent client for the purposes of establishing a media session, where the type of IP media session to be established between the user agents

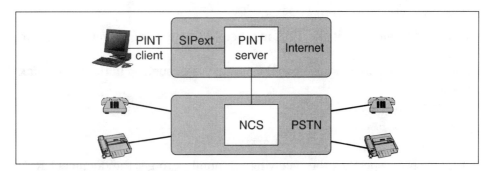

**Figure 13.1** The PINT model.

is described in the SDP message body of the `INVITE` request. In PINT, an `INVITE` request is generated by a PINT client to a PINT server which requests that the PINT server establish a PSTN telephone call, where the calling party, called party, and type of call are specified in the SDP message body of the `INVITE` request. This seemingly minor change in semantics represents a fundamental change in the purpose and interpretation of SIP messages. The additional methods were defined to allow a PINT client to request the completion status of a request using `SUBSCRIBE`, receive status updates using `NOTIFY`, and cancel subscriptions using `UNSUBSCRIBE`.

Other SIP methods also are changed slightly by PINT, including `REGISTER` and `BYE`. Refer to RFC 2848[1] for details.

## PINT Extensions to SDP

PINT introduces the notions of:

- **Network type.** "Telephone Network" or `TN`
- **Address type.** `RFC2543` (SIP)

Some examples follow:

```
c=TN RFC2543 +1-214-555-1234
```

is a global E.164 phone number characterized by the +1 prefix, North America in this example. The E.164 number can be dialed on a global basis. By contrast, some telephone numbers that are not E.164 have only local significance.

```
c=TN RFC2543 1-800-555-1234
```

 is only valid access to an 800 number within a geographic area.

The local context in circuit switched telephone networks depends on the type of local telephone network. This context is expressed by the PINT "phone-context" attribute:

```
c=TN RFC2543 123
a=phone-context: X-acme.com-98
```

specifies extension 98 at the PBX number 123 within the private acme.com PBX network.

The media type in SDP also can  have attributes, such as in the click-to-fax application:

```
c=TN RFC2543 +1-214-555-1234
m=text 1 fax plain
a=fmtp:plain uri: http://ietf.org/rfc/rfc2543.txt
```

This example specifies the receiving fax number to get the document RFC 2848 (PINT) from the indicated Web site.

We refer the reader to RFC 2848[1] for a complete text on PINT. RFC 2848 also has numerous options for dialing plans outside of North America and also for various applications. Examples for applications of PINT include:

- Request to a call center from an anonymous user to receive a phone call
- Request from a nonanonymous customer to receive a phone call from a particular sales agent
- Request to receive a fax back
- Request to have information read out over the phone
- Request to send an included text page to a friend's pager
- Request to send an image as a fax to a phone number
- Request to read out over the phone two pieces of content in sequence
- Request for the prices for ISDN to be sent to a fax machine
- Request for a callback
- Sending a set of information in response to an enquiry
- Sports-line "headlines" message sent to a phone/fax/pager
- Automatically sending someone a fax copy of a phone bill

These examples represent quite complex service requests that most users would not know how to formulate. The beauty of the PINT services lies in the fact that the embedded "click-to-" button on the Web page formulates these requests on behalf of the user.

## Examples of PINT Requests and Responses

1. Request to a call center from a customer to receive a phone call:

```
PINT Client -> PINT Server:

        INVITE sip:R2C@server.iron.com SIP/2.0
        Via: SIP/2.0/UDP 169.130.12.5
        From: sip:customer-1827631872@isp.net
        To: sip:+1-201-456-7890@iron.com;user=phone
        Call-ID: 19971205T234505.56.78@pager.com
        CSeq: 4711 INVITE
        Subject: Sale on Ironing Boards
        Content-type: application/sdp
        Content-Length: 174

        v=0
        o=- 2353687637 2353687637 IN IP4 128.3.4.5
        s=R2C
        i=Ironing Board Promotion
        e=customer-1827631872@isp.net
        t=2353687637 0
```

```
m=audio 1 voice -
c=TN RFC2543 +1-201-406-4090
```

In this example, the `INVITE` message is sent to the PINT server, server.iron.com. The username portion of the URL "R2C" indicates that the desired service is the Request to Call service. (Others defined in the PINT standard are R2F, Request to Fax and R2HC, Request to Hear Content.) The request is for a telephone call from a sales agent to be made to the telephone number :+1-201-456-7890. The telephone of the person who wishes to receive the call is explicitly identified as an internationally significant E.164 number that falls within the North American numbering plan (the "+1" within the `c=` line).

How does the customer know how to configure the `INVITE` message? All necessary parameters are sent from the PC client that enables the click-to-connect functions. This client is downloaded with the Web page from the ironing board promotion.

This `INVITE` will receive a `200 OK` response if the request is parsed and accepted by the PINT server. If the requestor wishes to receive confirmation that the telephone call was in fact placed to that number, the following `SUB-SCRIBE` message would be sent:

```
PINT Client -> PINT Server:

        SUBSCRIBE sip:R2C@server.iron.com SIP/2.0
        Via: SIP/2.0/UDP 169.130.12.5
        From: sip:customer-451827632@isp.net
        To: sip:+1-201-456-7890@iron.com;user=phone
        Call-ID: 71205T234505.56.77@pager.com
        CSeq: 4712 SUBSCRIBE
        Content-type: application/sdp
        Content-Length: 174

        v=0
        o=- 2353687637 2353687637 IN IP4 128.3.4.5
        s=R2C
        i=Ironing Board Promotion
        e=customer-1827631872@isp.net
        t=2353687637 0
        m=audio 1 voice -
        c=TN RFC2543 +1-201-406-4090
```

Note that the PINT server can match this `SUBSCRIBE` request to the `INVITE` even though the `From` and `Call-ID` headers are different—only the SDP message body is significant in determining the PINT call that is being referenced. This `SUBSCRIBE` message is similar to the use of this method in other contexts. However, in other applications, a `SUBSCRIBE` request will contain an `Event` header which indicates what the desired event is. When the `Event` header is not present in a `SUBSCRIBE` message, it is assumed that it is a PINT message and the SDP describes the event.

2.  Request to send an included text page to a friend's pager. In this exam-
    ple, the text to be paged out is included in the request:

```
C->S: INVITE sip:C2P@pint.pager.com SIP/2.0
      Via: SIP/2.0/UDP 169.130.12.5
      From: sip:friend@isp.net
      To: sip:C2P@pint.pager.com
      Call-ID: 19974505.66.79@isp.net
      CSeq: 4714 INVITE
      Content-Type: multipart/related; boundary=—next--next
      Content-Type: application/sdp
      Content-Length: 236

      v=0
      o=- 2353687680 2353687680 IN IP4 128.3.4.5
      s=C2P
      e=friend@isp.net
      t=2353687680 0
      m=text 1 pager plain
      c=TN RFC2543 +972-9-956-1867
      a=fmtp:plain spr:2@53655768

      --next
      Content-Type: text/plain
      Content-ID: 2@53655768
      Content-Length:50

      Hi Joe! Please call me ASAP at 972-555-1234.
```

These examples are taken from RFC 2848. The PINT draft standard specifies only the messages in the IP domain and does not specify, on purpose, anything specific on the PSTN side. This accomplishes the objective for PINT to
be independent of the implementation on the PBX or PSTN side of the control
elements, also called "executive system" in PINT. We use here the term NCS
(Network Control System) in Figure 13.1 instead. PINT services therefore can
be created without having to redesign anything on the circuit switched network side.

As can be seen from these examples, a number of very useful services can
be provided from the unidirectional action from the Internet to the PSTN.

PINT was the first specific application of SIP for telephony in the IETF.

The interest in PINT has led to proposals for the development of the SPIR-
ITS protocol.

# Introduction to SPIRITS

If an event on the Web can produce an action on the PSTN, why can't an event
on the PSTN produce an event on the Web, in the opposite direction? The two
directions of interaction are shown in Figure 13.2.

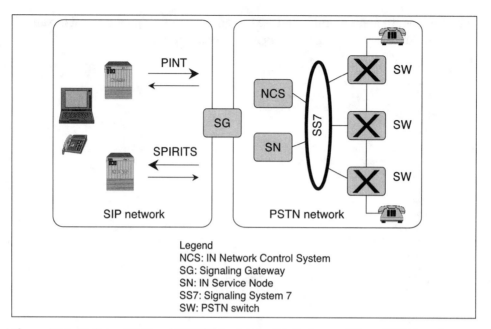

**Figure 13.2** Defining PINT and SPIRITS for interaction between SIP and PSTN services.

The SPIRITS IETF work also is based on SIP and allows access from the Internet to IN services [2]. The two-way interaction between the PSTN and the Web can support a large portfolio of services, such as will be shown here [3]. The best known SPIRITS service is Internet call waiting (ICW), mentioned earlier. Users with Internet dial access browsing the Web or using email can get a message on the PC that an incoming PSTN call is waiting. The user can have several choices of how to handle the call: accept the call, redirect the call to another destination (voice mail), or send a voice message, such as "please wait, ...."

## Call Flows for Internet Call Waiting

A high-level view of the call flows shown in Figure 13.3 is given here. User A has a SIP client on the PC. The SPIRITS client on the PC can be a thin client that is downloaded without the user intervention, the first time an incoming call has to be signaled to the user. The client registers with the registrar once user A gets online. (We will not show for simplicity how user A registers the SIP client with the registrar.) The main call flows are:

1. A telephone, user B, attempts a PSTN call to user A, who is occupying the phone line for Internet access.

2. The terminating PSTN switch alerts the network control system (NCS) of the incoming call and this alert is conveyed to the SPIRITS client on

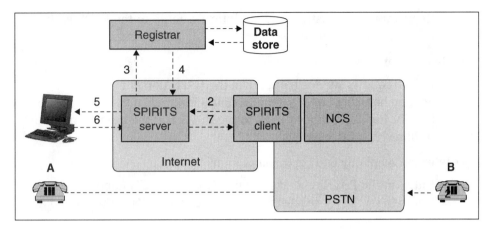

**Figure 13.3** Internet call waiting.

the Internet. (The implementation of the service on the PSTN side is beyond the scope of PINT and is not shown here.) The SPIRITS client makes a request for PINT service to the SPIRITS server to push a Web page on to the Web browser of user A.

3. The SPIRITS server queries the registrar if user A is registered and checks the IP address,

4. The registrar returns the IP address to the SPIRITS server,

5. The SPIRITS server pushes a Web page or panel to the PC of user A.

6. The PC user sends a reply to the SPIRITS server on the disposition for the incoming call. The user can decide how the call should be handled by the PSTN:

   ■ Accept the call via an IP telephony gateway using the PC as a SIP phone.

   ■ Forward the call to voice mail.

   ■ Play an appropriate announcement, from a given choice.

   ■ Refuse the call and provide a busy signal or no answer.

7. The disposition of the incoming call is transmitted to the PSTN via the SPIRITS client. This step is the reply to the client request.

Björkner and Nyckelgård [3] provide a list of possible SPIRITS functions. The word *possible* implies both (a) there can be more functions, and (b) some functions may be implemented by other means depending on the circumstances. Some of these functions are listed here:

■ Server and service registration:

- Registration/deregistration of an Internet entity to the PSTN entity.
- Registration of available services in the Internet domain.

- Request for service:
  - PSTN requests service handling in the PSTN domain.
  - Service handling handed back from the Internet to the PSTN.
  - Service handling handed back to the PSTN and the Internet monitors fulfillment.

- Internet telephony call leg manipulation:
  - Entity in the PSTN requests a call between two IP endpoints.
  - Entity in the PSTN requests a call between a PSTN endpoint and an IP endpoint.
  - Same as previous for several IP endpoints.
  - Transfer to another IP endpoint.
  - Hold/resume call to an IP endpoint.

- Spirits service monitoring:
  - Event notification requests sent from the PSTN to the Internet.

- Special resources functions:
  - Request an entity on the Internet to replay audio messages.
  - Collect information from the Internet such as voice browsing.
  - Set user data and service data from the PSTN in the Internet.

## IN-SIP Gateway and Services

Several implementations have been reported for interaction between the Internet and the PSTN [4]. Figure 13.4 shows the principle and implementation for an IN-SIP gateway [4], [5]. Examples for ITU Q.1211 services that could interwork with SIP via IN call triggers are:

- Abbreviated dialing (ABD)
- Call distribution (CD)
- Call forwarding (CF)
- Call rerouting distribution (CRD)
- Credit card calling (CCC)
- Destination call routing (DCR)
- Follow-me diversion (FMD)
- Free phone (FPH)
- Number portability (NP)

- Originating call screening (OCS)
- Terminating call screening TCS)

The gateway schema shown in Figure 13.4 is meant as an illustration only, since other designs also are possible.

Other telephony signaling protocols can be accommodated by gateways in this class, so as to encompass:

- SS7 for public PSTN networks
- ISUP for ISDN-connected enterprise networks
- Gateways for wireless networks
- INAP for interworking with ITU Advances Intelligent Network (AIN)-controlled networks

Commercial services have been reported using IP-SIP gateways [6], [7]. Gateway-enabled services include:

- Personal mobility within and between networks

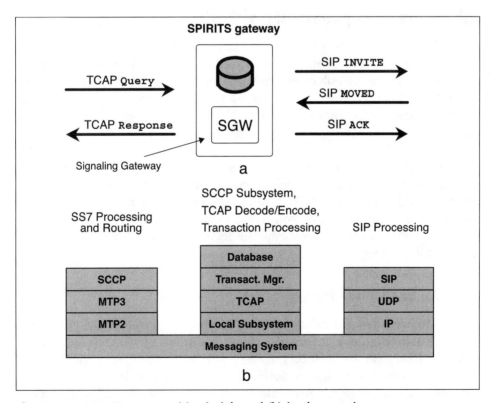

**Figure 13.4** SPIRITS gateway: (a) principle and (b) implementation.

- Self-managed incoming call screening
- Self-managed conditional call diversion
- Integrated enterprise communications
- Analog phones, mobile phones, PBX phones, IP phones, and call center applications
- Local and global number portability for fixed and mobile phones
- Service/customer broker for new business roles

An additional server connected to the local gateway provides number portability. We discuss in greater detail such types of services in Chapter 14, *DNS and ENUM*.

Similar to PINT, SPIRITS is defined entirely on the IP network side and makes no assumptions on the implementation of the "executive system" that controls the circuit switched network side. Given the rich portfolio of services however, engineers active and familiar with the PSTN IN world have defined the mapping from the IN call state model to the states of SIP [2].

## Enhancing or Replacing IN with SIP

Since SIP network control gateways to circuit-switched networks allow the creation of IN services and many other mixed IP-PSTN services, it makes sense to consider moving the enhancement work for IN to SIP, and even to replace the IN entirely with SIP servers for circuit-switched networks. An interesting design proposal by J. Björkner and S. Nyckelgård actually shows how to accomplish this [3].

At the time of this writing, interest in circuit-switched networks seems to be fast fading due to the emergence of IP networks, so this potential for reengineering the IN may not be of much practical value. We believe, however, that the interworking between PSTN central control systems and SIP is of great importance for the transition from telecom networks to the Internet. Many innovative services are possible from the IN-SIP interaction such as personal call control services.

## SPIRITS and INAP Interworking

So far, we have not provided any details on how the implementation on the PSTN side may look for interworking with Internet. The IN Application Protocol (INAP) can be used on the PSTN side and a number of IETF contributions elaborate on the interaction between SIP and the IN for fixed PSTN and mobile circuit switched networks [8]–[10]. We show for easy comparison two roles for the IP telephony gateway in Figure 13.5.

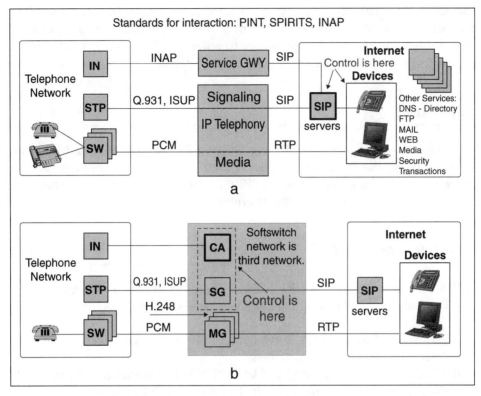

**Figure 13.5** Interworking between the PSTN and the Internet; a. Direct interworking using gateways, and b. Intermediate softswitch network.

Figure 13.5a. shows the direct interworking model between the telephone network and the Internet. Two types of gateways are deployed:

1. IP telephony gateway, without assuming any specific gateway decomposition. The IP telephony gateway does only the media and signaling conversion between the two networks.

2. Service gateway, linking the SIP control network with the IN using INAP.

Control for services resides on the Internet side, either in SIP servers or in SIP devices, as discussed in Chapter 17. This allows the service provider to freely introduce IP communication services that may or may not have a replica on the PSTN, such as presence, unified and instant messaging, and multimedia conferencing, while still preserving compatibility with traditional services and features available on the PSTN.

Figure 13.5b shows for comparison the interworking using an intermediate softswitch network, where the control for services resides in the call agent.

The softswitch network is, in effect, a third network, besides the IN/PSTN network and the SIP network. This third network (softswitch) is an unnecessary burden for the service provider. Chapter 17, *The Component Server Architecture*, discusses this alternative in more detail.

## Summary

This chapter has shown how SIP can be used for mixed PSTN and Internet services. Using the PINT specification based on SIP, PSTN services can be invoked using the Internet. Using the SPIRITS specification, SIP can be used by the PSTN to invoke services in the Internet.

## References

[1] S. Petrack and L. Conroy. RFC 2848: "The PINT Service Protocol: Extensions to SIP and SDP for IP Telephone Call Services," IETF, June 2000.

[2] V. Gurbani. "Accessing IN Services from SIP Networks," IETF Internet draft, May 2000, work in progress.

[3] J. Björkner and S. Nyckelgård. "A SPIRITS Solution Based on Virtual SIP User Agents," IETF Internet draft, July 2000, work in progress.

[4] L. Conroy and J. Buller. "A List of Possible SPIRITS Functions," IETF Internet draft, January 2001, work in progress

[5] H. Lu, et al. RFC 2458: "Toward the PSTN/Internet Inter-Working, Pre-PINT Implementations," IETF, November 1998.

[6] Sören Nyckelgård. "Fixed-Mobile-IP Convergence," presentation at the VON Fall 2000 conference, session 31.

[7] Ed Reaves. "SIP Enabled Unified Networks," presentation at the VON Fall 2000 conference, session 31.

[8] I. Faynberg, J. Gato, H. Lu, and L. Slutsman. "IN- and PINT-related Requirements for SPIRITS Protocol," IETF Internet draft, 1999, work in progress.

[9] H. Schulzrinne, L. Slutsman, I. Faynberg, and H. Lu. "Interworking between SIP and INAP," IETF Internet draft, 1999, work in progress.

[10] L. Slutsman. "Framework and Requirements for the Internet Intelligent Networks (IIN)," IETF Internet draft, September 2000, work in progress.

CHAPTER
14

# DNS and ENUM

This chapter introduces DNS, Domain Name Service, and ENUM, a telephone number mapping system to Internet resources.

## Introduction: DNS and Directories

Readers will easily recall how their Web browser finds the IP address for a Web site. For example, when entering for the first time (the Web site address and the Web pages were not yet cached by the browser) the Web site name:

ietf.org

the browser will first display, usually in the bottom left hand panel, a message such as

Finding site: ietf.org

Since the built-in DNS client will talk to one of the pre-configured DNS servers in the local IP stack, when the DNS returns an IP address, the browser will then display

Contacting: ietf.org

followed by

Web site found. Waiting for reply...

The Web page content is transferred to the browser after the Web server has responded. The speed of the response may sometimes make it difficult to follow this message sequence. The high speed of the above process, given reasonably fast Internet access, shows the power of the global Internet DNS system.

SIP is closely related to Web technology and can make similar use of DNS-based directory services and also make use of LDAP-based directories. The end user may not know or even care how it is done, but the practical result is powerful enterprise or global directory services can be integrated into SIP clients such as phones, PCs, or portable devices.

# Addressing and DNS

Understanding the Domain Name System (DNS) and directories requires a brief review of Internet and Web addressing that we provide here. Readers familiar with this topic can proceed directly to the section on DNS.

## URIs and URLs

We will present in this section a summary overview of addressing used on the Internet and the World Wide Web and related addressing methods for telephony and SIP. The material is only meant to give the reader a first contact with the topics. The associated references are intended for further in depth information. The examples given here use fictitious addresses and names that have no relation to existing ones.

We will show the involvement of SIP servers and gateways in the following examples. SIP end devices like phones or computers can, however, use SIP URLs and perform address resolution to initiate a communication all by themselves, true to the end-to-end control architecture of the Internet.

## The Domain Name System

We will provide here a summary of DNS concepts [1] that is limited only to the scope of explaining how the DNS is used for SIP services. Interested readers are referred to the large number of IETF RFCs and Internet drafts on the topic.

| | |
|---|---|
| **URI (RFC 1630)** | The *Universal Resource Identifier* is a name associated with a universal set of names in a registered naming space, such as Internet domain names registered with IANA or host names registered for a specific domain. URI's are independent of the location (a specific host) of the named object. |

For example:

firstname.lastname@company.com

is a URI associated with e-mail. Note the mail URI does not specify any specific host.

URI schemas are associated with various protocols and services, such as: FTP, HTTP, Mail, News, SIP, Telnet and other.

In SIP, a Request-URI is defined in RFC 2543 as a type of URI used to indicate the name of the destination for the SIP Request (INVITE, REGISTER, etc.) As a SIP Request is forwarded by proxies, the Request-URI can be changed as database lookups and feature invocations change the final destination of the request.

| | |
|---|---|
| **URL (RFC 1738)** | The *Universal Resource Locator* describes the location of a resource available on the Internet. Contrary to URI schemas, the schemas for URLs are associated with specific protocols and services. |

Example:

https://www.wcom.com/cgi-bin/WebObjects/olab

is the secure http address for an online address book, associated with the HTTPS service (secure HTTP) and refers to a specific host and file path.

A number of URL schemes are described, as follows.

| | |
|---|---|
| **mailto:** | The *mailto:* URL schema designates an Internet mailing address of an individual or service. It does not represent an actual Internet location, but serves only to route Internet mail. |

Example:

mailto: firstname.lastname@company.com

The mailto: URL appears frequently in Web pages for providing email feedback. In addition, the values of certain SMTP headers can be pre-populated by the URL. For example, clicking on the URL that follows in a Web browser will bring up a blank email message addressed To:

*continues*

webmaster@company.com and with the Subject: header set to "Feedback"

mailto:webmaster@company.com?Subject=Feedback

A mailto: URL can appear in a SIP message as part of a list of Contact headers.

| | |
|---|---|
| **Tel URL (RCF 2806)** | The *Telephony URL* schemas specify the "tel," "fax," and "modem" locations of a terminal in the phone network and the connection types that can be used to connect to that entity. Telephony URLs can be used for fixed and mobile phone calls and for fax. |

Examples:

tel:+358-555-1234567

points to a terminal in Finland able to receive phone calls, while

fax:+358.555.1234567

points to a fax machine in Finland.

Digit separators can be either "-" or "." or neither; the separators are removed by parsers and are ignored. The grouping of 358 as the country code for Finland is done for human readability—no Internet device needs to have knowledge of telephone numbers and their context specific flavors.

SIP URLs can also handle telephone numbers. In fact, the entire set of parameters specified for the tel URL can be used in the username portion of a SIP URL.

An example of a parameter in a tel URL is described for the *phone-context*.

| | |
|---|---|
| **phone-context (RFC 2806)** | The *phone-context* specifies under what circumstances a phone number can be used. |

Example:

tel:1-800-123-4567;phone-context=+1 972

refers to an 800 number valid only for the North American numbers for the 972 calling area. Note the absence of a + in the URL. Any digits in a tel URL which do not begin with a + are assumed to be a local, not global, number. If a phone-context tag is not present in the URL, then some other context (typically geographic) must be used to interpret the digits. Since the Internet does not have the kind of geographic isolation typically present in the PSTN, this is a difficult thing to do.

*continues*

Note: In the PSTN, a Class 5 telephone switch in a North American Rate Center covered by only a single numbering plan area code (NPA) may safely assume that any 7 digit number uses the default area code and country code. This is possible because of the structure of the PSTN and the limited connectivity that this switch has to other switches in the PSTN. In a SIP network on the Internet, a proxy is theoretically accessible to any SIP User Agent in the world and may not make such assumptions.

| | |
|---|---|
| **SIP URL (RFC 2543)** | *SIP URLs* are used within SIP messages to indicate the originator (From), current destination (Request-URI), final recipient (To), and redirection address (Contact). |

When used with a hyperlink, the SIP URL indicates the use of the INVITE method. SIP URL hyperlinks allow the embedding of links that when opened can initiate a phone call, for example.

Examples:

> sip:firstname.lastname@company.com

may be used to send a call to a voice mailbox.

> sip:+1-214-555-1212@gateway.com;user=phone

indicates how to address a call from the Internet to the PSTN E.164 phone number :+1-214-555-1212 via the IP telephony gateway having the domain name gateway.com. The user=phone tag is a hint to parsers that a telephone number is present in the username portion of the URL, and not just a numerical name.

The host portion of a SIP URL containing a telephone number does not always indicate a gateway. This is because the creator of the URL may not know the location of the gateway and may instead be relying on a proxy to locate an appropriate gateway. In this case, the URL would look like:

> sip:+1-214-555-1212@proxy.gateway.com;user=phone

where the proxy server at proxy.gateway.com will determine the gateway and forward the request.

> sip:firstname.lastname@registrar.com;method=register

is used to register a user at the SIP registrar server registrar.com.

The Internet Domain Name System (DNS) is a scalable name space used to refer to resources. DNS names avoid specifics such as network identifiers, addresses, or similar information.

Scalability for the huge size data in the DNS is due to its distributed nature and the use of caching. A root server for the DNS system only contains a single entry for the top level domains such as com, org, edu, gov, etc. and the complete list of country specific domains such as us, au, ca, it, etc. The DNS server for each of these top-level domains contains pointers to the authoritative DNS server for that particular domain, company.com, for example. The actual DNS records of host names, servers, etc., for the company.com domain is the responsibility of and under the complete control of the owner of the company.com domain. For example, the Address records, or A records that contain the IP addresses of servers within the domain, such as mail.company.com, www.company.com, ftp.company.com, etc. are maintained there. The creation and deletion of names is fully distributed and delegated to lower levels of the DNS in this way.

Without caching, every DNS query would have to begin at the root DNS server, continue to the top-level domain server, then end at the authoritative DNS server. Very efficient caching schemes employed in DNS makes this the rare exception rather than the rule. Most DNS queries only traverse one or two DNS servers. However, the price paid for this efficient caching is DNS changes (updates) do not happen in real time but take significant time to propagate throughout the Internet. As a result, DNS is not suited for roaming and other mobility services.

The DNS is designed to support many applications, such as referring to host addresses, mailbox data, and as shown here is also used by SIP servers. Address formats differ for various protocols and the DNS is designed to support various protocols with their notion of an address, such as FTP, HTTP, mail, or SIP.

> RFC-2219 specifies the protocols and services, some of them of interest here are:
>
> File Transfer Protocol—FTP (RFC-959)
>
> Lightweight Directory Access Protocol—LDAP (RFC-1777)
>
> Network Time Protocol—NTP (RFC-1305)
>
> Post Office Protocol—POP (RFC-1939)
>
> Session Initiation Protocol—SIP (RFC-2543)
>
> SMTP mail (RFC-821)—SMTP
>
> World Wide Web, Hyper Text Transport Protocol—HTTP (RFC-1945).

The DNS is independent of the underlying transport system for the data and can work with datagrams or virtual circuits. The DNS is also designed to be used by computers of all sizes, from small personal devices to large computers. RFC 1034 is the basis for the DNS system design. Several other RFCs have introduced various improvements. We limit here the discussion of the DNS to the information required for the understanding of SIP services that use DNS.

Most data in the DNS system are assumed to change very slowly, for example, mailbox addresses or host name-address bindings. Current IETF work aims at providing faster, dynamic updates [2]. Lower levels of the DNS may however accommodate faster changes, such as in the order of minutes or even seconds.

### A Partial DNS Glossary

We provide in Table 14.1 a summary overview of some DNS terminology, with special emphasis on the use of DNS with SIP where we believe most of the telephone number directory applications will reside.

## DNS and Directory Security

Readers of the public DNS data stored in both the first and second tiers of the ENUM service must be assured that they will receive valid information. Hence, the core underlying security considerations for the ENUM service focuses on add, change, and delete security at both the first and second levels of the solution.

Clients who have authority to add, change, and delete entries in the ENUM system must be assured that they:

- Are updating data in the correct directory service.
- Have uninterrupted access to the data.
- Are allowed to update the data based on presenting valid credentials.

Service administrators for both the First and Second tiers of the ENUM service have the responsibility to protect their physical and network resources as well as to ensure the validity of the DNS data entered in the system.

Level 3 of the architecture, implemented either as a 2nd-tier DNS server or directory server, needs to have secure communications between the PSTN telephone service provider that owns the phone numbers and its subscribers. If, for example, a phone is disconnected or the number is changed, a secure update has to be made in the DNS or directory server.

When preparing to prevent security breaches, the following types of attacks must be considered.

### Impersonation

Clients attempting to add and update entries in an ENUM service must be able to unequivocally prove their identity to the DNS system. Spoofing or misrepresentation of the identity of the originator of the information could allow unauthorized updates to the database. Invalid or missing data could in turn cause malicious redirection and denial of service, which are discussed later. The update facility of each ENUM system is responsible for preventing impersonation attacks.

**Table 14.1** Summary Overview of Some DNS Terminology

| | |
|---|---|
| Domain Name | The Domain Name is a list of labels on the path from the node to the root of the tree. |
| | For example: |
| | ipcom.worldcomnet.com |
| | is the name of the host ipcom in the worldcomnet network registered in the com top level domain (TLD). |
| Resource Record (RR) | Resource Records associated with a particular name, such as for hosts, mail exchanges, Web servers, SIP servers. |
| | For example: |
| | ipcom.worldcomnet.com   IN    A    166.15.21.14 |
| | provides the IP address on the Internet for the host ipcom, |
| | mail2.worldcom    MX    worldcomnet.com |
| | gives the name of the mail server for wolrdcomnet, |
| | SIP3.worldcom   SIP   worldcomnet.com |
| | refers to a SIP server. |
| A Record (A) | A RR that designates a host address. A records are the most commonly used DNS records for translating a domain name into an IP address. |
| Service Record (SRV) | A RR that contains the locations for services and their protocols. |
| | For example: |
| | SOA    root.wcom.com (see below for SOA) |
| | NS    ns1.wcom.com |
| | NS    ns2.wcom.com |
| | This part of a RR shows the names of the root DNS server and of two additional name servers. A complete RR would list other services as well. The use of SRV records to locate a SIP Proxy server for a particular domain is described in RFC 2543. |
| Mail Exchange Record (MX) | Identifies a mail exchange in the domain. |
| Name Server (NS) | Authoritative name server for the domain. |
| Pointer (PTR) | Pointer to another part of the domain space. These records are used for backwards DNS lookups—resolving an IP address into a domain name. |

**Table 14.1** (*Continued*)

| | |
|---|---|
| Naming Authority Pointer (NAPTR) | The Naming Authority Pointer [3] is a RR written according to specific rules, so that the address lookup can be delegated to a lower level DNS server. |
| | For example, the E.164 phone number |
| | +1-770-555-1212 |
| | can be converted for lookup in the DNS of the e.164.arpa domain to |
| | 2.1.2.1.5.5.5.0.7.7.1.e164.arpa |
| | A query sent to 164.arpa may produce the NAPTR records with the hosts that can process this address: |
| | sip:information@wcom.com |
| | mailto:information@wcom.com |
| Start of zone of Authority (SOA) | Start of zone for Authority for a given domain. |

## Eavesdropping

If the privacy of the information that is being transmitted between a client application and the ENUM service (first or second level) is compromised, then registrant-sensitive information such as the registrant's username and password, could be obtained by a malicious intruder. The DNS system must be able to prevent eavesdropping attacks.

## Data Tampering

During the transmission of directory records, valid URIs could be replaced by invalid URIs, in turn causing malicious redirection as discussed below. Since a high percentage of security breaches, such as data tampering can be caused by "insiders," physical and network security must be addressed. The widest range of network and physical security features must protect servers.

## Malicious Redirection

Malicious entries into the database will cause clients to retrieve wrong URI's that point to fraudulent or damaging content. This can be accomplished in two ways: first, by data tampering as discussed previously; and second, through server impersonation whereby a malicious server is masquerading as a valid ENUM server.

### *Denial of Service*

There are several ways that a client could be denied access to the desired network resources, which may include access to the DNS data as well as access to physical DNS servers. First, a malicious intruder could remove the URIs from the database, using the data tampering methods discussed above, thus making it impossible for the client to access the correct information. Another way to cause a denial of service to customers is to flood the DNS servers with enough data to prevent further communication with that server. This is done by either downloading gigabytes of information to the server all at once, or by maliciously flooding the server with bogus requests. And finally, by breaching the physical security of the servers by, for example, cutting off electricity to the facility, clients would be denied access.

Finally, the security of the DNS responses as they route through the public Internet must be considered. A third party could intercept and modify a DNS SRV record by deleting or modifying URIs.

Extensive work on DNS security is in progress. Interested readers are referred to the document roadmap [4] or the IETF DNSEX working group [5].

Example of security procedures for authentication and data integrity [6]:

**The NetNumber Inc. implementation.** Employs two-factor authentication that requires username and password as well as a client certificate, utilizing public-key cryptography along with the Secure Socket Layer protocol, or SSL. This approach addresses each of the security concerns described earlier. First, it reduces the possibility of impersonation by the parties who are attempting to update the DNS. The identity of the sender of the data, as well as the identity of the Authoritative Directory Service operator, is assured using SSL and mutual authentication. Further security of the database is assured by giving users access only to their own data. Once the identity of a user is established through two-factor authentication, the user cannot change or enter data that does not belong to them. Finally, the use of SSL eliminates the risk of data tampering as well as providing privacy through encryption of sensitive information.

**Physical security.** The facilities in which the DNS servers reside are protected by physical security measures including 24×7 secured access, video camera surveillance, security breach alarms, and secured equipment cabinets. State-of-the-art firewall appliances, VPN equipment, and hardened server operating systems provide network security.

# DNS-Based Directory Services Using SIP

There are some problems with personal addresses: With the proliferation of communication services provided by the PSTN, wireless phone systems, and various Internet services, it becomes quite difficult to track the increasing number of addresses for contacts we are interested in. The frequent changes by the desired contact of service providers and services make this problem even harder.

Contacting a called party is a difficult problem due to the number of communication devices, such as: Home PCs and home fax, palmtop computer, laptop, office PCs and fax, pager, cell phone, IP printers, vehicle, boat, in-conference device, etc. It is thus possible to require a choice among up to 10 devices or more, to reach the called party.

Users may also want to indicate temporary contact addresses, such as the phone of a secretary, restaurant, or a hotel phone number when traveling. Besides the contact address, users may also want to indicate the mode by which they are contacted. A user attending a meeting may indicate for example that text chat is appropriate to convey urgent messages in a non-intrusive manner.

## Single Contact Address

Could a single address be used to contact a person, no matter what devices they may have? There are two main choices:

### SIP URI

A SIP URI in the form of sip:alice@wonderland.com is a very powerful single address since it can support user pre-call mobility [7] as well as user preferences.

The Swedish service provider Telia using the Golden Gate service for its employees has first implemented a SIP URI service [8].

SIP URI requires, however, that the called party has subscribed to a SIP service.

### Phone Number

In the transition period where most users still have PSTN and/or mobile telephone service only, another solution is to provide an E.164 phone number as the single contact address on the business card. When a PSTN telephone number includes a country code, it is known as an E.164 number, which refers to the ITU document that describes telephone number structure. Phone numbers, especially the home phone number, change less frequently and are thus well suited as stable contact addresses.

The predominant availability of phones with 12 digit keypads (10 numerical digits plus the special characters "#" and "*") makes this the most practical near-term option for address entry.

If there is a desire not to give out the home phone number, another phone number, such as a work number could be given as the single contact address.

Thus by knowing just one telephone number, all the other communication addresses can be found.

## Three-Level Directory Systems

Internet-PSTN directory systems using ENUM and SIP have a three-level architecture, as shown in Figure 14.1.

**Level 1**. The Internet Domain Name Systems (DNS) root: e164.arpa

**Level 2**. National ENUM delegation authority, such as for +1, +44, etc. country codes

**Level 3.** SIP proxy server for call routing and for user preferences.

Here is a short description of the DNS-based directory system levels.

### First Level: DNS TLD

The name of the Top Level Domain (TLD) for the DNS for telephone numbers has been defined to be:

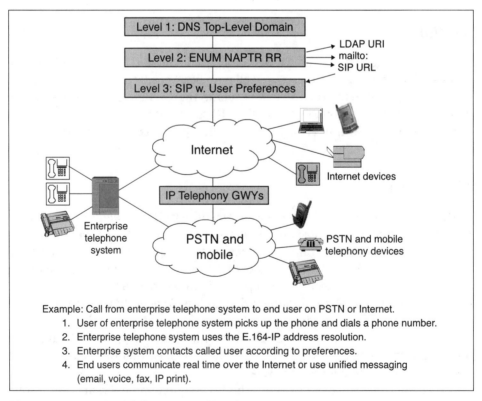

Example: Call from enterprise telephone system to end user on PSTN or Internet.
1. User of enterprise telephone system picks up the phone and dials a phone number.
2. Enterprise telephone system uses the E.164-IP address resolution.
3. Enterprise system contacts called user according to preferences.
4. End users communicate real time over the Internet or use unified messaging (email, voice, fax, IP print).

**Figure 14.1** DNS-based directory service using SIP.

e164.arpa

in the IETF ENUM RFC 2916 draft standard. Technically speaking, *e164.arpa* is a subdomain of *arpa*, but is referred to in ENUM documents as the top-level domain (TLD).

Any standard DNS client can make a DNS query to the TLD after some internal processing by an application of the telephone number to translate it in DNS syntax. The resolution of E.164 phone numbers to URLs has been specified in RFC-2916. Here is an example how a client application processes a phone number to make a DNS query:

1. Start with the complete E.164 phone number:

    +1-972-555-1212

2. Remove all characters that are not digits:

    19725551212

3. Reverse the order of the phone number:

    21215552791

4. Insert dots between digits and at the end:

    2.1.2.1.5.5.5.2.7.9.1

5. Append the DNS top-level domain: e164.arpa:

    2.1.2.1.5.5.5.2.7.9.1.164.arpa

The client is now ready to make a DNS query using the result from step 5.

Zones under e164.arpa are delegated by E.164 country codes to servers as designated by national regulatory authorities. Note that in keeping with standard DNS practice, this can be further partitioned in many ways, such as down to area codes, if required.

## Second Level: ENUM

The DNS client makes the first query to the TLD and is redirected to the second level for address resolution, to an ENUM DNS server. ENUM uses NAPTR

RR to input the DNS query as shown in step 5 for an E.164 phone number and gets the output in the form of a URI. Together with the phone number, the desired service can also be specified.

Examples of NAPTR Service Specification are as follows:

Specification of Service: E2U

Name: E.164 to URI

Mnemonic: E2U

Depending on the service specified in the query, the results in Table 14.2 will be returned.

The client now has the URL to the desired endpoint, or in the directory case, the pointer to the directory where user information resides. For example, the result of the query using the DNS RR is the SIP URL, the tel URL, or the mail-to:address.

It should be noted from this example that NAPTR is a service and application independent DNS capability and can be used directly to return URLs pointing to any type of server. NAPTR can return the URLs for directory servers, such as in the last line in the above example.

ldap://ldap.wcom.com:389

In this case an LDAP directory client can now make a directory query using the LDAP protocol. The number 389 indicates the port on the LDAP host.

### Third-Level Directory or SIP Servers

A directory server, as an alternative to a DNS server, can also accomplish third-level ENUM operation. The directory server uses another step to append as a prefix the desired service protocol, for example:

Add the service protocol:

6. sip. 2.1.2.1.5.5.5.2.7.9.1.e164.arpa

**Table 14.2** Query Results

| QUERY | EXAMPLE RESULT |
|---|---|
| "sip+E2U" | sip:henry@com.com |
| "mailto:+E2U" | mailto:henry@wcom.com |
| "tel+E2U" | tel:+1-972-555-1212 |
| "ldap+E2U" | ldap://ldap.wcom.com:389 |

The directory client will make the query and get the result.
Examples for queries and results from LDAP [9] databases:

Query:   sip. 2.1.2.1.5.5.5.2.7.9.1.tel

Result:   sip:user@company.com

Query:   smpt. 2.1.2.1.5.5.5.2.7.9.1.tel

Result:   mailto: user@company.com

The second-level address resolution has to determine the service registrar. The second-level DNS can be delegated to a second-tier DNS server or to an authoritative directory service that is the name server.

A second-tier DNS could be the country code for ITU E.164 address.

Examples for ITU country codes as second-level domain are given in Table 14.3.

In this example "phone.net" for the respective country codes is the authority to which the phone numbers are delegated [10]. Note the "+1" code for North America extends to Canada, USA, and Mexico, for which no single administrative authority exists [11]. The North American Numbering Plan (NANP) in the USA is currently delegated to NeuStar, Inc. [12].

### Implementation Issues

We have so far considered the second-level address resolution using the ENUM NAPTR approach. Lower level address resolution could also be implemented as an LDAP directory server. Several considerations have to be taken into account when choosing an implementation alternative:

**Client complexity.** The NAPTR solution requires mores complex regular expression processing and parsing to obtain a result, but a single DNS client is required. When using an LDAP directory, more simple queries are used, but an additional LDAP client is required.

**Real-time updates.** Present DNS technology may introduce 15-minute to 4-hour update delays. LDAP supports real-time updates. Current DNS work aims however to reduce the update delay.

**Provisioning complexity.** Implementation of provisioning of NAPTR or lower level LDAP records.

**Table 14.3** Examples for ITU Country Codes

| | | |
|---|---|---|
| 1.e164.arpa | ns.nanp.phone.net | for the North American Numbering Plan (NANP) |
| 3.3. e164.arpa | ns.fr.phone.net | for France |
| 2.7.9. e164.arpa | ns.il.phone.net | for Israel |

**Other considerations.** May include the storage of supplementary information, such as security data and spoken names (audio wave files), or the flexibility of queries.

More detailed implementation issues go beyond the scope of the present paper. The IETF in keeping with its tradition of choosing scalability, simplicity, and state of the art technology; together with allowing for only one option, has decided to use DNS NAPTR RR for the second-level address resolution.

## Third-Level SIP Address Resolution

The third level for address resolution is service specific. For IP communications, using SIP servers enables the following features:

- Security of the database by giving users access only to their own record. Users have to be authenticated and registered to the SIP server before getting access to the data.

- User data can change rapidly under user control in real time, for example, by uploading an XML script from the user device.

An example of a contact list for SIP is as follows:

```
Contact:  sip:henry@wcom.com
          ;service=IP,voice mail
          ;media=audio ;duplex=full ;q=0.7
Contact:  phone: +1-972-555-1212; service=ISDN
          ;mobility=fixed; language=en,es, ;q=0.5
Contact:  phone: +1-214-555-1212; service=pager
          ;mobility=mobile
          ;duplex=send-only ;media=text; q=0.1; priority=urgent
          ;description="For emergency only"
Contact:  mailto:henry@wcom.com
```

This contact list for Henry shows the most preferred contact to be voice mail, followed by an ISDN phone number to call, pager, and email in that order.

### SIP User Preferences and Precall Mobility

Besides contact preferences, SIP also allows users to specify preferences so as to route incoming calls depending on who the caller is, time of day, location of the user, etc. These preferences can be updated or changed in real time by the user.

Contact preferences for phone, e-mail, and other addresses can also be hosted in the second-tier DNS or directory servers though we believe this to be a less scalable approach, since user preferences can slow down such servers. DNS and LDAP directories are also less suited for frequent real-time updates. Finally, there are at present no standard facilities to register and authorize users and to provide standard contact data formats as specified in SIP. SIP servers that support CPL [13] can accommodate fast changing user preferences.

SIP adds the following value-added features to ENUM:

- User preferences
- Personal, service, and precall mobility
- Frequent and secure access by end users

These features simply may not make sense for ENUM and directory services.

Implementers of SIP clients can use the above to considerably enhance the value and indeed "stickiness" of their products. Intelligent SIP phones [14] and PC clients, for example, can display the directory information and use it in combination with other applications.

A number of interesting issues for implementing SIP call routing using ENUM for Freephone calls and number portability are discussed in [15].

It is important to note the SIP provides the ability of a User Agent without access to any DNS or LDAP database to place SIP calls. The configuration of a default SIP outgoing proxy server allows an extremely simple User Agent to simply take a telephone number or URL input from a user and forward the SIP Request to a proxy. The proxy then performs directory services described in this chapter and the call completes in the same way.

The default SIP proxy can be configured in a SIP User Agent Client, or automatically configured using DHCP (Dynamic Host Configuration Protocol) at the same time the device is assigned an IP address.

Outgoing calls can be handled by the SIP User Agent Client (UAC) several ways using ENUM:

- UAC takes phone number and performs ENUM DNS query to get the URL.
- UAC puts phone number in tel URL and forwards to a gateway or proxy.
- UAC puts phone number in SIP URL and forwards to gateway or proxy.
- UAC performs DNS SRV query on domain in URL to get IP address.
- UAC uses cached IP address from previous call/transaction in new request.
- UAC forwards URL to default proxy, which performs either 1-5, or queries a location service. This last option is the most preferable, as it relieves SIP devices of DNS transactions required for ENUM.

## Application Scenarios for SIP Service Using ENUM

We will provide here high level call flow examples for an end user in an enterprise network, such as a broker in a financial institution, trying the reach a customer who may be accessible on either the PSTN/mobile telephone network, Internet, or paging network.

### PBX Enterprise Voice Network

The caller in the enterprise network on the left in Figure 14.1 tries to reach a client having the phone number 214-123-4589. Suppose there is some urgency and using voice mail or e-mail is not desirable. There are several scenarios:

■ The enterprise PBX has not been upgraded for ENUM service. The called party can only be reached if they can answer on the dialed phone number.

■ The PBX has been upgraded for access to ENUM service, using a service provider. In this case when dialing the phone number:

■ The called party can be reached at any PSTN/mobile phone, without the calling party having to notice the difference. If the called party has also the benefit of SIP service, the caller may be notified where the call has been redirected. This option is, however, under control of the called party and can be made dependent on who the caller is, on location, time of day, etc.

■ The called party is not available. A voice announcement can inform the caller of the alternative contact options. If paging is an option, the called party can be paged and a text message sent by the caller, for example, using the Internet access to the paging system. If both the caller and called party have a bidirectional text paging system, they can communicate sending text pages.

### Enterprise System with IP Communications

The PBX has been replaced with a SIP-based IP communication system. The caller can be reached anywhere on the PSTN/mobile network or on the Internet, without the need for other systems, such as a separate paging system. The ENUM system will provide a URL for routing the SIP call to any destination.

The SIP phone user will be connected to the called party for a voice call, if the called party is reachable on any PSTN/mobile phone or by an IP phone.

If the called party is in a meeting and has the laptop computer connected to the Internet, the call will be redirected to the instant messaging client, and both parties can use text chat in a non-intrusive manner. The caller in the enterprise network can also push Web pages or transmit other documents to the client during the conversation.

We notice here that the caller can have also the benefit of the SIP presence service. In this case, the presence service would not only notify the caller of the availability of the called party anywhere on the PSTN/mobile or Internet, but could also convey additional information about the willingness to accept calls, and other information, such as being already in a call, and even who the other party in the conversation might be. Displaying such information is also subject to the preferences of the called party.

### Residential User with ENUM Service

A residential user wishing to print only one residential phone number (may have separate phone numbers for the home office) on the business card has the following options:

- Request ENUM service from the local phone company. If the local telephone company has ENUM service, the incoming call will be routed by the *Intelligent Network (IN)* control system. The IN will use ENUM and SIP to route the call, depending on the script for SIP called party preferences to:

  1. A PSTN phone or fax device.
  2. The nearest IP telephony gateways for forwarding the call to any IP device the called user may prefer.

- If the local phone company does not offer ENUM service, the users can request to have the telephone service moved to another service provider that offers ENUM service. *Local Number Portability (LNP)* will ensure the user keeps the same phone number. Incoming phone calls to the user will now be diverted to the other service provider (the ENUM service provider), using the *Local Routing Number (LRN)* to designate the alternate terminating switch of the ENUM service provider. The ENUM service provider will route the call as described above in option 1.

Notice that if the called PSTN device happens to be outside the local switch calling area (the called user is traveling and wishes to get incoming phone or fax calls directed to some remote place), the ENUM service provider can divert the call from the PSTN network and route the call over the IP network, thus reducing the cost of the call. This operation, known as *PSTN call diversion* will therefore also benefit from ENUM.

## Summary

We conclude from these discussions that ENUM service is extremely valuable for users of the existing switched telephone systems. ENUM remains valuable even in an end-to-end IP communications environment. Since there will be a long transition time to universal IP communications, if and when this happens, ENUM remains a powerful service that is also application independent.

# References

[1] P. Fallstrom. RFC 2916: "E.164 Numbers and DNS," IETF, September 2000.

[2] P. Vixie, S. Thompson, Y. Rekhter and J. Bound. RFC 2136: "Dynamic Updates in the Domain Name System (DNS Update)," IETF, April 1997.

[3] M. Mealing and R.D. Daniel. "The Naming Authority Pointer (NAPTR) DNS Resource Record," IETF draft, work in progress, August 2, 2000.

[4] S. Rose. "DNS Security Document Roadmap," Internet draft, August 2000, work in progress.

[5] http://ietf.org/html.charters/dnsext-charter.html

[6] From the procedures of the NetNumber directory service; http://www.netnumber.com

[7] H. Schulzrinne. "SIP Registration," Internet draft, work in progress, IETF, October 5, 2000.

[8] Sören Nyckelgård. "Fixed-Mobile-IP Convergence," VON Fall 2000 conference presentation.

[9] M. Wahl, S. Kille, T. Howes. RFC 2253: "Lightweight Directory Access Protocol (v3)," IETF, December 1977.

[10] A. Brown and G. Vaudreuil. "ENUM Service Specific Provisioning: Principles of Operation," Internet draft, work in progress, July 13, 2000.

[11] P. Pfautz. "Administrative Requirements for Deployment of ENUM in North America," Internet draft, work in progress, August 13, 2000.

[12] http://www.neustar.com

[13] H. Schulzrinne and J. Lennox. RFC 2824: "Call Processing Language Framework and Requirements," IETF, May 2000.

[14] http://www.pingtel.com

[15] S. Lind. "ENUM Call Flows for VoIP Interworking," IETF, July 2000, work in progress.

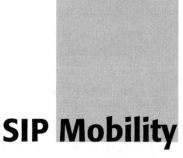

# SIP Mobility

SIP mobility has found increasing attention in both the IP communications and mobile services communities. There are a number of papers on SIP mobility available at the SIP Web site http://www.cs.columbia.edu/sip/papers, and we have been guided in this chapter by a recent presentation on mobility by Professor Henning Schulzrinne [1].

## Mobile Networks

Mobile phone networks have shown even higher growth rates than the Internet, according to several news reports. We explain this by a confluence of several factors, such as a satisfactory service for telephony (though not exactly a 100 percent replacement of wired telephony for features and quality of service), a real need for wireless services, and most of all, mobile telephony has no equivalent from existing wired telephony networks.

Marketers and business planning experts did not take long to figure out that the intersection of mobility and the Internet may be an even better combination of two already excellent ingredients. Several approaches are being pursued to make this happen:

- Add Internet-style services to present circuit switched mobile networks, such as the Short Messaging Service (SMS) and Web access. An attempt for what is marketed as Web access is the Wireless Access Protocol (WAP), although WAP is quite different in nature, reach, technology and performance from the World Wide Web [2]. The WAP Forum Web site is http://wapforum.org/index.htm.

- Design "next-generation" mobile networks that can accommodate both voice and data. One of the most prominent of such designs is the Third-Generation Partnership Project (3GPP) initiative. 3GPP is a complex project that has both a circuit switch domain and a packet (IP) domain [3], and also features the Internet Protocol Multimedia (IM) subsystem that uses SIP for call setup [4]. The 3GPP Web site is http://3gpp.org/.

- Pure Internet-based mobile network designs such as the proposal for Internet Technology Supporting Universal Mobile Operation (ITSUMO) [5]–[7].

- Commercial wireless networks for portable devices such as laptops and palm-sized computers. Such networks extend in variety from IEEE 802.11b (and emerging IEEE 802.11a) wireless LANs to metropolitan and national-sized networks. Surprising technology and market developments may make some of these the real winners in future wireless services.

Various mobile networks have very different approaches to mobility. We will try to shed some light on the meaning of mobility to better understand the various approaches taken in the design of mobile networks.

## Dimensions of Mobility

Mobility has several dimensions, which we will explore here for a more precise definition of mobile services. The five types of mobility are listed in Table 15.1.

The most interesting distinction with regard to SIP is terminal mobility, also referred to as *network-level mobility*, since network elements are required to support it. The main feature of network-level mobility is the fact that the IP device keeps its IP address and port numbers intact while moving, thus keeping applications unaware of mobility. TCP connections are also kept intact, so that a file transfer can be conducted, or a Web page can be downloaded while moving. Network-level mobility does not, however, support roaming users, personal mobility, and service mobility. Network-level mobility duplicates some functions necessary for the other forms of mobility such as registration for AAA services. Also, packet routing is sometimes not optimal for the shortest delay, as required for real-time communications.

**Table 15.1** Types of Mobility

| Terminal mobility | Also called network-level mobility. User device changes the point of attachment to the same network, such as in mobile telephony or in networks supporting Mobile IP [8]. |
|---|---|
| Roaming users | Logging into different IP networks away from home. |
| Personal mobility | Using different IP devices while keeping the same IP address. |
| Service mobility | Keeping personal services while moving between networks. |
| Session mobility | Keeping the same session while changing IP devices. |

SIP mobility, on the other hand, does not require any network mobility support, as in mobile IP, since it works at the application level. SIP mobility is, therefore, independent of the terminal and can support roaming users, personal mobility, and service mobility, as will be shown here. SIP mobility also could support continuous handoff for keeping TCP sessions alive on the move between subnetworks, as discussed in Vakil, et al. [7] on "Supporting Mobility for TCP with SIP."

It is arguable, however, to what degree TCP sessions for fast-moving users are of wider interest, since, in most cases, people who drive, for example, should not do file transfers or browse the Web. For drivers it may be actually more appropriate to use VoiceXML-based Web browsing for such applications as driving directions or to get traffic reports.

# Mobility Examples

We will illustrate here the mobility concepts with specific examples. The discussion on mobility also requires a short explanation of mobile IP.

## Mobile IP

The mobile IP protocol is a network layer protocol and is an important concept in understanding mobility. Figure 15.1 shows the operation of mobile IP.

Mobile IP maintains the IP address of the *mobile host* when away from home. It works in the following way: The *mobile host* has a permanent IP address assigned in the *home network*. A router in the *home network*, called the *home agent*, will route IP packets to and from the host using its IP home address, while the host is still in the *home network*. When away from home, the

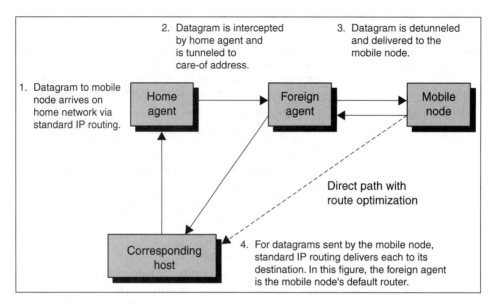

**Figure 15.1** Mobile IP operation.

mobile host will register with a local router, called the *foreign agent,* and will receive a temporary *care-of address.* The foreign agent will do the following for the mobile host:

1. The *care-of address* is communicated to the *home agent.*

2. An IP tunnel is used to forward IP packets (datagrams) from the *mobile host* to the *home agent.*

Mobile IP works with both UDP and TCP transport and keeps the applications unaware of mobility.

The flow of IP packets in both directions, between the mobile host and a corresponding host on the Internet, is shown in Figure 15.1. Note that communications between the mobile host and the corresponding host always go via the home network, although this route may not be optimal.

If, for example, the two hosts are quite near geographically, but the home network is far away, the nonoptimal routing becomes a problem. Route optimization for mobile IP is described in [9] and provides extensions to mobile IP for the corresponding host to cache the care-of address of the mobile host and to bypass the home network, so that packets use normal IP routes to the mobile host. Packets from the mobile host to the corresponding host, however, will still take the longer route via the home network.

The nonoptimal routing, at least in one direction, may introduce undesirable delay for interactive communications. The encapsulation in the IP tunnel shown in Figure 15.1 also adds to the overhead for RTP/UDP/IP packets.

Mobile IP requires two addresses for the mobile host and has problems with firewall transversal. Firewall transversal problems are not unique to mobile IP. SIP mobility also needs firewall transversal support, as we will show later in this chapter.

SIP mobility has none of these drawbacks, as we will see in the following examples, except for the "TCP tracking agent" as described in Vakil, et al. [6] for TCP-based applications.

We are not aware of any major deployments of mobile IP by service providers. This may be due to the fact that the first service providers to implement mobile IP have little incentive to do so, since they would only serve users belonging to other networks that just happen to visit their own networks.

## Roaming Users

Users away from home in a foreign network require several registration steps. The first registration step is at the network layer to get an IP address. For example, to log on in hotels and airline lounges, a Web page is first presented to the user, requesting credentials to use the service, after which an IP address is assigned, using standard DHCP. We presume devices, such as mobile SIP endpoints, may have to use a similar registration process, if the device is a mobile computer, or some other procedure, not yet standardized, if the device is a mobile SIP phone.

If the visited network has a firewall, the SIP device also will need to register with the local SIP proxy that controls the firewall transversal for UDP packets. Finally, the SIP device will register with the home SIP registrar, as shown in Figure 15.2, so that calls arriving at the home SIP server can be routed to the visited SIP server. SIP devices that support mobility will need to execute the registrations shown in Figure 15.2.

## Remote Registration

Repeated double registrations for roaming users (Figure 15.2) can be avoided by using a local registrar that covers the traveled domains, as shown in Figure 15.3. The mobile user needs to register only once in the visited domain, while keeping the home registrar unaware of the exact location in the visited domain. The home registrar and proxy will redirect incoming calls to the proxy server in the visited network.

## SIP Precall Mobility

Precall SIP terminal mobility is shown in Figure 15.4. For simplicity no firewall is shown in Figure 15.4 in the visited network. If there is a firewall, the roam-

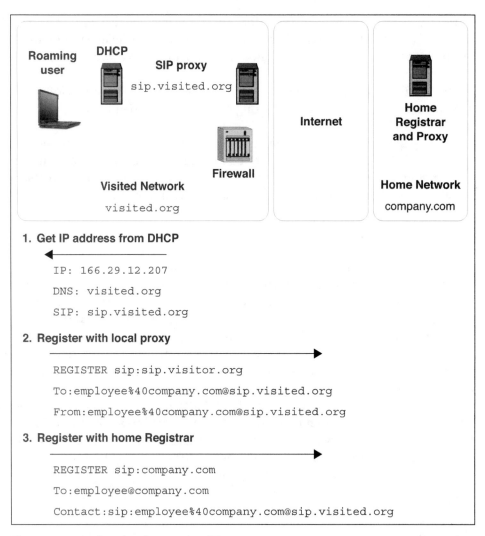

**Figure 15.2** Registration for roaming SIP users.

ing user will have to register, as shown in the previous paragraph and in Figure 15.3. Back to Figure 15.4, the caller initially sends the INVITE (message 3) to the SIP server that handles the company.com domain, probably located using DNS SRV records:

```
INVITE sip:henry@company.com SIP/2.0
Via SIP/2.0/UDP host.internet.org:5060
To: <sip:henry@company.com>
From: <sip:user@internet.org>
Call-ID: 4712374917@host.internet.org
CSeq: 63424 INVITE
```

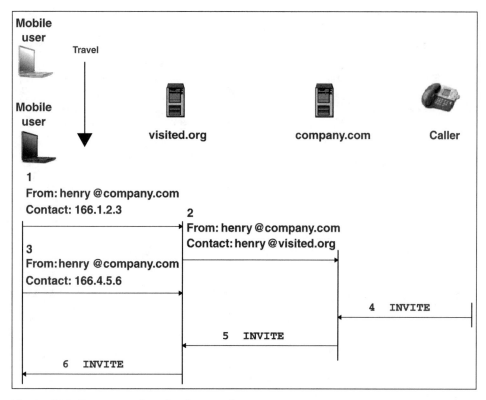

**Figure 15.3** Remote registration for roaming users.

```
Contact: <sip:user@65.64.63.62>
Content-Length: ...
```

where the SDP message body of the INVITE is not shown for simplicity.

The SIP server redirects the caller directly to the roaming user with a 302 response (message 2 in Figure 15.4):

```
SIP/2.0 302 Moved Temporarily
Via SIP/2.0/UDP host.internet.org:5060
To: <sip:henry@company.com>
From: <sip:user@internet.org>
Call-ID: 4712374917@host.internet.org
CSeq: 63424 INVITE
Contact: <sip:henry@166.4.5.6>
Content-Length:
```

where Henry's new address is contained in the Contact header of the 302 response. The resulting INVITE (message 6 ) would then look like:

```
INVITE sip:henry@166.4.5.6 SIP/2.0
Via SIP/2.0/UDP host.internet.org:5060
```

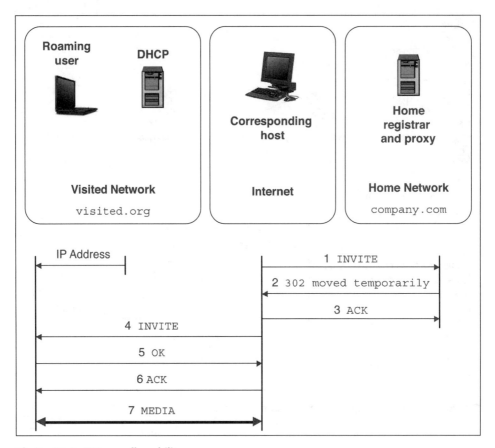

**Figure 15.4** SIP precall mobility.

```
To: <sip:henry@company.com>
From: <sip:user@internet.org>
Call-ID: 4712374917@host.internet.org
CSeq: 63425 INVITE
Contact: <sip:user@65.64.63.62>
Content-Length: ...
```

This type of redirection happens frequently in HTTP, where a Web server redirects a request to another Web server. However, if a secure Web server redirects to a nonsecure URL (that is, an HTTPS redirects to an HTTP URL), a typical Web browser, such as Netscape, will pop up a dialog box and warn the user that he is she is being redirected to a nonsecure site. It is likely that this will also be the case with SIP, where most redirects will be processed by the user agent without the knowledge of the caller. However, if there is a potential security issue, such as being redirected to a type of call involving charging, it is likely that the caller will be notified.

## SIP Midcall Mobility

SIP midcall mobility is required to support mobile users moving from one visited network to another or changing their point of attachment and getting a new temporary IP address.

Unless there is a different firewall to encounter, no new local registration is required. The SIP device has only to re-INVITE, as shown in Figure 15.5, and provide the new IP address in the SDP SIP body part.

## Personal Mobility

Personal mobility is one of the unique features of SIP and is basically a by-product of the similarity of SIP with HTTP and SMTP. The notion of personal mobility is illustrated in Figure 15.6. As can be seen, by redirecting incoming calls to any of the user devices, users can be reached on any network, in any geographic location. SIP is thus fulfilling the basic Web and e-mail-like requirements for users to be reachable irrespective of location and device. In addition to this property, SIP mobility can also be combined with called party preferences, as discussed in Chapter 7, *User Preferences*, so as to have different fil-

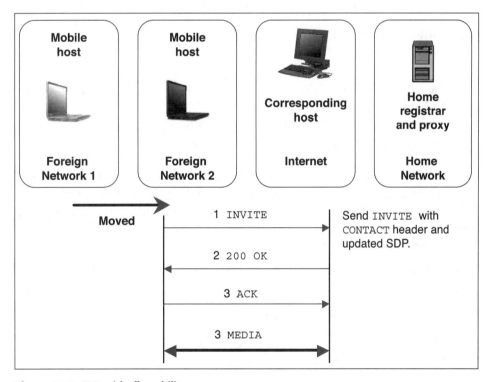

**Figure 15.5** SIP midcall mobility.

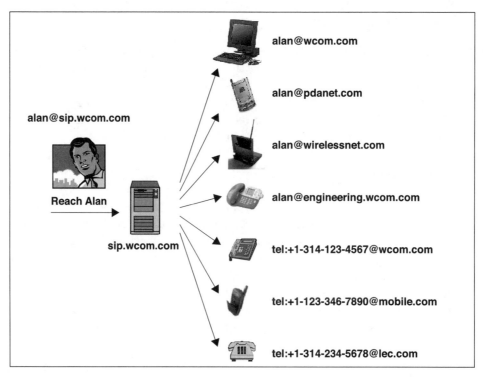

**Figure 15.6** SIP personal mobility.

ters as appropriate for specific devices and locations, from where, from whom, and at what times to receive calls.

## SIP Service Mobility

As the previous examples have shown, SIP can support terminal and personal mobility, but users can ask: What happens to my highly personalized services when traveling? SIP service mobility can address the desire of users to keep some or most of their services in a mobile environment. Examples of services "not to leave home without" are:

- Personal address book and speed dialing
- Media preferences
- Incoming call-handling preferences
- Buddy lists
- Special features such as voice mail, do-not-disturb
- Other features on the home network server

Service mobility is independent of terminal or the services in visited networks and can be designed to be available even on pay phones or Web kiosks and in Internet cafes.

The key to service mobility is SIP registration, as has been shown in the preceding paragraphs in Figures 15.2 and 15.3.

## Summary

SIP mobility provides a uniform solution for both wired and wireless mobile users and can support a rich set of mobility dimensions such as terminal, personal, and service mobility. Such features cannot be provided by IP network-layer mobility or by other means in a similar consistent way as by using SIP. Moving the functionality of mobility from the network layer to the application space, all types of IP communications and customized services, from text to voice to rich multimedia, can be supported across geographic, network, and service provider boundaries, and also across an unlimited range of suitable terminal devices.

## References

[1] Henning Schulzrinne. "SIP for Mobility," Presentation at the International Conference SIP 2001, Paris, France, February 21, 2001.

[2] Rohit Khare. "W* Effect Considered Harmful," *IEEE Internet Computing*, vol. 3, no. 4, IEEE, July-August 1999, pp. 89-92.

[3] Third-Generation Partnership Project; Technical Specification Group Services and Aspects; Network Architecture (Release 5), 3GPP TS 23.002 (2000-12).

[4] Third-Generation Partnership Project; Technical Specification Group Services and Aspects; "IP Multimedia System—Stage 2", 3GPP TS.23.228 (2000-11).

[5] F. Vakil, et al. "Supporting Service Mobility with SIP," IETF Internet draft, December 2001, work in progress.

[6] F. Vakil, et al. "Supporting Mobility for Multimedia with SIP," IETF Internet draft, December 2001, work in progress.

[7] F. Vakil, et al. "Supporting Mobility for TCP with SIP," IETF Internet draft, December 2001, work in progress.

[8] Charlie Perkins. RFC 2002: "IP Mobility Support," IETF, 1996.

[9] C. Perkins and D. Johnson. "Route Optimization in Mobile IP," IETF Internet draft, November 2000, work in progress.

[10] H. Schulzrinne. "SIP Registration," IETF Internet draft, October 2000, work in progress.

CHAPTER

16

# AAA and QoS for SIP

This chapter introduces concepts of authentication, authorization, and accounting (AAA), along with Quality of Service (QoS) as they relate to SIP.

## Options to Achieve QoS

At the time of this writing, the authors are conducting frequent long-distance calls in the United States and transatlantic calls of excellent quality over the Internet using SIP phones from both the office and home. This experience has led us to give credence to the following argument, sustained by some Internet engineers.

IP telephony QoS impairments are very unlikely on high-speed IP backbone networks and also are unlikely in well-designed enterprise LANs. With the passing of time, IP telephony will account for an ever-smaller percentage of bandwidth usage, compared to e-mail, Web, and other data applications.

The most likely network congestion occurs on access links to the Internet. From a practical perspective, the following three choices are available:

- Provide adequate access bandwidth on the access line.
- Provide a simple QoS mechanism on the access line, such as using Type of Service (TOS) bits from the user router to the first router in the ISP

network. Wireless Internet access is a special case that may require such a solution.

- End-to-end QoS using standard IETF protocols for QoS combined with SIP signaling.

Implementing QoS for IP networks is not a simple task. Table 16.1 shows the main IETF standards for QoS, although the table is not exhaustive on all QoS-related standards.

The decision on such choices as when to just use bandwidth and when to use which IP QoS mechanisms, as shown in Table 16.1, will play out in the marketplace, but from a technical point of view, the option to use IP QoS is the most challenging and will be presented here. We present the following two models for end-to-end QoS: (1) single-service provider domain and (2) interdomain QoS across the Internet, between various service providers and enterprise networks.

## Separation of Network and Application Signaling

The QoS architecture of the Internet separates IP-level signaling for QoS, as described for IP services in Chapter 4, *Internet Multimedia and Conferencing*, from application-level signaling such as SIP. This enables a single IP QoS infrastructure for all applications, be they real-time communications, financial transactions, games, or other. The QoS approach is similar to

**Table 16.1** Overview on IP QoS Standards

| QoS FOR LOW-BITRATE SERIAL LINKS | |
|---|---|
| RFC 2689 | Providing integrated services over low-bitrate links |
| RFC 2508 | Compressing IP/UDP/RTP headers for low-speed serial links |
| RFC 2686 | The multiclass extension to multilink PPP |
| RFC 2688 | Integrated services mappings for low-speed networks |
| **QoS MAPPING TO DIFFSERV** | |
| RFC 2998 | Integrated services operation over diffserv networks |
| **IP INTEGRATED SERVICES AND RSVP** | |
| RFC 2211 | Specification of the controlled load network element service |
| RFC 2212 | Specification of guaranteed quality of service |
| **QoS IN IP LANS AND NETWORKS** | |
| RFC 2816 | Providing integrated services over IEEE 802 LAN technologies |
| RFC 2382 | Framework for integrated services and RSVP over ATM |

the approach taken for security, where the common security tools of IPSec are used regardless of any particular application. This eliminates duplication of functionality and reduces overall cost.

SIP would be ill-suited for QoS signaling also for another reason: SIP messages can take different paths than the media and, as a consequence, SIP servers have no access to the media path.

The separation of signaling at the application layer, SIP in our case, from the QoS signaling at the IP layer does not, however, reduce the interaction between the two signaling layers, as we will show in the following examples. There is actually a close coupling between SIP signaling and QoS signaling, such as RSVP. This close coupling leads to complex message flows as will be shown.

# Network Models for QoS

There are a number of models for QoS in general as shown in Table 16.1 and also specifically for SIP. The SIP specific models are for the single service provider domain and for the Internet-wide interdomain case as will be shown here.

## Single-Domain QoS

It is easier to implement QoS within the domain of a single service provider than it is across the whole Internet. Within their domain, service providers can support QoS-assured phone calls, similar to the PSTN, where if no adequate network resources exist, the call will not be completed [1]. A diagram illustrating the single service provider domain is shown in Figure 16.1.

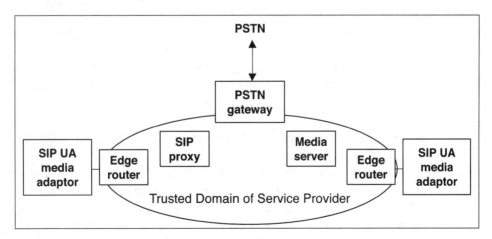

**Figure 16.1** Single domain QoS network model.

Edge routers bordering the domain act as gates. They provide access control so as to permit end users to complete phone calls only if certain preconditions for QoS are met and if access is granted by AAA mechanisms. If end-to-end QoS cannot be supported, the edge router will reject the RSVP request and, as a consequence, SIP signaling will not complete the call. Depending on service policy, the end user could also be alerted that no QoS could be provided for the call, providing the end user with the option to proceed or end the call. There are instances, such as emergencies, where a call without QoS is preferable to not getting through at all. The SIP endpoints also could retry the call using a lower bandwidth codec.

The originating SIP endpoint uses the attributes in the Session Description Protocol (SDP) to convey the conditions that must be met for QoS, such as:

- **The direction for QoS support.** Send, receive, or bidirectional (send-receive)

- **A "strength parameter."** Optional or mandatory

The destination SIP endpoint will send a confirmation message of "conditions for QoS are met" (COMET) if the required QoS has been set up, after which the end users will be alerted and the voice call will proceed. We will illustrate SIP and QoS signaling for a success scenario, as shown in Figure 16.2.

The initial INVITE is confirmed by a provisional response 183 Session Progress that has the SDP body confirming the agreement for the required QoS support. This confirmation is acknowledged by the provisional response acknowledgment (PRACK). The three-way handshake is concluded with a 200 OK response for PRACK and now both endpoints proceed with QoS signaling for resource reservation, as shown by the Reservation arrows. If the resource reservation for QoS has been successful, the endpoints will transmit the SIP extension COMET and the called party can be alerted. The 180 Ringing message is transmitted to the caller and will be acknowledged by another PRACK. The transactions are complete after the user picks up the phone and the 200 OK and ACK messages end the SIP transactions that have set up the call. More details about PRACK and COMET can be found in Marshall, et al. [1]. Complete call flows with messages have been published by the Distributed Call Signaling Architecture group of Cablelabs PacketCable [2] project and AT&T labs in Marshall, et al. [3].

Note that the call flows in Figure 16.1 are somewhat complex, although the details of the QoS signaling, such as RSVP, are not shown. Multiple media flows, such as for video and data, may complicate the call flows even more.

Since QoS calls require the use of significant resources in the service provider's network, it is necessary that all signaling relating to QoS must have appropriate security. For example, since a QoS session is likely to have a per-minute charge associated with it, a service provider must know who to bill for

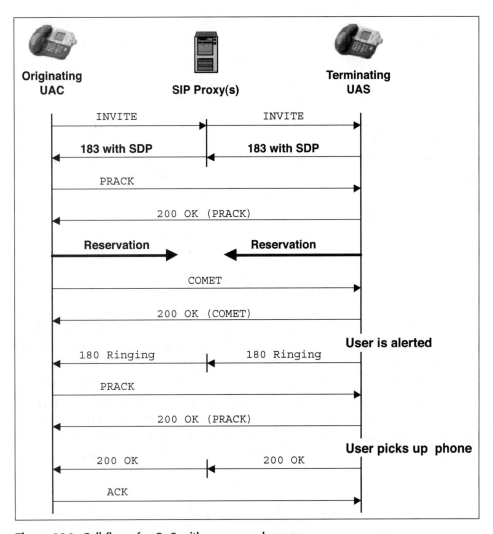

**Figure 16.2** Call flows for QoS with COMET and PRACK.

this session. Security mechanisms described in Chapter 8, *Security, NATs, and Firewalls*, such as authentication, firewalls, and IPSec tunnels, can be employed to design a secure network.

## Interdomain QoS

Interdomain QoS is of interest for providing SIP-based IP communications across several service providers on the Internet. It is, however, a much more complex problem compared to the single domain case due to several factors.

- QoS requires valuable network resources that have to be agreed and accounted for between all participating parties. Therefore, QoS and interdomain AAA cannot be separated.

- The Internet has many thousands of service providers, so a scalable solution has to be found for both QoS and AAA.

Figure 16.3 shows the model for interdomain QoS as has been proposed in Sinnreich, et al. [4].

The model shows two Internet access networks that can belong to ISPs or can be enterprise networks and one or more transit networks in between. The QoS and AAA functions are taken care of in the following way:

Edge routers (ER) in the access networks shape traffic delivered to the transit networks so as to stay within the services-level specification (SLS). Border routers (not shown) in the transit network police the incoming traffic from the access networks and deal with any extra QoS traffic by either remarking packets from QoS to best effort traffic or by discarding packets.

Different service provider networks may have a trust relationship for AAA functions by using a common clearinghouse. The clearinghouse solves the scalability problem for AAA, since it reduces the number of relationships required for AAA from a square of the number of ISPs to a linear one.

The transit networks in Figure 16.3 are not aware of any individual QoS flows, since that would contradict the requirements for scalability. End-to-end transparency for individual QoS flows, such as for RSVP over Differentiated Services networks is treated in detail in Bernet, et al. [5].

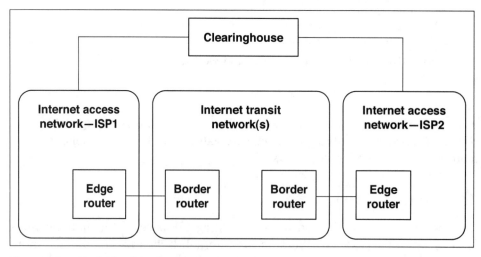

**Figure 16.3** Model for interdomain QoS.

After presenting the 50,000-foot view of the interdomain model, let's zoom in to the access networks for the coupling between QoS and AAA functions. Since transit networks are not aware of individual flows, all the details for SIP, QoS, and AAA coupling reside in the access networks.

## The Application Policy Server

Though many approaches are possible to solve the coupling between SIP, QoS, and AAA, it is desirable to choose a generic approach that is applicable for a wide range of applications, some of them not related to SIP. The network element that can support local policy for a wide range of applications is the Applications Policy Server (APS) described in Gross, et al. [6]. Figure 16.4 shows the place of the APS in the access network.

Several functional layers exist in the network diagram in Figure 16.4:

- Layer 2 network elements (L2) such as Ethernet switches. QoS is invoked from the IP layer 3 using appropriate protocols defined in the IETF ISSL Working Group and are available at the Web site http://ietf.org/html.charters/issll-charter.html. For example, the Subnet Bandwidth Manager (SBM) [7] protocol is used to control IEEE 802.3–style networks (Ethernet).

- IP network layer 3 elements such as the media agent in a SIP endpoint and IP routers, including the edge router (ER). QoS at the IP layer shown here is RSVP, since RSVP is a generic method for applications to

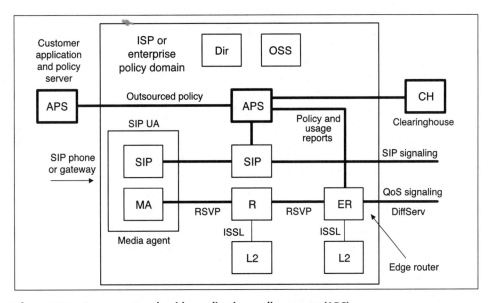

**Figure 16.4** Access network with application policy server (APS).

communicate their QoS requirements to the network and individual RSVP requests can be traced back to the user for accounting. The edge router (ER) aggregates all RSVP requests in the access network into a specific Differentiated Services Point Code (DSPC) for transmission across the transit network on the right.

- Application layer SIP signaling between the SIP user agent (UA), the local SIP proxy server, and SIP servers outside the access network.

- The AAA layer consisting of Applications Policy Servers (APSs) and one or more clearinghouses.

The APS in the access network has a number of "stakeholders" that have a "say" in the policy decisions taken by the ASP. Examples of policy stakeholders shown in Figure 16.4 are:

- The directory (Dir) of individual users having service accounts.

- The directory of corporate accounts in the operational support system (OSS).

- External APSs of corporate customers. If an end user belonging to a corporate account makes a request for QoS, the local ASP will outsource the policy decision to the external ASP shown on the left.

- An external clearinghouse (CH) that approves the interdomain QoS request, as we will show, and provides a token to be presented at the far end to complete the RSVP setup process.

Upon receiving an INVITE message from a SIP UA, the SIP proxy (SIP) will ask the ASP if it is OK to proceed with the call. The ASP first consults with its local stakeholders and then informs the clearinghouse of the request. The clearinghouse will return a token that the ASP delivers to the SIP proxy as confirmation to proceed with the call.

The ASP will also install policy in the edge router to accept and pass the RSVP request from the SIP endpoint that originates the call. The Common Open Policy Service (COPS) [8] protocol is used between the ASP and the edge router [9].

Figure 16.5 shows the lifecycle of the AAA token.

In step 1, the local SIP proxy will consult with the ASP if to proceed with the call. In step 2, the ASP requests authorization from the clearinghouse, after which the token from the clearinghouse is transmitted in the INVITE message to the far end in step 3. The SIP server at the remote end will forward the token to its ASP in step 4. The remote end may not have a trust relationship with the calling side, but will use the token to decide to accept the call.

1. The call can be accepted, since the token is recognized as from a clearinghouse with whom a trust relationship has been established.

2. The token will be used in logging QoS usage for accounting with the clearinghouse.

The use of SIP to carry the token is described in Johnston, et al. [10].

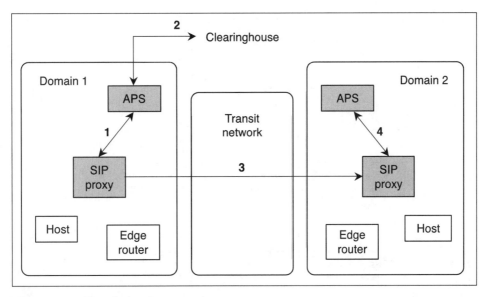

**Figure 16.5** Lifecycle for the AAA token.

### SIP QoS and AAA for Mobile Users

The interdomain models shown in Figures 16.3 and 16.5 can be extended for mobile users, by making the distinction between the home domain and the visited domain for the mobile user, as shown in Figure 16.6.

The mobile caller is shown here in the visited domain and may attempt to place a call to a domain where the usual clearinghouse is not recognized. In this case, similar to using a different credit card, the user may chose to try a second clearinghouse, as shown in Figure 16.6.

## Interdomain Signaling for Quality of Service

There are several models for policy-controlled QoS for IP telephony. The various models result from the type of QoS and the type of policy implementations that will be explained here.

## QoS Options

We consider here three main classes of service for IP telephony:

**Best effort packet delivery.** Such service can be acceptable in high-bandwidth networks and in other networks during non-peak traffic times.

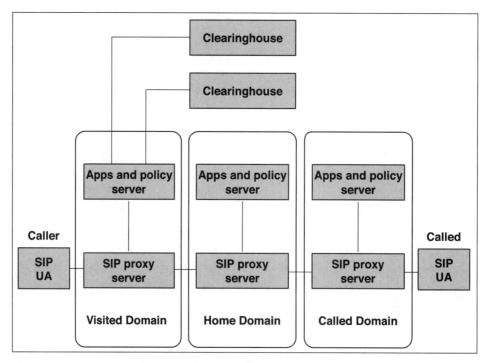

**Figure 16.6** SIP QoS and AAA model for mobile users.

Best effort service may be unsatisfactory, however, on slow access links (less than 1 to 2 Mb/s) when voice packets may be delayed due to other types of long data packets.

**QoS Assured.** The telephone call will complete only after all the network resources required for a specified QoS are assured by such means as a successful RSVP reservation end-to-end. QoS Assured mimics the behavior of the PSTN in that QoS is guaranteed before a call goes through.

**QoS Enabled.** When only partial or no QoS is available, the caller could receive messages such as, "Sorry, we cannot guarantee complete quality for this call due to <reason code>. Would you like to continue anyway?" Reasons to inform the customer could be that no end-to-end guarantee QoS is possible, or there is a temporary high network load.

## Policy Implementation Options

The application policy server (APS) can preinstall policy for a specific call in the edge router, in which case we have a *push approach* to policy. Upon receiving an enquiry from the SIP server to see if the call can proceed, the APS will not only provide a positive response (as the case may be) to the SIP server, but will also send a COPS message to the edge router to install policy to allow the RSVP request for the call to be honored.

The APS may receive a policy enquiry from the edge router if it is OK to proceed with an RSVP path set up from a certain endpoint. In this case we have a *pull approach* to policy.

There are some interesting implications when choosing between the push and pull approaches for policy implementations such as the number of messages required and total system delay for QoS setup at the beginning of the call. These options are discussed in detail in Sinnreich, et al. [11].

### Call Flow Example for SIP-QoS-AAA

The detailed message flows for SIP, QoS, and AAA depend on the combination for QoS usage, such as QoS Assured or QoS Enabled and the implementation for policy; using the push or pull approach to install policy in the network elements. Figure 16.7 shows the call flows for QoS Enabled and policy push implementation. We chose this example, since it has the least coupling between SIP and RSVP.

The initial INVITE message (1) from the SIP phone is temporarily halted in the SIP server, who requests an OSP token (2) from the policy server. This request is forwarded to the clearinghouse (3) and if granted, the OSP token will be carried in the INVITE message (6) to the called Domain 2. The SIP server in Domain 2 will decide if the token is acceptable and forward the INVITE to the gateway on the right side, in message (7). Upon receiving a provisional response, the SIP server in Domain 2 will request Local Decision Policy (LDP) from the APS in the COPS message (9). The APS will install policy for the flow in the edge router with message (10). On confirmation from the edge router (messages 11 and 12), the SIP server in the called Domain 2 will transmit the provisional response to the calling SIP server in (13), after which policy is installed in the edge router of Domain 1 as well with the message sequence of 14 through 17. End-to-end SIP signaling will complete call setup with messages 18 through 27.

RSVP signaling in both directions takes place at the same time, as shown at the bottom of Figure 16.7. No exact timing relation exists between call setup and RSVP QoS setup, since the RSVP setup can proceed as soon as the APSs in both domains instruct the edge routers to honor the RSVP requests. Timers in the endpoints, not shown in Figure 16.7, assure that RSVP setup starts with a small delay after the SIP call setup messages are sent.

The example in Figure 16.7 shows the somewhat complex message exchange required for interdomain QoS setup with accounting for network usage. Other scenarios, such as for QoS-assured calls are somewhat more

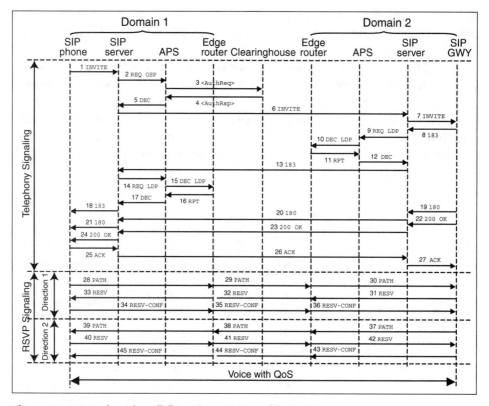

**Figure 16.7** Interdomain call flows for a QoS-enabled call.

complex, since the coupling between SIP, AAA, and RSVP messaging is more intricate.

Figure 16.7 shows only the call flows for call setup. Call flows for call and QoS teardown are not shown here, but are also somewhat complex.

### Accounting for QoS

At the end of the call, the APS reports the usage to the clearinghouse and the reports are confirmed, as shown in Figure 16.8.

The clearinghouse has now all the required data for settlements of accounts between the calling and the called domains.

## Summary

Providing QoS for IP telephony and other interactive communications requires complex technology and has been avoided so far by ISPs in favor of providing

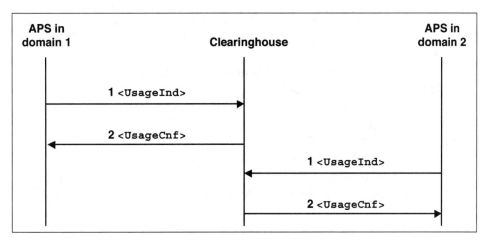

**Figure 16.8** Usage reporting to the clearinghouse.

ample bandwidth. Signaling to set up end-to-end QoS is closely coupled with SIP signaling and also with AAA functions, requiring a clearinghouse when the number of possible ISPs is large. The complexity of SIP, QoS, and AAA functionality resides in the access networks on the periphery of the Internet. Application policy servers are required for such functions in ISP access networks.

# References

[1] W. Marshall, et al. "Integration of Resource Management and SIP," IETF Internet draft, February 2001, work in progress.

[2] "Packet Cable Distributed Call Signaling Specification," PKT-SP-DCS-D03-000428.

[3] W. Marshall, et al. "Architectural Considerations for Providing Carrier Class Telephony Services Utilizing SIP-based Distributed Call Control Mechanisms," IETF Internet draft, February 2001, work in progress.

[4] H. Sinnreich, D. Rawlins, A. Johnston, S. Donovan, and S. Thomas. "AAA Usage for IP Telephony with QoS," IETF Internet draft, July 2000, work in progress.

[5] Y. Bernet, et al. "A Framework for Integrated Services Operation over Diffserv Networks," IETF RFC 2998, November 2000.

[6] G. Gross, et al. "QoS and AAA Usage with SIP Based IP Communications," IETF Internet draft, November 2000, work in progress.

[7] R. Yavatkar, et al. "SBM (Subnet Bandwidth Manager): A Protocol for RSVP-based Admission Control over IEEE 802-style networks," IETF RFC 814, May 2000.

[8] D. Durham, et al. "The COPS (Common Open Policy Service) Protocol" IETF RFC 2748, January 2000.

[9] G. Gross. "COPS Usage for SIP," IETF Internet draft, November 2000, work in progress.

[10] A. Johnston, et al., "OSP Authorization Token Header for SIP," IETF Internet draft, November 2000, work in progress.

[11] H. Sinnreich, S. Donovan, D. Rawlins, and S. Thomas. "Interdomain IP Communications with QoS, Authorization and Usage Reporting," IETF Internet draft, March 2000.

# The Component Server
# Architecture

Value-added services in the PSTN are implemented using the Intelligent Network (IN) [1]. The IN is a collection of servers and other resources used to control call setup and to provide media services such as announcements, voice mail, etc. IN services have benefited from a large amount of standards work in the ITU and in regional telecom standards bodies to ensure multivendor and internetwork interoperability. In hindsight, IN services seem rather frugal compared with the emerging communications on the Internet. Other architectures, such as H.323 or the so-called softswitches based on IP telephony gateway decomposition [2], have similar central control approaches to the IN for enhanced services, although they are less completely standardized compared to the IN. In this chapter, we will show how value-added services using SIP can be implemented, using application servers [3] in an open, distributed, and loosely coupled architecture that is highly scalable.

## Services for IP Telephony Gateways

The earliest implementers of IP telephony gateways used monolithic and highly proprietary approaches for auxiliary functions such as tone announcements

## DEVICE CONTROL PROTOCOLS

Device control protocols can be found in proprietary IP PBX designs and also in various proposed standards such as MGCP, MEGACO, and H.248. The decomposition of an IP telephony gateway using a device control protocol is shown in Figure 17.1a. Device control protocols are master/slave protocols where every detail of the device operation is controlled from a central server. Master/slave protocols are also sometimes called "stimulus protocols," since every event or stimulus experienced by the terminal must be relayed to the controller using the protocol. In this model, every event, such as a hook flash, has to be reported to the central controller and every action of the device has to be controlled, such as how to display a number or a message.

How does the controller know if the device has a display at all? The answer is, it does not know, unless it has been preconfigured with a so-called package (Figure 17.1b) that is written for that particular device, such as, for example, for a specific phone model that may or may not have a display with certain capabilities.

Since the package in the control device has to know every detailed feature of the controlled device, and is also dependent on product version, it is practically impossible to have them made by different and possibly competing vendors, in spite of the standard control protocol between the controller and the device.

In the case of media gateways, packages have to be written and provisioned, depending on the particular circuit switch network signaling of the media gateway such as channel-associated signaling (CAS), Q.931, and SS7 in its various national variants.

This is in stark contrast to the Internet model, where the implementation of networked devices does not need to be known by other devices to interwork and even more, where interworking devices have to be developed in an independent manner by designers around the world. One can communicate with an Internet-connected device without caring if, at the other end, there is a palmtop computer or a powerful server farm in a data center. Also, when using FTP, email, or browsers, no consideration has to be given how the remote IP device is configured. Furthermore, device control protocols have no notion of redirection and a controlled device cannot refuse a request, unless it reports an error, and cannot offer alternate destinations to honor a request.

Master-slave protocols such as MEGACO are "lossy" in that they strictly limit the information that can be exchanged between the device and the controller. This limits the ability to rapidly develop new services and features, since extensions to the package must be defined. In comparison to SIP, new headers to implement new services and features can be implemented by endpoints without the knowledge or support in the SIP network.

Master/slave protocols, such as MEGACO, only succeed in reducing infrastructure costs if the simplification of the extremely "dumb" terminals offsets the increased costs of additional protocols and distributed intelligent network elements. However, when a requirement is added to the "dumb" terminals to be able to act autonomously under certain circumstances (for example, complete an E911 call when no controller is available), most of the lower-cost benefits of a master/slave protocol will be lost.

and IVR functions, for example, for credit card number input. Small gateways can be built using application programming interfaces (APIs), depending on the particular product and operating system. However, such monolithic designs proved to be undesirable for both vendors and service providers as they tried to scale the systems in size and across the network and to add various new services.

The abundance of services and features in the competitive marketplace led service providers especially to search for unbundled systems, so as to benefit from products by multiple vendors, specialized to be the best of the breed.

A first attempt to provide unbundled IP telephony gateways was the decomposition of the gateway into a gateway controller (GC) and one or more media gateways (MG), as shown in Figure 17.1a. The link between the GC and the MG has undergone numerous developments, starting with APIs and later giving birth to protocols with names such as IPDC, SGCP, MGCP, MEGACO, and H.248. As of this writing, the de facto industry standard is the Media Gateway Control Protocol (MGCP). The IETF and the ITU have coordinated the development of another protocol standard, called MEGACO in the IETF and H.248 in the ITU. These standards were developed with some broader aims, such as to accommodate both SIP and H.323 and to be used for the control of gateways

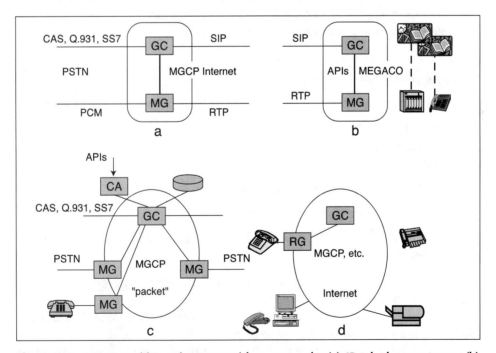

**Figure 17.1** Decomposition using master/slave protocols: (a) IP telephony gateway, (b) application server, (c) IP telephony gateway network with central call agent (CA), and (d) residential gateway (RG) for telephony.

to ATM networks and, last but not least, for the control of ATM circuit switches for voice. MEGACO and H.248 are thus considerably more complex than MGCP, without offering any more functionality. All of the preceding protocols have one feature in common: They are master/slave protocols, where an "intelligent" central master controls every action in detail of the "dumb" slave devices, such as media gateways, media servers, and slave telephones.

The gateway controller is also sometimes called a "softswitch." Various designs have started out with the model in Figure 17.1a and have added proprietary APIs for third-party developers to add new services and also APIs to control the MG itself, as shown in Figure 17.1b. Since each system has its own APIs, third-party developers would have to learn all the APIs for all the various proprietary designs. Full-featured multivendor interoperability between the media gateway (MG) and gateway controller (GC) is more difficult to achieve, the more APIs there are. Complete interoperability has not been accomplished in the industry, to our knowledge, at the time of this writing, and there are companies that have found a niche in writing code to for GCs to interoperate with various MGs.

As the number of required services increases, the need for separate service platforms becomes evident. Figure 17.1b shows the decomposition of the service platform between a service controller and media servers using one of the previous master/slave protocols. This decomposition has, however, the well-known drawbacks of central control, such as:

- Single point of failure.
- Proprietary service logic.
- Heavy control traffic between master and slaves leads to very lengthy and complex call flows.
- Details in implementations by vendors and APIs make interoperability unlikely.
- Bundled services inhibit third-party application providers.
- New services are difficult to introduce due to tight coupling of features.
- Integration with Web, e-mail services, presence, and instant messaging is very difficult.

We believe the last item to be the most restrictive for the architecture shown in Figure 17.1b for application servers.

The decomposition using master/slave protocols, such as MGCP or MEGACO/H.248, has constraints for service providers. Figure 17.1c shows a network composed of IP telephony gateways to bypass the PSTN network or to avoid PSTN trunking for PBXs in enterprise networks. The GC is controlled by a Call Agent (CA) where the service logic resides, and has access to the necessary database to control call setup. The central control, the proprietary controller, and the control protocol now have produced a network that is neither the PSTN/PBX network nor the Internet, but, in effect, a third type of network. This new network can provide voice services only. Service providers have enough work cut out for them to manage existing circuit switched networks and the IP network and need not trouble themselves with the managing a third type of network. Such a PSTN or PBX bypass network cannot support any services that do not exist already on the circuit switched side, thus taking away the main rationale for a third, new network.

The residential gateway (RG) shown in Figure 17.1d is another example of the use of master/slave protocols such as MGCP and MEGACO/H.248. This time it is the end user who is deprived of three main benefits available on the Internet:

1. Free choice of any server such as is the case on the Web.

2. Free choice of any communication application, since all applications reside in the central office of the service provider.

3. Telephony is segregated from all other Internet applications.

Residential gateways for voice as shown in Figure 17.1d are negating the requirements for equal access to public service providers, since competing service providers cannot have access to control the phones behind the residential gateway.

We will show by contrast how these problems can be avoided using an Internet and Web-centric architecture for the application environment.

# The Integrated Applications Environment

The integrated applications environment is based on the distributed Internet and Web architecture and is not dependent on any proprietary APIs and operating systems for interworking of multiple servers, since it is based on simple SIP and HTTP message flows. The open architecture is especially well suited for third-party service providers across IP networks or across the Internet.

Figure 17.2 shows the integration of communications with applications and transactions, as is required for e-commerce. The real-time communications part is emphasized here with the main communication servers logically clustered around the capability to exchange SIP and HTTP messages. The various components are loosely coupled, in the sense that once their functions have been invoked by simple call flows, the details of operation are left to each server, without affecting the operation of other servers.

**USEFUL INTERNET TELEPHONY GATEWAY DECOMPOSITION**

Central control of distributed media gateways, as shown in Figure 17.1c may be useful, however, in such cases where many smaller IP telephony gateways from an ISP have to interface with the PSTN using SS7 signaling. Since SS7 interconnection points are quite expensive, and no other services than voice are possible anyway over the PSTN part of the call, a central controller combined with an SS7 interconnect point makes good sense. However, ISPs have to be careful not to have any service features provided by the central controller, since such services would be difficult to extend across the rest of the IP network, where multivendor compatibility will be required. This example is an exception to the rule in our opinion to avoid central control-type IP telephony gateway networks.

The main types of communication servers are:

- General-purpose SIP server (center, with database access) acting as registrar, redirect server, and for QoS admission in conjunction with the AAA and location services, such as directory or ENUM. The redirect server also can implement private dialing plans for enterprise networks.

- Service controller for delivery of services in conjunction with specialized communication servers, as will be shown. The service controller uses SIP third-party call control [4] to orchestrate the interaction between the various servers.

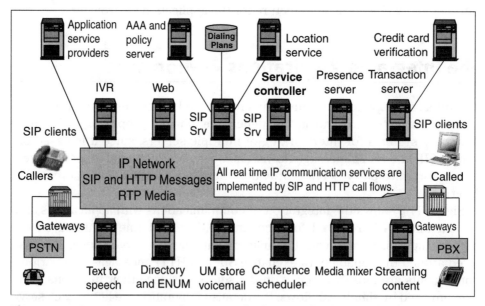

**Figure 17.2** Component servers for communications, applications, and transactions.

- Voice portal using VoiceXML technology for voice control and voice browsing. This is also acting as an interactive voice-response (IVR) server.
- Web server for provisioning and control by end users.
- Presence server.
- Text to speech server.
- Voice recognition server.
- Universal messaging (UM) server.
- Conference scheduler.
- Media mixer for audio conferences.
- Content server for streaming multimedia, such as stored presentations, shows, etc.
- In addition to servers for communications, other servers are rounding up the portfolio:
  - Transaction server for credit card transactions.
  - Application service providers (ASPs) such as productivity software. This allows the integration of office applications (document editors, spreadsheets, presentations, databases) and personal information managers (PIMs) with real-time communications.

Really interesting applications for outsourcing, however, go beyond the generic services shown here, for such as:

- Services of general interest such as travel and weather
- Highly specialized services such as security by voice recognition or PKI systems
- Virtual communities for business and nonprofit organizations

Service providers offering such an open and integrated environment for Web, e-mail, and voice also can be referred to as Application Infrastructure Service Providers (AIPs).

How does it work? Users can provide inputs to the service controller either via the Web servers, the DTMF digit collector, or the voice portal using speech recognition with VoiceXML, or simply DTMF input. This allows invoking services using a wide variety of devices, ranging from plain PSTN phones to PCs and palm computers. The user input can be either by voice channels or using Web pages.

Open peer-to-peer Internet and Web protocols are used exclusively. As a consequence, servers can be distributed across the network and can be provided and operated by various parties, using appropriate Internet security procedures. All real-time communication servers use only SIP and HTTP to communicate, as will be shown later in this chapter. No APIs are required. This makes the architecture completely open and allows easy outsourcing for specialized or high-performance services, such as unified messaging, instant messaging, or conferencing.

There is a loose coupling between service components. The service controller only invokes various service components by providing call control and leaves the detailed operation to the respective servers.

Dedicated servers also allow the use of application switching in high-traffic service hosting centers such as routing Web, e-mail, and various SIP and RTP communication flows to the appropriate servers.

The architecture is completely distributed. Internet-style alternate servers provide a high degree of reliability. Single points of failure can be thus avoided.

Two or more levels of authentication are required in this architecture. Users need to authenticate themselves to the controller and controllers need to authenticate themselves to the various servers, especially if some of the services are outsourced.

## Integration of Web, Email, and Voice

Figure 17.3 shows the logical view of integrated services for an Internet service provider or e-commerce site using the Web, e-mail, and voice. Various user devices can access the service provider via Web, e-mail, or voice portals, depending on the device. On the right side of Figure 17.3 are various services that may have some or all of the three interfaces: Web, e-mail, and voice. The directory service on the right may have, for example, Web, email, and voice interfaces.

We will focus here only on voice services enabled by SIP signaling and show only the lines for SIP message paths. Similar message paths exist also for the Web and e-mail functions, but are not displayed so as not to complicate the diagram. As shown on the left side of Figure 17.3, users may deploy PSTN phones, mobile phones, PBX phones, and IP voice devices such as SIP phones or computers. An incoming call to the service provider will first be routed by default to a voice portal. The voice portal can have the URL 800.isp.com, or a phone number, 1-800-yourisp.

The voice portal will collect dialed digits for input from PSTN phones using dual-tone multi-frequency PSTN signaling (DTMF), or may have voice recognition capability to avoid interactive voice response system (IVR) menus that can be annoying to users. Depending on the user input, the voice portal will then route the call further to the appropriate service to handle the call to any of the servers shown on the right side. More detailed call flows are illustrated in the following paragraphs.

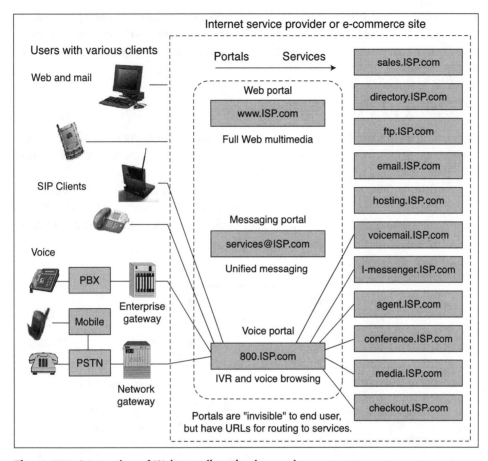

**Figure 17.3** Integration of Web, email, and voice services.

The existence of a distinctive voice portal is invisible to the caller, but the portal itself and the various other servers have distinct URLs so as to route calls, HTTP, and email messages during a service session. A service session consists of all the processes required to handle the call, such as moving the call from the initial link to the sales server and eventually to the successful completion of checkout at the end. During a service session, an incoming call, e-mail, or Web request will be routed to the various servers shown on the right side of Figure 17.3.

# Examples of Integrating Component Services

We will provide examples to illustrate some basic services. The examples are simplified so as only to explain the operation. Real production call flows are more complex due to the need to accommodate various service options and error conditions. For simplicity we will not show the various authorization messages between users and the controller and between the controller and the various servers.

## Collecting of DTMF Digits

Figure 17.4 shows the basic call flows for the plain collecting of dual-tone multifrequency digits, without voice recognition. We will discuss how SIP third-party call control is used for this application.

The initial `INVITE` (message 1 in Figure 17.4) from the caller is directed to the service controller. The Request-URI in the `INVITE` message identifies this service, so various SIP servers in the network, not shown here, know to route the call to the controller.

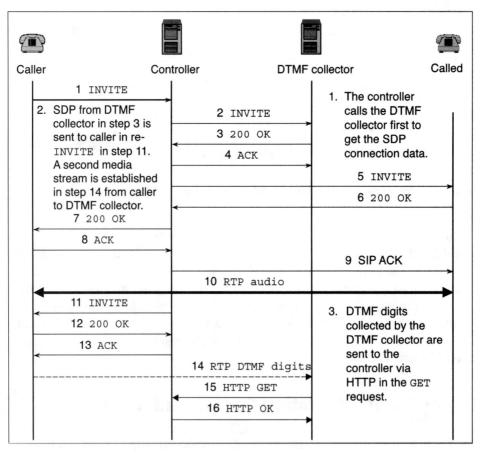

**Figure 17.4** Call flow for collecting DTMF digits.

The controller first forwards the `INVITE` to the DTMF collector (message 2) with the connection address in the SDP body set to 0.0.0.0. This creates an initial media stream on hold. The DTMF collector answers with its own SDP body in the reply `200 OK` (message 3). The controller uses the reply (message 3) to capture the data in the SDP body from the DTMF collector. It then proxies the call to the desired called party in message 5 and gets, in return, a `200 OK` (message 7) in case of success. This response has the form:

```
SIP/2.0 200 OK
Via: SIP/2.0/UDP 100.101.102.103
To: User A <sip:UserA@here.com>
From: User B <sip:UserB@there.com>
Call-ID: a5-32-43-12-77@100.101.102.103
CSeq: 1 INVITE
Contact: sip:UserB@there.com
Content-Type: application/sdp
Content-Length: ...

v=0
o=UserA 289375749 289375749 IN IP5 110.111.112.113
s=-
c=IN IP4 110.111.112.113
t=0 0
m=audio 5004 RTP/AVP 0
```

After message 9 in Figure 17.4, the caller and called party can communicate.

The controller then initiates a re-`INVITE` (message 11) to instruct the caller's UA in the `INVITE` message where to direct the DTMF media stream using the SDP connection data to the DTMF collector acquired in message 3. This re-`INVITE` has the form:

```
INVITE sip:UserB@there.com SIP/2.0
Via: SIP/2.0/UDP 100.101.102.103
To: User B <sip:UserB@there.com>
From: User A <sip:UserA@here.com>
Call-ID: a5-32-43-12-77@100.101.102.103
CSeq: 1 INVITE
Contact: sip:UserB@here.com
Content-Type: application/sdp
Content-Length: ...

v=0
o=UserB 289375749 289375749 IN IP5 100.101.102.103
s=-
c=IN IP4 100.101.102.103
t=0 0
m=audio 5004 RTP/AVP 0
m=audio 53000 RTP/AVP 96
c=IN IP4 200.201.202.203
a=rtpmap:96 telephone-event
```

Note that this SDP now has a second media m= line for the DTMF digit transport with a new connection c= line with the IP address of the DTMF digit collector. The caller can now send DTMF digits in midcall to the digit collector, since it knows the connection data to the DTMF controller.

The called party may instruct the caller to input data using the telephone keypad. The resulting DTMF digits are captured by the DTMF collector and sent to the controller in the HTTP GET message (15).

Plain DTMF service is useful for simple applications such as two-stage dialing, where the user first dials an access number for the respective service, gets a prompt tone, and then dials an identification such as the calling card number. A new dial tone invites the user then to dial the phone number. As we will see, DTMF digits can also be collected by more complex interactive voice response systems.

## Interactive Voice Response

State-of-the-art IVR can be implemented with voice recognition and voice prompts generated using pages marked up with the Voice Extensible Markup Language (VoiceXML). Figure 17.5 shows the call flows for IVR service.

The service starts with an interactive voice response (IVR) exchange to determine the wishes of the caller. The controller, therefore, first proxies the call to the IVR server, so the caller can interact directly with the IVR server. As in the previous example, the initial INVITE message (1) from the caller has the Request-URI pointing to the controller for this particular service.

After the establishment of the media stream, the IVR will generate a voice prompt to the caller, along the line of:

Welcome to our <name> service! Please speak your ID.

The answer from the caller is transformed from speech to text and returned in message (6) of Figure 17.5, HTTP GET, to the controller. The next VoiceXML script is sent from the controller in the HTTP 200 OK (message 7) to further prompt the caller for information regarding his or her request. After the IVR process comes to an end, the last message HTTP 200 OK (message 9) carries an empty VoiceXML script. The call to the IVR is terminated with a BYE (message 10) and the call is forwarded to some other destination with the INVITE in message 12.

## Scheduled Conference Service

A large variety of conference types are possible on the Internet, from spontaneous initiated conferences using presence, such as in instant messaging, to telecom-type scheduled conferences. However, for most types of network-based conferences a mixing voice bridge is necessary, such as discussed in

**VOICEXML**

VoiceXML was introduced in Chapter 6, *SIP Service Creation*. Interactive voice response systems based on VoiceXML technology can support several features for voice services:
- Text to speech (synthesized speech)
- Output of audio files
- Voice recognition
- DTMF input
- Recording of spoken input

VoiceXML servers also have some telephony features, such as call transfer and disconnect, but these may not be always necessary in the presence of a service controller as discussed here. The following example reproduces a sample dialog from the VoiceXML specification [5] that shows the power of IVRs using VoiceXML.

Computer:   Welcome to the weather information service.
                    What state?
Human:      Help
Computer    Please speak the state for which you want the weather.
Human:      Georgia
Computer    What city?
Human:      Tblisi
Computer    I do not understand what you said. What city?
Human:      Macon
Computer:   The conditions in Macon, Georgia are sunny and clear at
                    11 AM...

Chapter 12, *SIP Conferencing*. Therefore, it makes sense to separate the conference-scheduling servers from the voice-mixing bridge, since they are so very different in functionality and technology. Figure 17.6 shows an example of the call flows for a scheduled conference using separate scheduling and mixing servers. In this example we assume the scheduling server is also the controller.

The conference is scheduled and set up on the Web server, which, in turn, informs the scheduler using an HTTP POST message (1). The controller confirms the conference is possible and will be scheduled in the 200 OK message (2) to the Web server. Email or some other means can also be used to inform the users of the scheduled conference.

At the scheduled time, the controller will connect the users successively to the voice mixing bridge. Only two users, A and B, are shown here for simplicity, since all additional users would have the same call flows for call setup with the conference bridge. Note that an alternative service would be the controller could call the participants A and B and use third-party call control to connect them to the mixing bridge.

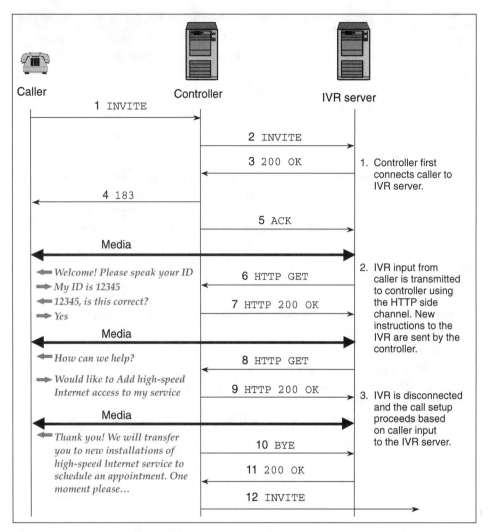

**Figure 17.5** Call flows for interactive voice response service.

## Voice Mail

Users can control services either by voice or using forms on Web servers. We will show in this example how a user can invoke voice mail using the Web server. The call flows are shown in Figure 17.7.

The caller uses a Web page to click on the URL of the called party intended to receive the voice message. The Web server requests in message 1 the controller to connect the caller with the voice mail server. The controller then connects the user's SIP client with the voice mail server using SIP third-party

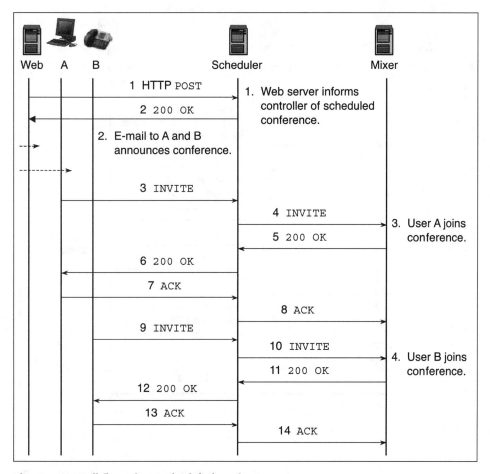

**Figure 17.6** Call flows for a scheduled conference.

call control. The call to the message server is accepted in message 7 and the SDP data from the message server is conveyed in the re-INVITE of message 9, giving the SIP client the necessary information where to send the audio.

# Summary

IP telephony gateways decomposition using master slave protocols such as MGCP, MEGCO or H.248 with service packages in "softswitches" and close, proprietary coupling between components have limitations for nontelephony services. They also have the disadvantage of proprietary bundling and introduce added complexity for network operators.

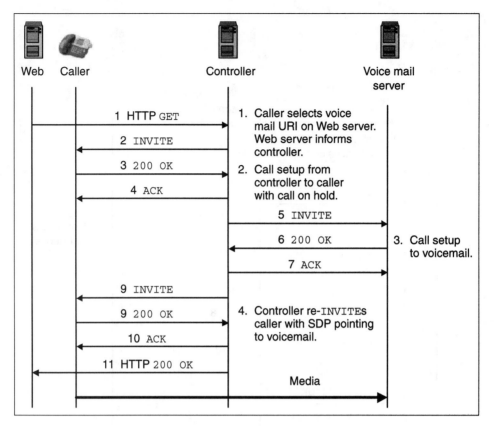

**Figure 17.7** Call flows for voice mail.

By contrast, the component server architecture allows Web-style interaction between large numbers of loosely coupled, specialized servers across the Net. The component server architecture can provide access to all services using the web, email, and voice, relying only on the basic standard Internet protocols HTTP, SMTP, SIP, and RTP. IVR or VoiceXML service call flows are straightforward using third-party call control to direct incoming calls to the appropriate servers.

# References

[1] I. Faynberg, L. Gabuzda, M. Kaplan, and N. Shah. *McGraw-Hill Series on The Intelligent Network Standards, Their Application to Services,* McGraw-Hill, New York, 1997.

[2] F. Cuervo, N. Greene, C. Huitema, A Rayan, B. Rosen, and J. Segers. "Megaco Protocol Version 0.8," IETF RCF 2885, August 2000.

[3] H. Rosenberg, P. Mataga, and H. Schulzrinne. "An Application Server Component Architecture for SIP," IETF Internet draft, November 2000, work in progress.

[4] H. Rosenberg, J. Peterson, H. Schulzrinne, and G. Camarillo. "Third Party Call Control in SIP," IETF Internet draft, May 2000, work in progress.

[5] Voice Extensible Markup Language (VoiceXML™) Version 1.0, The World Wide Web Consortium (W3C), May 2000. http://w3.org/TR/voicexml.

CHAPTER
18

# Conclusions and Future Directions

This chapter will discuss some of the future directions of the SIP protocol and standards in new application areas for SIP.

## The Future of SIP

As of IETF-50 (March 2001), SIP is defined by RFC 2543. However, an Internet draft containing clarifications, bug fixes, and minor changes is being maintained by Henning Schulzrinne. It is known as RFC 2543bis.[1] All of the changes in RFC 2543bis are either backward compatible with 2543 or are considered a bug fix. Most of the important changes between RFC 2543 and RFC 2543bis have been covered in this book, but a few more may be introduced before "bis" moves to RFC. This is likely to happen in late 2001 or early 2002, and will result in the assignment of a new RFC number, which will "obsolete" RFC 2543. At this time, SIP could move from *proposed* to *draft* standard.

[1]"Bis" is Old Latin for "repeat." When used in context with a standard, RFC 2543bis means the second version of the document. If a third version is produced, it would be RFC 2543ter since "ter" is Old Latin for "three times" (from the dictionary at whatis.com).

Many SIP working group Internet drafts are scheduled to be submitted to the Internet Engineering Steering Group (IESG) to reach RFC status. Some of these documents are referenced in this book. Some may be revised as a result of this important protocol review process. The schedule and progress of this work may be tracked at the SIP and SIPPING working group charter pages in the listed references.

The SIP extensions for instant message and presence Internet drafts are also scheduled for submission to the IESG in 2001. The progress of this work can be followed at the following address: http://ietf.org/html.charters/simple-charter.html

The use of IPv6 by the 3GPP wireless project will be the first major use of IPv6 with SIP, and may produce some minor changes in the protocol address handling.

# Future Services

The authors believe that new applications of SIP will be developed in the future and that the SIPPING working group will be extremely busy. Areas of current interest include:

- Firewall traversal:
  - Firewall control protocol
  - Extend SIP and SDP
  - Enhance firewalls and NATs

- Spatial location and services

- Emergency services: 911

- SIP phones:
  - Server location
  - Configuration
  - Management

- SIP use in third-generation wireless networks

- SIP for the hearing impaired

- Legal intercept of SIP calls

- Internet appliances

SIP may also find use in the "Invisible Internet Telephony" [1] such as in Internet appliances, home security systems, 3G mobile devices, interactive multiplayer games, and proximity sensors that trigger a call.

# Summary

SIP has evolved rapidly over the past few years. Although the base specification will remain fairly stable, a whole set of extensions will soon be implemented widely. It is likely that in a few years, the protocol will find a whole new set of applications.

As with the World Wide Web, the uses and applications of SIP are only limited by our imagination. The vision of simple, rich and secure communications over the Internet is steadily moving to become a reality.

The topics still in development and their progress can be followed at the following Web sites:

**SIP Working Group**: http://ietf.org/html.charters/sip-charter.html

**SIPPING Working Group**: http://ietf.org/html.charters/sipping-charter
.html

**SIMPLE: SIP Instant Messaging Working Group**: http://
ietf.org/html.charters/simple-charter.html

**Internet Appliances Web Page (Telcordia)**: http://
argreenhouse.com/iapp/

Readers may also look up the other Web sites mentioned in Chapter 1 (see the section "References in This Book").

# References

[1] H. Schulzrinne. "Why SIP?" Keynote address at the SIP Services Conference, Washington, DC, April 18–20, 2001.

# Glossary

**3GPP**  third-generation wireless mobile Partnership Program

**3pcc**  third-party call control

**802.11b**  IEEE (Wi-Fi) wireless LAN protocol

**AAA**  authentication, authorization, and accounting

**ACD**  automatic call distributor

**ACK**  SIP method for Acknowledgment of final response to INVITE

**AIN**  Advanced Intelligent Network

**AIP**  Application Infrastructure Service Provider

**ALG**  application layer (or level) gateway

**API**  application programming interface

**applet**  small Java application program

**APS**  application policy server

**ASP**  Application Service Provider

**AVP**  audio-video profile for conferencing using RTP

**AVT**  IETF Audio Video Transport WG

**B2BUA**  Back-to-Back User Agent, used to implement some features in SIP

**BGP**  Border Gateway Protocol, binding association made between a private IP address and a public IP address by a NAT

**bis**  Old Latin for "repeat," RFC 2543bis is the Internet draft which is an updated version of the RFC standard that will receive a new RFC number in 2002

**BYE**  SIP method for termination of session

**CA**  Call Agent

**call leg**  The unique identifier for a SIP call consisting of the `To`, `From`, and `Call-ID` headers including any tags

**CANCEL**  SIP method for cancellation of pending session

**CAS**  circuit-associated signaling

**CGI**  common gateway interface

**CNAME**  DNS canonical name Resource Record

**COMET**  SIP method for notification of preConditions MET

**COPS**  Common Open Policy Service

**CPIM**  Common Profile for Instant Messaging

**CPL**  Call Processing Language

**CRM**  customer relations management

**CS-1, CS-2**  ITU-T capability sets 1 and 2 for the AIN

**CTI**  computer telephony integration

**DHCP**  Dynamic Host Configuration Protocol

**DiffServ**  Differentiated Services QoS architecture

**digest**  type of authentication supported by both HTTP and SIP

**DNS**  domain name system

**DSL**  digital subscriber line

**DTD**  document type definition

**DTMF**  dual-tone multifrequency PSTN signaling

**E.164**  global standard for telephone numbers using country codes

**e164.arpa**  TLD root for ENUM

**ENUM**  E.164 number and DNS-based service

**escaping**  process in which headers or bodies can be included in a URL

**ETSI**  European Telecommunications Standards Institute

**firewall**  network element, IP packet filter to protect private IP networks

**Fork**  process in which a single SIP request is sent to multiple locations

**Forking Proxy**  A SIP server which forks requests

**FTP**  File Transfer Protocol

**GET**  HTTP method for retrieving information

**GSM**  Global System for Mobile Communications

**GUI**  graphical user interface

**H.248**  ITU-T recommendation for media gateway control, known as MEGACO in the IETF

**H.323**  ITU-T recommendation for packet based multimedia communications systems

**headers**  fields in a SIP request or response

**HTML**  HyperText Markup Language

**HTTP**  HyperText Transport Protocol

**HTTPS**  Secure HTTP

**IAB**  Internet Architecture Board

**IANA**  Internet Assigned Names Association

**ICMP**  Internet Control Message Protocol

**ICW**  Internet Call Waiting feature

**I-D**  IETF Internet draft document

**IESG**  Internet Engineering Steering Group

**IETF**  Internet Engineering Task Force

**IM**  Instant Message

**IMPP**  IETF Instant Messaging and Presence WG

**IN**  Intelligent Network defined by the ITU-T

**INAP**  IN Application Part

**INFO**  SIP method for the transport of application level information along the signaling path

**INVITE**  SIP method for session setup in SIP

**IP**  Internet Protocol

**IPP**  Internet Printing Protocol

**IPSec**  IP Security Protocol

**IPTEL**  IETF IP Telephony WG

**ISDN**  Integrated Services Digital Network

**ISP**  Internet Service Provider

**ISSLL**  Integrated Services for Specific Link Layers

**ISUP**  ISDN user part

**ITU-T**  International Telecommunications Union—Telephony

**IVR**  interactive voice response system

**JAIN**  Java-IN programming APIs for Integrated Networks

**KEA**  key exchange algorithm

**key**  cryptographic string used for encoding or decoding encrypted messages

**LAN**  local area network

**LDAP**  Lightweight Directory Access Protocol

**LDP**  local decision policy

**LNP**  local number portability

**location servers**  database of registration information accessed by a proxy or redirect server

**LRN**  Location Routing Number for PSTN LNP

**MAC**  media access control

**maddr**  multicast (or secondary server) address

**MAP**  mobile application part

**MBONE**  Internet multicast backbone

**MCU**  multipoint control unit., used to mix media in a conferencing session

**MD5**  Message Digest 5

**media**  session established using SIP Payload in IP packets for communications

**MEGACO**  Media Gateway Control Protocol, IETF Working Group

**MGCP**  Media Gateway Control Protocol

**MESSAGE**  SIP method for the transport of a short instant message in the body of SIP

**message body**  attachment of SIP message

**method**  type of SIP request

**MF**  multifrequency PSTN signaling

**MG**  media gateway

**MGC**  media gateway controller

**MIB**  management information block

**MIDCOM**  Middle Box Communication Protocol, IETF Working Group

**MIME**  Multipart Internet Mail Extension

**MMUSIC** Multiparty Multimedia Session Control IETF Working Group

**MPLS** multiprotocol label switching

**MSC** mobile switching center

**MTU** media transmission unit

**multicast** packet broadcast protocol over the Internet

**MX** DNS Mail Exchange Record

**NAPT** Network Address and Port Translator

**NAPTR** DNS Naming Authority Pointer Resource Record used for ENUM telephone number mapping

**NAT** network address translator

**NCS** network control system

**NGN** next-generation network, a.k.a. the Internet

**NNI** network-to-network interface

**nonce** string used by MD5 to encode response

**NOTIFY** SIP method for transport of an event notification

**NPA** telephone number "area code" in the North American numbering plan

**NS** DNS authoritative name server for a domain

**NTP** Network Time Protocol

**NXX** telephone number prefix used in local routing of calls in the North American numbering plan

**OPTIONS** SIP method for query of options and capabilities

**OSP** Open Settlement Protocol

**OSS** operational support systems

**PBX** private branch exchange

**PC** personal computer

**PCM** pulse coded modulation for voice used in the PSTN

**PGP** pretty good privacy

**PINT** PSTN and INTernetworking

**PIM** personal information manager

**PKI** public key interchange

**POP** Post Office Protocol

**Port** logical number used by UDP or TCP to demultiplex packets between applications

**POST** HTTP method for posting information

**POTS** plain old telephone service

**PPP** Point-to-Point Protocol

**PRACK** SIP method for Acknowledgment of Provisional response ACKnowledgment

**presence** service showing the state of connectivity of a user

**presentity** software that provides presence information to a network

**PRI** primary rate interface

**Proxy** logical function of SIP server

**PSTN** public switch telephone network

**PT** payload type—codec in RTP packet.

**PTR** DNS Pointer Record

**PUA** presence user agent

**Q.931** ITU Call Control Protocol

**QoS**  Quality of Service

**Q.SIG**  ITU-T signaling standard for private ISDN networks

**REFER**  SIP method to transfer a user in a call to another URL

**REGISTER**  SIP method for registration of a user's URL

**Request-URI**  indicates the recipient of the SIP request

**RFC**  request for comments

**RG**  residential gateway

**RLC**  release complete message

**RPC**  remote procedure call

**RR**  DNS Resource Record, or RTCP Receiver Reports

**RSVP**  Resource reServation Protocol

**RTP**  Real-Time Protocol

**RTP/AVP**  Real-Time Protocol—Audio Video Profile

**RTCP**  Real-Time Control Protocol

**RTSP**  Real-Time Streaming Protocol

**S/MIME**  secure MIME encryption

**SAP**  Session Announcement Protocol

**SCIP**  Simple Conferencing Invitation Protocol, forerunner of SIP protocol

**SCTP**  Stream Control Transport Protocol

**SDES**  RTCP Source Description

**SDP**  Session Description Protocol

**SDPng**  SDP "next generation," the successor protocol to SDP being developed by the MMUSIC WG of the IETF

**servlets**  Java applications

**SGML**  Standard Generalized Markup Language

**SIGTRAN**  Signaling Transport Working Group of the IETF

**SIMPLE**  SIP for Instant Messaging Protocol Leveraging Extensions

**SIP**  Session Initiation Protocol

**SIPit**  the SIP interoperability test formerly known as a Bakeoff

**SIPPING**  SIP Protocol INstiGation (of applications) Working Group

**SIP-T**  SIP telephony, carrying of PSTN ISUP message attachments in SIP messages

**SIP URI**  addressing schema defined for SIP

**SLS**  service level specification

**SMIL**  Synchronized Multimedia Integration Language

**SMS**  short messaging service

**SMTP**  Simple Mail Transport Protocol

**SNMP**  Simple Network Management Protocol

**SOA**  start of authority DNS record

**SOAP**  Simple Object Access Protocol

**softswitch**  marketing term for media gateway controllers (MGC)

**Spam**  unwanted emails, messages, or media

**SPIRITS**  servers in the PSTN Initiating Requests to InTernet Servers, IETF Working Group

**spoofing**  imitation of one user by another

**SR**  RTCP sender report

**SRV**  DNS Service Resource Records

**SS7**  ITU-T Signaling System #7

**SSRC**  RTP synchronization source indicator

**SUBSCRIBE**  SIP method to request, the notification of an event

**T1**  SIP timer 1, default value 500 ms

**T2**  SIP timer 2, default value 4 s

**tag**  pseudorandom string used in SIP as part of a call leg, or element of a markup language such as XML or HTML

**TCAP**  Transaction Capability Application Part in SS7

**TCP**  Transmission Control Protocol

**TDM**  time division multiplexing

**Tel URL**  addressing schema used by SIP

**TFTP**  Trivial File Transfer Protocol

**TIPHON**  Telecommunications and Internet Harmonization body run by ETSI

**TLD**  DNS top-level domain

**TLS**  TransmissionTransport Layer Security, also an IETF WG

**TOS**  type of service bits in IPv4 header

**TR**  RTCP transmit reports

**TRIP**  Telephony Routing over IP Protocol

**TTL**  time to live

**TXT**  DNS text record

**UA**  user agent

**UAC**  user agent client

**UAS**  user agent server

**UDP**  User Datagram Protocol

**UM**  unified messaging

**UNI**  user to network interface

**Unicast**  point-to-point packet delivery mechanism common on the Internet

**UNSUBSCRIBE**  SIP PINT method to cancel the subscription for a notification of an event

**URI**  uniform resource indicator

**URL**  uniform resource locator

**VoiceXML**  Voice Extensible Markup Language

**VoIP**  voice over IP

**VON**  Voice On the Net conference

**VPN**  virtual private network

**W3C**  World Wide Web Consortium

**WAP**  Wireless Access Protocol

**Watcher**  software that requests presence information

**WG**  IETF Working Group

**WWW**  World Wide Web

**XML**  Extensible Markup Language

# Index